RACE TO THE POLAR SEA

Elisha Kent Kane, age thirty-five, with telescope

KEN McGOOGAN

RACE

TO THE

POLAR SEA

THE HEROIC ADVENTURES
AND ROMANTIC OBSESSIONS OF
ELISHA KENT KANE

HARPERCOLLINS PUBLISHERS LTD
A PHYLLIS BRUCE BOOK

Race to the Polar Sea
© 2008 by Ken McGoogan. All rights reserved.

A Phyllis Bruce Book, published by HarperCollins Publishers Ltd

First Edition

HarperCollins books may be purchased for educational, business,
or sales promotional use through our Special Markets Department.

HarperCollins Publishers Ltd
2 Bloor Street East, 20th Floor
Toronto, Ontario, Canada
M4W 1A8

www.harpercollins.ca

Library and Archives Canada Cataloguing in Publication

McGoogan, Kenneth
Race to the Polar Sea : the heroic adventures and romantic obsessions
of Elisha Kent Kane / Ken McGoogan. — 1st ed.

"A Phyllis Bruce book".
ISBN 978-0-00-200776-4

1. Kane, Elisha Kent, 1820–1857.
2. Fox, Margaret, 1833–1893.
3. Arctic regions—Discovery and exploration—American.
4. Explorers—United States—Biography.
I. Title.

G635.K2M33 2008   910'.92   C2008-901851-6
HC 9 8 7 6 5 4 3 2 1

Printed and bound in the United States
Text design by Sharon Kish

For Sheena

Afoot and light-hearted, we take to the open road . . .

{ CONTENTS }

MAPS

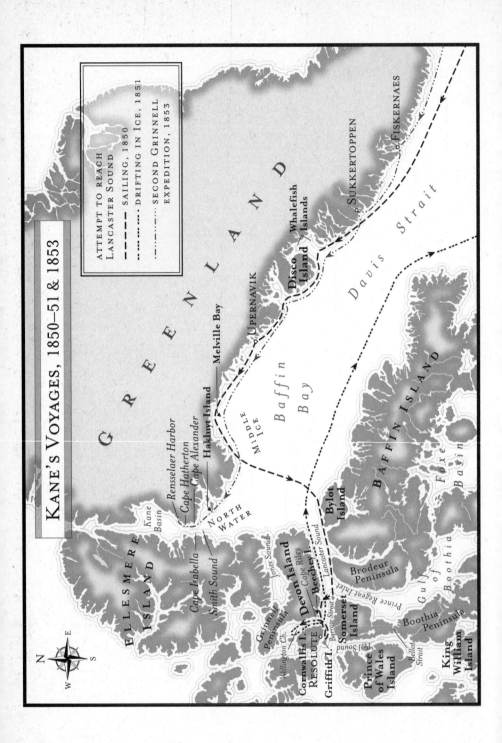

KANE'S VOYAGES, 1850–51 & 1853

ATTEMPT TO REACH
LANCASTER SOUND

------ SAILING, 1850
-·-·- DRIFTING IN ICE, 1851
-··-·· SECOND GRINNELL
       EXPEDITION, 1853

N
W E
S

G R E E N L A N D

Kane
Basin

Rensselaer Harbor
Cape Hatherton
Cape Alexander
Haklurt Island

NORTH
WATER

Cape Isabella

Smith Sound

ELLESMERE
ISLAND

Jones Sound

Grinnell
Peninsula

Wellington Ch.

Devon Island
Cape Riley
Beechey I.

Cornwallis I.
RESOLUTE
Griffith I.

Barrow Strait

Lancaster Sound

Somerset
Island

Peel Sound

Prince
of Wales
Island

Bellot
Strait

Boothia
Peninsula

King
William
Island

Gulf
of
Boothia

Brodeur
Peninsula

Prince Regent Inlet

Bylot
Island

BAFFIN ISLAND

Foxe
Basin

Baffin
Bay

MIDDLE
ICE

Melville Bay

UPERNAVIK

Disco
Island

Whalefish
Islands

SUKKERTOPPEN

Davis Strait

FISKERNAES

TODAY & YESTERDAY

One afternoon in August 1850, as Arctic explorer Elisha Kent Kane stood talking with several fellow naval officers on the icy, snow-covered shores of Beechey Island, a sailor came stumbling over a nearby ridge. "Graves!" he shouted. "Graves! Franklin's winter quarters!"

Searchers for the lost expedition of Sir John Franklin had found what has since become the most famous historical site in the far north—the graves of the first three sailors to die during Franklin's final voyage. At this desolate spot in 1846, while hoping still to discover a Northwest Passage, the long-winded Franklin conducted three sonorous funeral services.

Four years later, the American Kane led searchers in scrambling over the ice to the makeshift cemetery. "Here, amid the sterile uniformity of snow and slate," he wrote later, "were the headboards of three graves, made after the old orthodox fashion of gravestones at home."

Flash forward 157 years. Late in August 2007, as a resource person aboard an expeditionary cruise ship, I stood gazing at those three graves while a Scottish bagpiper played "Amazing Grace" and a light snow fell and instantly melted. Certainly, I felt moved by what I heard and saw: the skirling of the pipes, the desolate loneliness of the landscape.

Yet as I read the wooden headboards, facsimiles of the originals, I felt more shaken by what I did not see—by the absence of ice. We had arrived at Beechey two weeks later in the season than Kane, and yet, where he encountered heaps of ice and snow, both in Lancaster Sound and on shore, we found nothing but open water, naked rock, and scree.

The contrast shocked me. Satellite images from the European Space Agency had recently revealed that, for the first time in recorded history, the Northwest Passage lay open to commercial traffic. The retreat of the polar ice cap, I knew, had revived an ancient dream in altered form. Business interests were looking forward not to carrying real gold from Cathay, as in the beginning, but to transporting black gold from the Alaskan oil fields.

Yet to see Beechey Island free of ice drove home the new reality of the twenty-first century, if only because, thanks to Elisha Kane, I knew how the area looked in 1850. As I stood at the three graves, I realized that the opening of the Northwest Passage brought a centuries-old saga to a surprising conclusion, one that shed new light on the history of Arctic discovery, and especially on Elisha Kent Kane.

All through the twentieth century, historians portrayed the Arctic as a harsh world that hardly changed at all. The Arctic represented months of winter darkness and stupefying cold; it included pack ice, icebergs, and countless polar bears, walruses, and seals; and it featured "Esquimaux" hunters who lived in igloos—or could at least build them.

Suddenly, we realize that this picture is obsolete. And that brings a corollary surprise. The hundreds of pages that Elisha Kane devoted to describing the High Arctic—people and animals as well as glaciers, ice fields, icebergs, and the Greenland ice cap—have become invaluable. They enable us to compare and contrast, and so to appreciate the scale of what is happening in the far north.

The supremely literate Kane, easily the most articulate of northern explorers, wrote of sailing among upraised tables of ice fourteen feet thick.

He described hummocks, forced skyward by the pressure of pack ice, rising "in cones like crushed sugar, some of them forty feet high." He would leave off hunting to sketch a glacier, describing it as "a stupendous monument of frost." So vivid is Kane's depiction of the mid-nineteenth-century Arctic that, for today's readers, his work constitutes an irreplaceable touchstone.

Similarly, Kane's descriptions of Arctic wildlife resonate with contemporary meaning. The explorer describes hunting birds, seals, and walrus, all now seriously depleted in numbers, and waxes eloquent about polar bears. He relates, for example, how several bears ravaged a cache of provisions, smashing open iron caskets of pemmican and tossing aside boulders that had tested the strength of three men. Today, these magnificent creatures are nearing endangered status.

But above all, Kane's writings about the Inuit, with whom he forged a singular alliance, have taken on new significance. His detailed depictions of clothes, sledges, weapons, housing, and habits provide a unique opportunity to juxtapose today and yesterday. Unlike many others, this gentleman from Philadelphia proved humble enough to learn from hunter-gatherers who had been born into a tradition of Arctic survival. "I can hardly say how valuable the advice of our Esquimaux friends has been to us upon our hunts," he would write. He marveled at how they observed every movement of ice, wind, or season and "predicted its influence upon the course of the birds of passage with the same sagacity that has taught them the habits of the resident animals."

By creating an unprecedented cross-cultural alliance, Kane not only saved the lives of most of his men, but set an example that would be remembered among the Inuit for thirteen decades. In the 1980s, after criticizing several explorers for their arrogance and insensitivity, the Frenchman Jean Malaurie would hail the "extraordinary agreements" Kane made with the Inuit and observe that "the favorable memory that Kane has left among my Eskimo friends is vague, certainly, but tenacious."

Yet all this, I realized on Beechey, accounted for only half the sense of urgency I felt about Elisha Kent Kane. The other half came from a discovery

3

I had made a few months before, when from my home in Toronto I visited Calgary, Alberta, to view some Kane-related artwork at the Glenbow Museum. Afterward, acting on impulse, I hiked up a hilly street to visit my friend Cameron Treleaven, the antiquarian-adventurer with whom I had visited the Arctic in 1999 while working on my book *Fatal Passage*.

When I told Treleaven how I had spent the morning, he said, "You do realize that the Glenbow got those images from me?" The sketches and paintings at the museum derived from a collection he had acquired from descendants of Thomas Leiper Kane, the explorer's dearest brother—some of it at a 2003 auction in Kane, Pennsylvania, a town I had already visited. Treleaven said he had retained the most important material, and that it included journals as yet unseen by any biographer.

This I could not ignore. And three months later, I revisited Calgary to investigate. At his bookstore, Aquila Books, and later at his home, Treleaven produced an astonishing array of journals, documents, letters, drawings, photos, and memorabilia. As I sifted through this material, slowly the truth began to emerge: I was making one of those discoveries that invariably happen to somebody else.

Some of the material was interesting, but not useful—for example, a handwritten copy of the autobiography of the explorer's father, Judge John K. Kane, a work readily available as a printed book. Other documents proved disappointing, like the "boat journal" that appeared to cover Kane's Arctic escape, but turned out to be a handwritten copy of the final, anticlimactic section of a journal kept by seaman George Stephenson, who lacked anything approaching his leader's sensibility and expressiveness. Nor could many of the illustrations and memorabilia, some hitherto unknown, be regarded as more than potentially enhancing—not even the original marble bust of Kane from which a plaster copy was taken, a facsimile now kept at the American Philosophical Society.

Still, that left three items of note: three handwritten, large-format journals that Kane produced in the Arctic. Two of these are clearly significant: first, a 161-page journal from Kane's 1850 expedition in search of Sir John

Two items from the collection of antiquarian Cameron Treleaven:
the telescope Elisha Kane used in the Arctic during his second expedition
(compare frontispiece) and a marble bust of the explorer. A plaster copy of
the bust is held at the American Philosophical Society in Philadelphia.

Franklin, during which he visited Beechey Island; and second, a 239-page "natural history journal" from his 1853 expedition, containing detailed observations on everything from the seal fishery to scurvy, loons, wolves, and "Esquimaux."

The third constitutes what I believe to be the most important primary material to surface in the field of Kane studies in 150 years: a 376-page log-book from that second expedition, covering the period May 31, 1853, to March 23, 1854. This is the long-lost Volume One of Kane's private journal, which opens at the beginning of the voyage with the explorer describing, from on board the *Advance,* the experience of sailing out of New York to go in search of Sir John Franklin and an Open Polar Sea.

Kane evokes crowded wharves and "salutes, bell ringings and huzzas" wafting over the water in a continuous clamor: "To men bound for the Arctic region, sailors with undigested shore habitudes, officers with heads full of home thoughts and disrupted associations, this big response came very cheeringly." Those words have never before seen print. No scholar or author has even read them in more than fifteen decades. The explorer continues: "I had lived for the past two years as, I suppose, all men live—with much to regret and something to cherish. I had followed one preponderating motive directly connected with my better nature; but had marred it by a host of interludes uncomfortable to recall."

That "preponderating motive" was to find out what had happened to the lost Franklin expedition. To the less salubrious "interludes" we shall come in good time. Kane would write and reflect in this private journal for two years. In his neat handwriting, while leading one of the most dramatic and arduous polar expeditions ever mounted, he would churn out more than 700 pages, filling two large-format volumes (8 1/2 by 14 inches) with roughly 350,000 words.

The continuation of this journal, Volume Two, takes up where this newly discovered manuscript leaves off, on March 24, 1854. The original is housed at Stanford University in California, and is rightly regarded as the single most important item in the Elisha Kane archive. Several biographers—notably George Corner, who wrote in the 1960s—have put it to excellent use, comparing journal entries with more polished renditions in Kane's published, two-volume masterpiece, *Arctic Explorations*. Microfiche copies of Volume Two are available in several archives and collections.

But with the possible exception of William Elder, who wrote a biography in the 1850s, I am the first author to have read Volume One. The manuscript covers the tumultuous period during which two of Kane's men lost their lives as a result of a controversial sledge journey. But, like its Stanford-held extension, this journal sheds light on the whole expedition—and, indeed, on Kane's entire life.

That light, I realized on Beechey Island, had changed the way I viewed Elisha Kent Kane. Taken together with the opening of the Northwest Passage, it showed this forgotten American to be not only the most articulate and tragically neglected of Arctic heroes, but also the explorer most relevant to the twenty-first century. And that, I felt, demanded expression.

{ I }

Call to Adventure

In Search of Franklin

On July 27, 1853, three years after his visit to Beechey Island, Elisha Kent Kane stood at the railing of the *Advance,* telescope in hand, and peered eastward across the pack ice at Greenland. The fog had lifted at last, but now Kane perceived that the ice belt along the coast was breaking up. The conventional route north looked unpromising.

To the west, on the other hand, in the direction of the Middle Ice, the floating pack looked loose, and a deep current drove the largest icebergs north, some of them towering over the ship. His most experienced officers had warned repeatedly against entering the Middle Ice, famously a graveyard for both explorers and whalers. And so Kane, an expedition commander at age thirty-three, faced a difficult choice. Should he follow the safe, slow route along the Greenland coast as far as possible, and forget about catching his English competitor, forget about making history by wintering farther north than any voyager yet? Or should he ignore his advisers and risk the Middle Ice?

To many back home in America, Kane well understood, this voyage in search of a lost British expedition seemed foolhardy, dangerous, quixotic, unnecessary. Yet he remained convinced that, while searching for the

Northwest Passage, Sir John Franklin had become trapped in an Open Polar Sea at the top of the world. He believed that even now, eight years after leaving London, Franklin and his men might be struggling to escape from behind a great barrier of encircling ice.

That was why, in the months before sailing out of New York, Kane had traveled the eastern seaboard to raise funds, arguing that his projected voyage could not be dismissed as a scientific curiosity; rather, it constituted a philanthropic effort to rescue John Franklin and his men, an enterprise that should engage "the sympathies of the whole civilized world."

Early in 1853, speaking to audiences of hundreds in Philadelphia, Boston, Washington, and New York, Kane repeatedly reviewed the historical record. For three centuries, geographers and mapmakers had speculated that a warm-water ocean, a polar basin teeming with fish and animals, might exist at the North Pole, ringed by an "annulus" of ice. He had cited expert after expert, starting with the testimony of voyagers from the sixteenth century and ending with the eyewitness account of British commander Edward Inglefield, who just last year had penetrated Smith Sound and established a new "farthest north" in the western hemisphere.

Before being driven back by a gale, Inglefield had seen nothing to the north but open water. Had he glimpsed a passage to the fabled Polar Sea? Kane argued that he had. Furthermore, this young American, so handsome, so eloquent, and already celebrated for heroic deeds in the service of his country, believed that the Franklin expedition, missing since 1845, had entered that polar basin by another route. He contended that, from Beechey Island, Franklin sailed north up the nearby Wellington Channel and got trapped behind the ice barrier. Who could say otherwise?

While drumming up funds to undertake this voyage, Kane had detailed his expeditionary plan to enthusiastic audiences. Having secured the brigantine *Advance,* the same sturdy vessel in which he had sailed to the Arctic three years before, Kane would proceed north along the west coast of Greenland into Smith Sound. As the weather turned cold and the ice grew thick, he would force the *Advance* "to the utmost navigable point."

During the ensuing winter, with the ship frozen fast, he would send dogs and sledges still farther north to create a chain of provision depots. The following spring, to rescue survivors of the Franklin expedition, he would take sledges and small boats and make for the Open Polar Sea. "Once there, if such a reward awaits us, we launch our little boats, and, bidding God speed us, embark upon its waters."

Now, on July 27, as he stood on the deck of the *Advance,* the young explorer wrestled with the biggest decision of his life. If he sailed north along the coast of Greenland, he risked getting trapped by pack ice before he reached the perennially open North Water and spending the winter far south of where he needed to be. If instead he steered westward into the Middle Ice, he could shorten the voyage by days or even weeks, and get much farther north—but that treacherous icefield had wrecked hundreds of whaling vessels and might make short work of the *Advance.*

Despite his youth, a weak heart, and recurring health problems, Elisha Kane had made countless tough decisions in difficult circumstances. He had descended into a volcano in the Philippines, infiltrated a company of slave traders in West Africa, grappled with thieves on the Nile River, and narrowly survived getting stabbed during hand-to-hand combat in the Sierra Madre. For the past six months—ever since the day he read, while recovering from illness in his hometown of Philadelphia, that Edward Inglefield was returning to Smith Sound to resume the search for Franklin—he had understood that he might face a choice like the one before him.

Inglefield had already come achingly close, Kane believed, to discovering the Open Polar Sea, and so to achieving a certain immortality. Last January, when he learned that Inglefield would return to those waters in a steam-powered vessel, Kane had responded viscerally. To John Pendleton Kennedy, who was both his friend and the secretary of the navy, he wrote that the mail "to my great mortification brings me the news that the British Admiralty have adopted my scheme of search and are about to prosecute it with the aid of steam. Nothing is left to me but a competition with the odds against me, and for this, even, I must hasten the preparations for my departure."

To another faithful correspondent, Jane Franklin, the wife of Sir John, Kane wrote seeking clarification. She responded from England with assurances that Inglefield would not enter Smith Sound. "You may probably have had the gossip that appears in our papers under the schedule of naval intelligence from Woolwich," she wrote. "There is no authority for any such assumption." Instead, she insisted, Inglefield would sail in a steamer carrying supplies to an expedition far to the west, through Lancaster Sound. She added: "he thinks he may fall in with you in Davis Strait, and if so how glad will he be to tow or help you in any way."

Kane had remained unconvinced. He knew that naval officers were given to reinterpreting their orders when it suited them—especially if the stakes involved national pride, American versus British. He suspected that Inglefield intended to race him to the Open Polar Sea and steal the glory not only of discovering that High Arctic phenomenon, but of rescuing survivors from the Franklin expedition.

Ten days before, on July 17, when he called in at the Greenland port of Proven to acquire more sled dogs, Kane learned that Inglefield had visited twelve days earlier. The Englishman not only enjoyed the advantage of a steam engine that could free him from pack ice, but had apparently taken a significant lead in their undeclared race to the polar sea. Since leaving Proven, Kane had worked furiously to make up time. Instead of sailing the *Advance* into ports to buy dogs, he visited a series of settlements in a whaleboat, rowing among icebergs that assumed fantastical shapes, some of them rising forty feet above the surface.

Now the *Advance* stood off the southern tip of Melville Bay, a crescent-shaped indentation that extends 150 miles north along the Greenland coast. To the west and northwest, in the heart of Baffin Bay, lay the Middle Ice, a floating agglomeration of ice floes and rolling "growlers" interspersed with massive icebergs. Whalers had long since determined that in mid-summer the main pack of the Middle Ice drifted some distance westward, opening a semi-navigable channel along the coast of Greenland. Through that waterway, they could usually proceed north under sail or, if necessary, by

This 1850s view of Melville Bay is taken from Kane's first book, The United States Grinnell Expedition in Search of Sir John Franklin. *Like most of the period illustrations in* Race to the Polar Sea, *it is based on a sketch by Kane himself. The artist James Hamilton turned Kane's drawing into a watercolour, and engraver John Sartain produced the finished work.*

"tracking" or man-hauling their ships with ropes.

The Middle Ice itself remained, almost always, dangerously impenetrable. Occasionally, in a good year, a few ships had managed to sail through it. When they did, as Kane knew from wide reading, they reached the North Water far more rapidly than they otherwise would have. As often as not, however, they got trapped in the pack—or else wrecked.

Elisha Kane would never describe the moment of decision. But his journals, letters, and published books show him to be the most introspective of all polar explorers. He emerges from those documents as profoundly aware of the judgment of history. Inevitably, he reflected on how posterity would regard what he did next. His notebooks and correspondence also attest that Kane, the scion of an illustrious Philadelphia family, would have felt the weight of family expectations and considered how people back home would respond.

Just a few days before, in a letter to his father, Kane had written that, looking out from the brig, he could see more than 200 icebergs—yet he could not bring himself to describe them: "Time was when I could have piled epithets upon such a scene, but that time has passed." Based on his knowledge of the ice, he added, he anticipated a safe and easy passage: "Say this to Mother, but to no outside person, as I do not wish to hazard an opinion." And tell Mother as well, he wrote, with the romantic, theatrical flourish that characterized his correspondence, that he had committed himself heart and soul to this project, and so remained "willing to meet like a man the worst that can happen."

On July 27, 1853, as he stood at the railing of the *Advance,* looking out at the Greenland coast, Elisha Kent Kane felt the gaze of posterity upon him. He lowered his telescope, turned to his first officer, and told him to summon all hands. He had a decision to announce.

THE PHILADELPHIA STORY

Two centuries ago, the foremost city in America—the wealthiest, most populous, most cosmopolitan, and most beautiful—was not New York City or Boston but Philadelphia. Founded on the site of a Delaware Indian village, and boasting a distinguished historical pedigree, the City of Brotherly Love had established more precedents than any other American center—among them, the first circulating library, first botanical gardens, first hospital, and first medical school. Closely identified with the Revolutionary War, Philadelphia spawned both the Declaration of Independence and the United States Constitution and served, during the 1790s, as the nation's capital.

By the turn of the century, when the Kane family arrived, the city (with suburbs) boasted a population of 68,000 led by an elegant aristocracy of businessmen, doctors, and lawyers. It had given rise to theaters, restaurants, bookshops, fine hotels, a natural history museum, an art museum, and the American Philosophical Society—the leading scientific institution on the continent, then under the leadership of Thomas Jefferson. For beauty, while Philadelphia could not compare with the centuries-old cities of Europe, an eminent French botanist called it "the most extensive, the handsomest and most populous city in the United States," while a Swedish baron declared it "one of the loveliest cities in the world."

Visiting Americans, according to art historian Edgar P. Richardson, proved still more effusive. One writer eulogized the cleanliness, the gas lighting, the plethora of trees, and the streets paved with pebblestones and bordered with raised footways. The cosmopolitan artist Gilbert Stuart, who lived in the city from 1795 to 1802, would ever afterward begin favorite anecdotes with the phrase, "When I resided in the Athens of America . . ."

In 1801, a six-year-old named John Kane arrived in Philadelphia from Albany, New York. He came with his father, Elisha Kane, a widower bent on establishing a new branch of Kane Brothers & Company, a window manufacturing concern. The boy's mother, who had died two years before, had sprung from the wealthy Van Rensselaer family of New York. On his father's side, John Kane could trace his lineage to one of the first settlers of Massachusetts, a Puritan Irish clergyman named Elisha Kent whose offspring had prospered.

During the next few years, as Philadelphia began transforming itself into an industrial city, the boy's businessman father would also prosper. By 1808, when John reached thirteen, the name Elisha Kane would appear on a published list of the city's principal manufacturers. By that time, too, his father had taken a second wife, a Miss Kintzing. Later, John Kane would describe her as "a fine-hearted woman, of strong mind not uncultivated, and in manners a lady of the old school. . . . I loved her sincerely." The youth added a middle name, becoming John Kintzing Kane.

As a middle-aged man, he would write an autobiography for his descendants, mentioning that he resolved to become a lawyer at an early age. Educated privately, first by a British remittance man who had attended Eton, he mastered Greek, Latin, and French at an early age, and later added Spanish. At fourteen, he went off to New Haven, Connecticut, to study at Yale, a residential college modeled on Oxford and Cambridge.

A strong-minded but immature young man, John Kane rebelled against a certain professor's foolish demand, then "idled away the remaining months, lost my habits of study, and contracted associations with the lazy wits of the upper classes." As a result, though he read the classics privately, wrote for the newspaper, and established a reputation as an outstanding public speaker, he graduated "without honor and without much profit."

At twenty, back in Philadelphia, he joined a law firm as an apprentice. The following year, from his mother's family, he inherited property in upstate New York. He visited the estate and then sold it, although later he wondered whether he should not have kept a rugged field or two as a memorial. "But I was very, very poor," he explained, "very, very much in love—and perhaps, a very, very little in debt. If I thought of family, it was as future, not as past."

In 1817, with a year to go before he could seek admission to the bar, John Kintzing Kane grew worried. "I was desperately in love," he later explained, "and I knew that till I had a profession I had no hope in that quarter; while a train of suitors, whiskered and epauletted, lengthening out it seemed to me like the revolving series of Banquo's issue on the stage, was striving to anticipate me." He resolved to take the bar admission examination one year early. And so, after working all day in a law office, he would go home and study for six hours.

As examination time approached, young Kane got wind that a well-prepared candidate had recently appeared before the three-person committee and failed to gain acceptance. He sought out his fellow aspirant, gleaned that he had been undone by a single complex question about "the law of distress," and applied himself to mastering that specialty. When the cruelly demanding examiner asked that same question, Kane wrote later, "I gathered myself up, and after a modest preface, gave him an answer that lasted forty minutes. . . . It closed the examination: he had no more questions."

Within a couple of weeks, John Kintzing Kane "kissed the book as a lawyer and paid my dollar to the tipstaff." Almost immediately, he went to court to defend "a Negro well known as a chicken stealer" who had been caught filching strings of half-dried herrings—and lost the case. He proved no more successful in the next cause he pleaded. For the past several years,

*As a young lawyer, John Kane courted and
married the Philadelphia beauty Jane Leiper.*

ever since he was sixteen, John Kane had been pining after Jane Duval
Leiper, a renowned beauty one year younger than himself.

Jane was the musical sister of a friend, and one of the daughters of
Thomas Leiper (1745–1825), a Revolutionary War hero who inspired
extravagant stories, according to one of his grandsons, "of bringing wagon
after wagon through the British lines to Valley Forge disguised as a Quaker."
A Scottish immigrant and a friend of Thomas Jefferson, Leiper amassed a
fortune as a businessman, first by manufacturing tobacco and snuff, then
by building flour mills and stone quarries on an estate eighteen miles west
of Philadelphia. Over the years, he served as a director of the Bank of
Pennsylvania and the Bank of the United States, as president of the common council of Philadelphia, and, without remuneration, as head of the
Democratic Party in Pennsylvania. But he was best known for creating a
"pioneer railway" that used cast-iron wheels and wooden rails. From around
1809, this horse-drawn tramway carried piles of stone three-quarters of a
mile from his quarry on Crum Creek to a dock on Ridley Creek.

At age forty, Leiper built a summer residence on his 800-acre property. John Kintzing Kane would describe visiting this home on April 15, 1817, when he "hired a bald-faced mare of Mrs. Engle at [the nearby town of] Chester, rode out to the Mills, and rode back again with my walking ticket in my pocket." The beauteous Jane Leiper, as mindful of the proprieties as any middle-class British woman, had declined his proposal.

Back in Philadelphia, qualified now to practice law, twenty-two-year-old John Kane rented an office, "got a huge book case and clumsy table built by my father's carpenter . . . bought eight chairs, second-hand ones, at a furniture warehouse, and with sundry books that I had picked up at auction, hung out my sign as an attorney at law."

That autumn, the young lawyer went again to the country house of the Leipers, this time to serve as best man at the wedding of his friend, James Leiper: "I had tried to get off from an old promise that I would do so; but he insisted, and I went down to the Mills to help him through his catastrophe." After the wedding, with numerous other guests, Kane stayed on overnight. The next day, while running in a footrace, he "had the good luck to break [his] head by a fall, and to be carried into the house, bleeding and senseless, before the ladies."

A normally obtuse friend "found out before I was roused from my stupor that Miss Jane had mistaken her feelings when she rejected me. I imagined a similar discovery myself, as we rode up to town, when I was well enough to share a seat with her in Mr. Leiper's carriage." On April 20, 1819, after an engagement that lasted a year, the young couple married.

A dozen years before, a home-builder of artistic taste, William Sansom, had bought a block of property on the north side of downtown Walnut Street between Seventh and Eighth streets. Here, influenced by the latest British fashion, he built a block-long row of houses, Sansom's Union Row, so distinctive that the style came to be known in the U.S. as "Philadelphia rows." The newly married couple acquired one of these houses on Walnut near Eighth.

Decades later, in his autobiography, John Kane would interrupt the narrative to address his wife: "We were very happy, Jeanie, when we found

Thomas Leiper House, in Delaware County west of Philadelphia, contains a room devoted to the memory of Elisha Kent Kane. The explorer's grandfather, Thomas Leiper, built the mansion in 1785 as a summer residence. Nearby, he created a "pioneer railway" to carry stone from his quarry. As a boy and a young man, Kane visited frequently.

ourselves in our snug, plainly furnished house in Sansom's Row, with our one woman-servant. There was no hopeful future before us; the present was enough. My nice little office in the front room, with the open Franklin stove, and your parlour back, with the piano, how we divided our time between them. I studied then as I have never studied since, and you played and sang for me by the hour every evening. Do you remember our first purchase, the breakfast table, at the auction in Fourth Street? Such a bargain it was, and so beautiful with its scrolled legs,—and the extravagance you reproached me with, when I bought the looking glass to hang above it!"

o   o   o

During the 1820s and '30s, the ferociously active John K. Kane became increasingly prominent in many spheres. He lectured on Shakespeare at the Athenian Institute, founded the Musical Fund Society, became master of a lodge of Freemasons (Franklin Lodge #134, Philadelphia), and served as secretary of the American Philosophical Society. In 1828, the sharp-eyed Kane made a crucial career move: he joined the Democrats, a party controlled locally by his late father-in-law until his death three years before.

As a lawyer, John Kane assisted Nicholas Biddle, easily the wealthiest, most powerful man in Philadelphia, in completing both a railroad (the Sunbury and Erie) and the Chesapeake and Delaware Canal. He was also elected to the legislature as a Federalist in that party's dying days, when most partisans "would have begged as creditably for a pair of breeches as for a nomination or a vote."

Now, as old party lines disintegrated, Kane supported the Democrat Andrew Jackson for president. Applying his well-honed ability to communicate, he wrote a pamphlet—*A Candid View of the Presidential Election*—so persuasive that it helped the Democrats win a major victory. Rewarded under the emerging spoils system, Kane became city solicitor to Philadelphia mayor George M. Dallas. His political acumen and powerful connections would resonate through the life of his son Elisha.

In the early 1830s, President Jackson—known as Old Hickory for his supposed toughness—brought John Kane to Washington to negotiate a "convention of indemnity" with France. In 1838, though not an elected politician, Kane stepped forward to lead the Democrats during the so-called Buckshot War, a political dispute that culminated in the calling out of the militia to protect the legislature against rioters. At that juncture, he inspired his allies by reading aloud, no fewer than three times, a letter sent to him in Washington by his wife. "They tell me that our house is threatened," she wrote, "that you are upturning Society, and are not far from treason; I thank God, I have a husband and a brother [William Leiper was also there] whose patriotism does not startle at words."

She also had a son old enough, at eighteen, to applaud his mother's example.

To Die in Harness

Elisha Kent Kane was the first-born son of this striving, prominent family—a reality that would prove both a blessing and a curse. Born in the Walnut Street home on February 3, 1820, he would become one of the best-traveled men of his times. He would roam the world from Brazil to China and Africa, and from Mexico to the Arctic Circle. Yet, in crucial ways, he would never leave the city in which he was born. Never would he sever the ties that bound him to his family, especially to his mother.

Evidence abounds in the archives of the American Philosophical Society in Philadelphia. The earliest exhibit would appear to be a lock of hair taken from the child, obviously by his mother, when he was two years old, and preserved under glass in a metal medallion. Chestnut in color, remarkably fine and curly, it looks as if it had been snipped only yesterday.

In 1826, Jane Leiper Kane kept a letter Elisha wrote home from boarding school, mentioning his brother Thomas, two years younger. "My dear mother," he wrote. "I hope you are well. How is Father? I am much pleased with the things which you sent me, and divided them with the boys. I am learning geography, writing, reading and arithmetic. . . . Thomas is very well and sends much love to you, Father and little brother. We have recess ten minutes in the morning and afternoon. . . . We have been weighed. Tom weighed 33 and I 34 pounds."

The boy's mother also preserved one of Elisha's notebooks from this period. It includes Latin exercises, a hard-to-read narrative entitled *Caesar,* and a charming pen-and-ink sketch of two soldiers fighting with swords, one of them driven onto his back, the other striking a lethal blow.

Late in 1824, when Elisha was four, his mother was chosen to open a costume ball in honor of the visiting Marquis de Lafayette—an aging hero of the American Revolution who, touring the United States at the invitation of Congress, inspired parades and celebrations and awakened historical interest in the Pennsylvania State House, soon to be known as Independence Hall. At twenty-eight, twice a mother, Jane Leiper Kane remained a beauty. She dressed as Mary, Queen of Scots. She danced a stately quadrille with the marquis, and so impressed the artist Thomas Sully (who had studied with Gilbert Stuart) that he insisted on painting her in costume.

Years later, a son-in-law would add dimension to the portrait by describing Jane Leiper Kane as a courageous woman "distinguished for the energy, nerve, elasticity, and warm-heartedness which became famous in her son." Through the 1820s and '30s, she gave birth not only to Elisha, but to five more children who lived—four boys and a girl. The children were raised in a home that valued education, hard work, discipline, order, literature, music, public service, and reputation.

Growing up, Elisha Kane would spend several weeks each summer in "Leiperville," roaming the countryside with his cousins and other local children, learning to hunt and ride. Until the age of eight, he rode the horse-drawn tramway built by his late grandfather (who died in 1825); then, he sometimes floated along the canal that superseded the tramway. His uncle Samuel moved into his grandfather's summer home, but more often Elisha stayed at "Lapidea," the grander residence of his uncle George Gray Leiper, who was ten years older than Elisha's mother. There, he grew especially fond of his aunt Eliza.

Young Elisha proved imaginative, active, and daring, and both here and at home he led his brother Thomas in countless escapades—scaling fences, climbing trees, and once, after elaborating a complex plan, scaling a sixteen-foot chimney at night. At boarding school, Elisha developed a reputation as a "bad boy," though today we might apply the term "hyperactive." He was also brave and protective. On one occasion, when the master ordered young Thomas up for punishment, he sprang from his seat and cried: "Don't whip him, sir. He's such a little fellow—whip me." The master replied, "I'll whip you too, sir." And apparently made good on his threat.

These early scenes derive from an effusive biography by Dr. William Elder, a friend of John K. Kane who had access to materials since lost. According to Elder, between the ages of eight and thirteen Elisha "manifested no extraordinary love of learning." He did read voraciously, however—everything from *Robinson Crusoe* to *Pilgrim's Progress* and the *American Journal of Science*.

The boy filled cabinets with collections of minerals and exploded chemicals in a Leiperville outhouse. As he grew older, he devoured *Ivanhoe* by Sir Walter Scott, the *Leatherstocking Tales* of James Fenimore Cooper, and *Astoria* by Washington Irving, a narrative of exploration and adventure in the northwest. Elisha also read about Meriwether Lewis and William Clark, who had purchased tobacco from his grandfather for their overland expedition through the Rockies to the Pacific.

Despite his father's urgings, the furiously active boy shunned serious study until he reached sixteen, when he realized too late the practical value of a classical education. His lack of Greek and Latin prevented him from getting into Yale. So, in the autumn of 1837, influenced by his grandfather's example, he entered the University of Virginia at Charlottesville to study geology and civil engineering.

During the previous couple of years, Elisha had been repeatedly driven to bed by sickness. He and his family shrugged off these setbacks, never dreaming that they might be the first indications of rheumatic fever and heart disease. Illness dogged Elisha through his first year at university. Still, setting aside his natural gifts for art, music, and literature—according to one contemporary, "he could have beaten [Daniel Defoe] in his own line of writing"—Elisha excelled in chemistry, mineralogy, and mathematics.

He worked closely with Professor William Barton Rogers, an outstanding geologist who later became the first president of the Massachusetts Institute of Technology, but who was then mapping the geological formations of the Blue Ridge Mountains. With Rogers, Elisha studied not only geology, but mineralogy, geography, and chemistry. He also accompanied the young professor on several rugged outings into the mountains. But then, in the autumn of 1838, while residing in the dormitory—which was so smoky from the coal fires that he had to keep the windows open—he fell seriously ill with rheumatic fever.

After recovering back home in Philadelphia, he resumed his studies. The university granted him special permission to live with Robert Patterson, his first cousin, in a vacant library room that was smoke-free and better heated than the dormitory. To this young man—whose father, Dr. Robert M. Patterson, had until recently been a professor of natural philosophy at the university—Elisha confided that he was "determined to make his mark in the world." And, by June 1839, Patterson could write his mother that Elisha spent every evening working in the science laboratory, and "stands among the best in all his classes."

That autumn, however, Elisha suffered such a severe attack of illness that his father had to bring him home wrapped in a blanket, making the journey in short stages because of the pain in his inflamed joints. Specialist doctors diagnosed endocarditis, an inflammation of the lining and valves of the heart that often accompanies rheumatic fever. For several weeks, Elisha lay in bed, critically ill. Whenever he tried to sit up, he endured spasms of pain that left him gasping for breath. One worried doctor warned that an incautious movement could prove fatal: "You may fall, Elisha, as suddenly as from a musket shot."

Not surprisingly, the sensitive youth took this to heart. Although he slowly recovered, regaining the ability to sit up and then walk without pain, he became depressed and languished in bed. His exasperated father, not the most patient of men, urged him to get out of bed: "If you must die, Elisha, die in the harness."

This remark galvanized the young man. To die in the harness became his unspoken credo. Elisha Kane would suffer through one debilitating illness after another. At times, he would become depressed. But he refused to remain in that condition. Nor would he acknowledge any physical limitations. From one sick bed after another, often incredibly, he would arise to resume a whirlwind life.

o   o   o

At nineteen, Kane assessed his professional options. The physical demands of civil engineering, which might include scouting out bridge sites in mountainous terrain, now appeared problematic—as they certainly did to his father. After some discussion, the young man decided to study medicine. This would lead to a viable living, and would also help him understand his physical condition and enable him to govern himself accordingly.

Late in 1839, Kane apprenticed himself to a Philadelphia doctor, William Harris, who would later report that he "prosecuted his various studies with so much zeal that he made rapid progress." The following spring, he enrolled in medicine at the University of Pennsylvania and began attending lectures and clinical demonstrations and making rounds at local hospitals. In his second year, he served as a resident physician at Blockley, now the Philadelphia General Hospital, under Dr. William McPheeters, and for six months shared rooms with him. He kept records, dressed wounds, cupped and bled patients, and assisted in operations.

A male nurse at the lunatic asylum would later describe him as universally popular, while a female ward attendant declared him "the handsomest young man she ever saw. Such a beautiful complexion and slender figure. . . . He was very kind in his manner and had a very soft voice when he spoke and was always familiar and ready to come in and sit down in a friendly way, not proud and haughty like some."

During this period, Kane more than once had to be helped to his home in pain. McPheeters wrote later that the slim young man "was laboring under a serious organic affliction of the heart-dilatation with valvular disease, which gave rise to a very loud *bruit de soufflet* [blowing murmur], accompanied by the most tumultuous action of the heart from any violent exertion."

The doctor added that Kane could not sleep in a horizontal position, but had to elevate his head and shoulders almost to a right angle with his lower body. While aware of the gravity of his disease, McPheeters wrote, Kane did not allow it to check his enthusiasm. "I have always thought that the uncertain state of his health had a good deal to do with his subsequent course of life, and the almost reckless exposure of himself to danger."

More than a century later, another medical doctor would suggest that Kane's "symptoms were caused by paroxysmal atrial fibrillation, a transient irregularity of the heart beat often associated with stenosis [narrowing] of the mitral valve. No doubt the severe attack of rheumatic fever with endocarditis a year before had damaged Kane's heart valves and had affected the atrial musculature to some extent, but as yet not enough to limit his restless activity. The heart was still a good pump."

By March 1842, when he graduated as the top student in his class, Kane had distinguished himself by placing an article with the *American Journal of the Medical Sciences*—a groundbreaking essay based on original research into kiesteine, a substance found in the urine that can indicate pregnancy. He had embarked on a career as a medical man—or so it appeared.

4

INTO THE VOLCANO

At age twenty-two, Elisha Kane had no intention of becoming a practicing physician in Philadelphia. His interest in medicine had always been theoretical rather than practical, and as he felt no financial pressure, he did not attempt to establish a medical practice. Instead, he dreamed of a grander destiny. Kane had been reading reports of the United States Exploring Expedition to the South Pacific, recently returned after a four-year, 90,000-mile voyage of discovery involving six ships and 490 men, all commanded by American navy lieutenant Charles Wilkes. The naval officer had seen the world—Rio de Janeiro, Cape Horn, Samoa, Borneo—and he had tried to capture the experience in words: "You feel an exultation, you are a conqueror, you have made a conquest of Nature, you are going to add a new object or a new page to science."

Elisha Kent Kane decided to join the U.S. Navy. As a naval surgeon, he could practice his profession while seeing the world. Fearing that his medical history might present a problem with the navy board, he asked his father for help. Initially, the older man resisted, arguing that Elisha should remain near home for the sake of his health. But he recognized the logic of the proposal, as well as the burning desire in his son, and so he acquiesced.

John K. Kane wrote to Abel Upshar, secretary of the navy, asking that Elisha be granted a warrant of examination for appointment as a naval surgeon. Upshar, formerly a Virginia judge, responded quickly to the influential Democrat. He directed Elisha to report to the Philadelphia Navy Yard to be examined for a commission. The young man prepared diligently and duly presented himself. When the testing was done, and he learned that he had been passed for naval service, Elisha felt honor bound to mention that he suffered from chronic rheumatism and cardiac disturbance. The board declined to re-examine him.

The navy had no immediate openings for an assistant surgeon, however. Rather than wait passively in Philadelphia, where he would almost certainly come under parental pressure, Elisha departed without telling anyone for Leiperville, where he was always welcome at Lapidea, the estate of his uncle George and aunt Eliza. To his father, he wrote that he hoped to return home a new man after spending six months focusing on his health, "living the life of the body that I may hereafter live that of the mind."

For entertainment, he had the company of his sixteen-year-old cousin Mary Leiper, who admired him tremendously. He flourished with the physical activity. But that autumn, when he returned to Philadelphia, he again fell ill, though he managed to attend lectures at Jefferson Medical College. By January 1843, tired of waiting for a naval commission, and certain that he would benefit from an active life at sea, Kane requested leave from the navy to join a merchant vessel.

But now a far more exciting opportunity arose: the American government, responding to changing political conditions abroad, had decided to send a first diplomatic mission to China. In settling the Opium War (1837–42), China had reluctantly agreed to open its markets to Great Britain at half a dozen "treaty ports." Now, the Americans hoped to gain access to the capital, Peking. To impress the Chinese, they would dispatch a fleet of four 200-gun ships. Obviously, these vessels would require surgeons.

At the urgent request of his son, John K. Kane pulled the requisite strings. Through an intermediary, a well-known professor of medicine, Kane solicited Secretary of State Daniel Webster. Webster was happy to gratify the political heavyweight and to appoint the well-qualified young man to the mission on an "honorary," or non-salaried, basis. On May 24, 1843, Elisha Kent Kane sailed out of Norfolk, Virginia, on the frigate *Brandywine,* bound for the Far East.

His young cousin Mary Leiper, writing from Lapidea, became one of the first to articulate feelings that would arise, again and again, in those who, having come to know Elisha Kane, would then have to watch him leave: "How much I still miss you, more than ever since my return home, for the last time I was here . . . we were together and walked up the creek over the falls, little dreaming that it would be the last time. . . ." In closing, Mary added that every time she wrote farewell, "a pang shoots through my heart."

o   o   o

To take advantage of the prevailing trade winds and avoid the doldrums, the *Brandywine* followed a commercial trade route. The frigate crossed the Atlantic to the island of Madeira off the northwest coast of Africa, then doubled back to the southwest, putting in at Rio de Janeiro. In a long letter to his uncle George at Lapidea, Kane described the scenery as "wild and highly picturesque, the mountain ridges having an air of rugged grandeur which contrasted admirably with the quiet waters around them."

While in port, together with the other members of the legation, Kane attended both the theater—"imagine me seated in private box . . . and around me six tiers of gilded boxes, contained some two thousand souls in full court dress"—and an elaborate royal wedding reception. Unlike most, he took notes on both occasions. Under the tutelage of his father, who had edited his youthful essays, Kane had learned how to wield a pen. Rather than fritter away this travel opportunity, and having concluded that Americans were eager to read stories of travel to exotic lands, the young man intended to write a book about his wanderings—and, not incidentally, to have as many adventures as possible. While docked in Rio, he explored the nearby eastern Andes mountains and filled a notebook with descriptions and sketches.

After leaving South America, the *Brandywine* rounded southern Africa and proceeded to Bombay. During this long voyage, which included "a true initiatory gale," Kane suffered from seasickness—a condition that would plague him every time he sailed. He hired a young midshipman to care for him, and mentored that youth, who would later become a doctor, in the rudiments of medicine. Meanwhile, he applied himself to studying geometry, algebra, navigation, and European languages. Fellow voyager Fletcher Webster, eldest son of Daniel Webster and secretary to the legation, would later describe Kane as "evidently annoyed when not engaged in something, and always restless unless busy—for hours in the stateroom buried in mathematics, and then next seen at the masthead or over the ship's side."

On October 25, 1843, the *Brandywine* reached Bombay, where the legation leader, statesman Caleb Cushing, was expected to come aboard. Cushing had been delayed in Gibraltar by the burning of a ship, however, and would not arrive for another month. Kane used the time to visit the nearby mountains, the Western Ghats, and the sculptured caves at Elephanta. And he followed this with an extraordinary 200-mile journey, traveling by palanquin to Ellora, crossing the mountains at Kandalah, and investigating the little-known caverns at Karli.

Kane then sailed to Ceylon, that lush island (now Sri Lanka) off the south coast of India. From the port city of Colombo, he traveled inland sixty miles to Kandy and joined in an elephant hunt. Here, according to a friend, "he picknicked in the summer palace among the hills, took his nooning under the taliput palms, and waked to the wild hazards of the chase."

On December 9, Kane rejoined the *Brandywine* when it called at Colombo with Caleb Cushing aboard. At last, on February 27, 1844, the legation reached Macao, a tiny island situated in the Bay of Canton and controlled by the Portuguese. The Chinese had agreed to discuss trade, but only under duress. They would not allow the Americans to set foot on their soil, and would negotiate only in Macao.

The island proved too small to interest Kane for long. His friend Fletcher Webster noted that the young doctor had "explored the whole town itself before we, of slower motions, had commenced," adding that he went alone on "excursions attended with a good deal of personal danger." Kane had no role in negotiations, and an eminent physician and medical missionary who had lived in the area for several years, Dr. Peter Parker, had joined the legation as an interpreter.

Kane ranged more widely, visiting Hong Kong and Canton, filling notebooks as he went. When he learned that the navy had ordered the *Brandywine* to sail to Manila on business, he obtained leave from Cushing to explore the Philippine Islands, then a little-known Spanish colony. Before leaving America, Kane had acquired letters from a variety of religious figures—Catholic bishops, the papal consuls of Spain, Portugal, and France, and sundry Presbyterians, Lutherans, and Moravians. After arriving in Manila on March 17, he used some of these references to gain acceptance as a scientist, and so extend his range of travel.

Manila, a bustling town of 140,000, served as a base from which to explore Luzon, the largest of the Philippine islands at about 40,400 square miles—roughly the size of Kentucky. Accompanied by a young German aristocrat, Baron Diedrich von Loe, Kane traveled 200 miles across the mountainous island to its Pacific coast and bathed in the forbidden waters of a thermal lake. He devoted careful attention to this volcanic region, Albay, intending to compare it, in his projected book, with parts of Sumatra.

Back in Manila, Kane learned of an active volcano forty miles away, at Lake Taal. From the surface of this enormous lake—ninety miles in circumference, ten miles across—the volcano soared a thousand feet into the sky. It had erupted three times in the last century, and again in 1808, just thirty-six years before. Only one adventurer had ever tried to descend into its mouth, and he had been forced to retreat.

To Elisha Kane, age twenty-four, the challenge proved irresistible. With Baron Loe, he journeyed through the bush to Lake Taal. He located a religious hermitage on the shore of the lake and convinced the worried monks to help him secure Tagalog-speaking guides. Kane, Loe, and half a dozen men eventually paddled out to the volcanic island, then climbed the increasingly steep slope to the open mouth. "Crawling upon our hands and knees," he would write, "the lava within six inches of our noses, suddenly our heads jutted up above the crest of the volcano, and the magnificence of the crater, literally a *coup d'oeil,* burst upon us."

One hundred feet below, spires of rock-hard lava protruded from a steamy, bubbling green lake. The volcano stank of sulfur. To Loe's dismay, Kane announced that he intended to descend into the crater to collect a sample of the water on the scientific pretext of ascertaining its sulfur content. The native guides, who viewed the volcano as sacred, protested. Kane tried and failed to reassure them, but carried on anyway, leading the heavy-set Loe in scrambling about twenty feet down the slope. The two men reached a ledge from which they could descend no farther without ropes or ladders. They clambered back to the top of the crater. Loe was ready to abandon the experiment, but Kane had a book to write, and this adventure had the makings of a climactic chapter.

He conceived the idea of making ropes out of the liana vines that grew everywhere here, so that the other men could lower him into the volcano. At this, even the adventurous Loe balked. Kane remained resolute, and agreed to write a note—which still exists today—absolving his friend of responsibility. He addressed it to his father, indicating that he wrote on April 14, 1844, at the Crater of Taal, Batangas: "Being about to descend into the Crater for the first time since its great alteration, I would exempt my friends from all participation in my attempt, and I beg that this may be forwarded to my friends at home."

Having woven a long rope, Kane instructed the agitated guides to dig holes in which to brace their feet as they lowered him into the volcano. Soon after he went over the side and began his descent, several of them dropped the rope and moved to abandon their stations. In a handwritten draft that survives, Kane describes how Baron Loe grabbed a pistol and waved it around, "and after an interesting jumble of Tagolog & Spanish succeeded in conveying the conviction that any man who spoke, or laughed, or changed his betel nut, or quit his hole, was to be instantly shot through the head."

The rope held, but proved too short. When he reached the ashy slope at the foot of the cliff, the young daredevil had to untie himself to reach the cauldron. He managed to dip a specimen bottle into the water, but then, as he scrambled back to the dangling rope, he slipped repeatedly in the scalding ash. The heat charred his boots so badly that one fell to pieces as he churned upward. A shifting wind wafted hot gas over him.

Perceiving that Kane had run into trouble, Loe ordered one of the guides, the light, muscular Isedro, into the volcano on a second rope. When Kane finally reached the first rope, nearly overcome by the sulfurous steam, Isedro helped to secure it around his waist. By the time he reached the surface, still clinging to his specimen bottle, Kane was almost senseless. The frightened Loe revived him by splashing water into his face.

While paddling back to the mainland, the guides grumbled menacingly. By descending into the volcano, Kane had committed sacrilege. An angry god had almost killed him. On reaching the shore, some of the guides disappeared into the bush. Before long, Kane and Loe found themselves surrounded by an angry, spear-wielding mob. Retreating into a thicket, they fired their pistols and threw up enough dust to keep their tormentors away. At the sound of gunshots, the monks came running. Speaking in Tagalog, they managed to pacify the locals, enabling the visitors to escape without further incident.

5

THE ROMANCE OF EGYPT

Back in Manila, Kane received a letter from his father assuring him that funds were available to maintain him through the Cushing mission—but that afterward he was to come home to Philadelphia: "No outer Island, no South American project, but home, home to us, and to such welcome as no man has a right to think coldly of." To this missive, his brother Thomas had added a few paragraphs of a different tenor. Elisha had enlisted this closest sibling to serve as editor and publicist for his projected travel book, and now Tom scolded him for having denied himself some crucial escapade: "Damn your 'resisting temptation'—damn and double damn your having lived so cheaply."

Specifics are lacking, but in Manila—far from the watchful eyes not only of his extended family, but even of the American legation—Kane had lived voraciously. Soon after he arrived back in Macao, in mid-May, he received a letter from Baron Loe: "Since you left me . . . I go on drinking gin and water from morning till evening and smoking again from twilight till dawning." Loe reminisced about a time when he and Elisha had been briefly imprisoned—an incident otherwise lost—and regretted his friend's absence during a recent escapade involving a fine "collection of Tuchan and

Mestizo women" that, however, had not been "equal to what we have seen on our trips."

In Macao, negotiations between the Americans and the Chinese were winding down. On June 24 and 25, Kane attended a final official dinner and then a dance. Bent on practicing his literary skills, and working actively to hone his style, he later produced a 10,000-word epistle detailing the pomp and ceremony of these festivities. In this communication, which clearly he intended to rework for his book, Kane showed off his writer's eye while touching on everything from Chinese costume and architecture to manners and political tactics.

He described the Chinese commissioner, Li-Kying, as "a man above the medium height, stout rather than corpulent, with an easy walk. . . . His face [wore] a rather sleepy expression; and yet the smile, though nearly sneering, was animated and expressive." He devoted much attention to the Chinese custom of drinking health, and after Cushing offered a well-expressed remark that the Chinese did not understand, "we toasted the Emperor of China, hip-hipped him, hurraed him, hiccupped him, and withdrew."

The following day, at Cushing's behest, Kane found thirteen American women around Macao and produced them for a final dinner and dance— though to no avail. The Americans were denied their fond wish of visiting the imperial palace "and seeing the Majesty of the Celestials in his own proper person." Kane remained unperturbed: "Two hours after [these festivities], I was in a chartered boat, armed to the teeth, and threading the ladrone dangers of the Canton River. I was a freed man."

Kane traveled upriver to Whampoa Reach (present-day Huang-Pu), a bustling harbor. He had no intention of returning home, as instructed by his father, but instead teamed up with a young British surgeon, Michael O'Sullivan, to run a hospital boat serving the crews of foreign vessels. The two put a notice in an English-language newspaper—"For the greater convenience of Vessels lying in the Whampoa and Blenheim reaches, the Hospital vessel is moored off the Bombay Creek"—and soon had more business than they could handle.

Thomas Leiper Kane, Elisha's nearest sibling, became a leading abolitionist and also assisted Mormons fleeing persecution. This likeness derives from the 1860s, when Thomas fought in the American Civil War.

Around this time, Kane wrote an exuberant letter home. During the past few months, he had earned nearly $3,000—the equivalent today of $80,000. Soon he would resume traveling—visiting new lands, meeting new peoples, pushing back the boundaries of knowledge. He invited his brother Thomas to join him in this adventure. From Philadelphia, Tom felt obliged to decline this "romantic" proposition. As the second oldest son, he had shouldered "the duty, which alone keeps me here, of taking care that Bess & Pat & John get in good society—of which without something being done there is at present no chance." A few days later, on December 9, 1844, in response to another effusive missive, Tom added, "I can see damned plain now that you have been freed from our cramping [and] are rebelling."

By the time he received this communication, however, Elisha had fallen seriously ill with "rice fever"—probably cholera. A Mr. Ritchie took the young doctor into his home in Canton. In a surviving fragment of journal or letter, Kane poured out his disappointment. Having at last "assumed the self-sustaining duties of a man," he had been improving in his profession, gaining in experience, and "looking forward with almost childlike delight to what? To day dreams. To publications which would advance my reputation and gladden dear father's heart. To collections which would secure me consideration at home. To a little fortune which if not a competence would at least show my capacity to *acquire* . . ."

Illness had struck him down: "I was delirious—for three weeks my life was despaired of, and when at last I awoke from the stupefaction of a frightful fever it was to feel, not that disease had crushed my energies, nor sickness broken down the pride of manhood, but that both were useless—Nature's frail instrument the carcass had broken down. My well-founded hopes were thus rendered completely visionary."

There was nothing left to do apparently, but to settle his affairs and sail for home.

o o o

Elisha Kane frequently fell victim to debilitating illness. Yet he showed an extraordinary resilience, rebounding again and again and again, regaining his sense of adventure each time he recovered his health. On this occasion, details are lacking. But what started as an ignominious trip home became a seven-month odyssey that began on January 25, 1845, when Kane sailed from Macao to Singapore. From there, he called in at Borneo and Sumatra before reaching Galle, in southern Ceylon, on February 19. He proceeded up the east coast of India to Madras. While in the subcontinent, he met a wealthy nobleman, Dwarkanath Tagore, who was leaving for England to visit the court of Queen Victoria. Tagore, whose grandson Rabindranath Tagore would become a world-famous poet, invited Kane to join his entourage.

With Tagore, after spending three weeks in India, Kane traveled by steamer to Egypt, arriving in Suez on April 3. He crossed the isthmus by rail to Alexandria, and here, having secured a glowing reference letter from Tagore, he struck out alone. Instead of continuing on to England in comfort, and then heading straight home, he decided to visit Cairo, to see the pyramids and then take a boat trip up the Nile River—a journey that, a dozen years previously, had been undertaken by Jane Franklin, a woman who would loom large in his future.

Now, in April 1845, while Lady Franklin helped her husband, Sir John, prepare to sail from England on an ill-fated Arctic expedition, the twenty-five-year-old Kane secured memberships in the Egyptian Society of Cairo and the Egyptian Literary Association. Like Jane Franklin before him—and thanks to Tagore—Kane had obtained from Pasha Mohamed Ali a safe-conduct to travel around Egypt. Scholars had only recently discovered and begun excavating the ruins of ancient Egypt, and the first traveler's guide to the area, Sir John Gardner Wilkinson's *Hand-book for travellers in Egypt,* would not appear for two years. Yet on April 15, the pioneering Kane hired a boat and a pilot and started up the Nile.

At Dendera came a first mishap. Intending to inspect the ruins at Tentyrus, six miles away, Kane went ashore to sleep, taking only a small bag and a few necessities for the hike. When he awoke the next morning, the boat was gone—along with his journals and collections. He discovered the craft two miles downstream, stuck on a sandbar, half-full of water but empty of contents. At first, although shaken, he believed this to be an accident—that the current had tilted the boat and swept away his possessions.

He wrote home that he felt heartsick and depressed. At least he had already sent his best clothes and his diplomas on to England. But gone were his papers, and "even Dr. Morton's skulls have sunk in the quicksands." Kane especially regretted the loss of his watch: "Remaining are dear mother's battered writing desk, containing my business correspondence and my money, my legation sword, valued for old associations, and a carpet-bag of shirts. No jackets, no boots, and no pantaloons."

He continued upriver. A few days later, while going ashore, he spotted his watch chain hanging round the neck of his interpreter. After a tussle, he retrieved both the chain and his watch, though the thief escaped. On May 2, having reached Thebes, Kane set up camp in the temple of Sesostris. To his father he wrote outlining his extensive reading on the antiquities and noting that he had crossed the river to visit the Egyptologist Richard Lepsius: "I met him, seated cross-legged in the great temple of Karnak, supping coffee and copying hieroglyphics." Kane reported that Lepsius had recently become an honorary member of the American Philosophical Society, and that he recognized the surname of the society's recording secretary: "It required a very tolerable strain of my tolerably plastic countenance to sustain myself in the scientific position which, by reflection or inheritance, I was supposed to occupy."

Reveling in the romance of Egypt, Kane described how, while drinking coffee in the temple of Sesostris, he "would scribble notes to my Karnak friend on the other side of the river, or pay running visits to a couple of Germans who lodged up the hill in an excavated tomb. My Thebes life is a very wild one; I am in native dress, with a beard so long that I have to tuck it in. My lodging is on the hot ground, and I walk on an average twenty-six miles a day."

From Thebes, over several weeks, Kane explored Luxor, Abydos, Saqqara, Serapeum, Masara, and the Valley of the Kings. A statue of Pharaoh Amenhotep III, seventy feet tall and known as the "Vocal Memnon," excited him enough to perform a characteristic stunt. Between the knees of the seated pharaoh hung a tablet, ten inches thick, printed with hieroglyphics legible from above. The underside of this tablet, thirty-three feet above ground, could not be seen from below. Surmising that this underside might also contain hieroglyphics, a hidden message, Kane insisted on finding out.

Waving aside protests, he stripped to his "pantaloons," braced his back against one stone calf of the statue and his feet against the other, and wriggled slowly upward. He got high enough to see that the underside of the tablet contained no inscription, but then found himself stranded, fully extended, unable to move up or down. His boatman went running for a local guide, who climbed the statue from the more accessible back side. The man made his way down onto the tablet, then swung his sash over the edge and hauled the adventurer to safety.

Kane began his return to Cairo by sending his boat downriver 125 miles to Girga. He hired two camels and a guide and went to visit the tomb of Osiris, an overland journey requiring three days and two nights. During this trek, he fended off an attack by Bedouin thieves, receiving a knife wound in the thigh. He rejoined his boat and carried on beyond Cairo to Alexandria, where a surgeon treated his wound. Soon afterward, probably as a result of infection, Kane again fell ill—so seriously that he suspected bubonic plague. While he lay feverish, near death, his collection of antiquities disappeared, including "two royal ovals in colors as fresh as my Chinese miniatures."

o o o

After two months in Egypt, almost fully recovered, Kane sailed for Greece. On June 10, he wrote his parents from Athens—and then, accompanied by a young British army lieutenant, set out on a walking tour of Greece. He visited Eleusis, Thebes, and Livadia, and felt well enough to climb the 5,000-foot Mount Helicon, where he cut a walking stick for his father. He visited Thermopylae and the Gulf of Corinth, traversed the Peloponnese peninsula and took a steamer from Patras to Trieste. He then traveled through Italy and Switzerland, devoting considerable attention to the geology of the Alps.

With his funds running low, Kane contemplated returning to the Philippines to work as a surgeon, and so finance further travels. From Paris, on July 13, he wrote his father asking him to have Washington Irving, then the American minister to Spain, seek permission for him to write his surgeon's examination in Manila instead of Madrid. This project came to naught. After briefly touring France, the traveler proceeded to London and, from there, booked passage for home.

6

CRIME & PUNISHMENT

During the early decades of the nineteenth century, Philadelphia became America's first major industrial city. Its location at the confluence of two rivers, the Schuylkill and the Delaware, provided ready access to steam power. By 1840, Philadelphia was producing more steam engines than any other city, with manufacturers servicing twenty-five types of mills that in turn generated everything from flour and carpets to beer and iron products. Turnpikes, bridges, and steamboats carried raw materials from the interior, creating jobs and attracting immigrants. During the 1840s, according to *Philadelphia: A 300-Year History,* the population of the city proper grew by 30 percent, from 94,000 to 121,000.

Inevitably, rapid growth and a changing economy created social problems. As living conditions deteriorated, workers occasionally began to strike, and racial tensions increased. During the 1830s, the vast majority of Philadelphians had opposed abolition; yet the city had also given rise to both the American Anti-Slavery Society and the Pennsylvania Anti-Slavery Society. In 1838 and 1842, abolitionist meetings and marches had drawn a fierce reaction, with anti-black rioters torching halls, recreation centers, and even a church. Before long, the issue of slavery would divide families, including the Kanes.

But for now, though some upper-echelon Philadelphians began moving to outlying regions, most remained insulated from the violence. Certainly, John Kintzing Kane continued to thrive. At one point, Andrew Jackson recommended him to the newly elected president, James Polk, for a cabinet position. This yielded nothing, probably as a result of politicking by rivals. Instead, in 1845, the state governor appointed John Kane attorney general of Pennsylvania.

The previous year, anti-Catholic riots and burnings had erupted in a predominantly Irish ward of the city, and according to a profile in *Lives of Eminent Philadelphians,* the attorney general would earn "an odium upon which he prided himself" by seeking to punish those responsible. John Kane was engaged in this when his eldest son arrived home from his travels.

Five years before, to accommodate their growing family, the Kanes had moved from Walnut Street into a large home centrally located at the corner of Seventh and Locust streets. Now, in 1845, Jane Leiper Kane presided over a household that included several servants and five offspring ranging in age from twenty-three (Thomas) to seven (Little Willie). Elisha had always enjoyed an especially close relationship with his mother, and on August 6, she welcomed him home joyously.

Over the past two and a half years, Elisha had traveled nearly 40,000 miles, sailing the Atlantic, Pacific, and Indian oceans, and cruising the Mediterranean, Red, and Adriatic seas. He had set foot on five continents and explored three of them. In the autumn of 1845, having arrived home in Philadelphia, he set up an office in the family's Walnut Street house and began practicing medicine.

He translated a French medical text into English, kept an eye out for more such projects, and started writing a book about his travels. With his parents, he discussed resigning from the navy, which had yet to call him to active duty. He hesitated because the United States had been at loggerheads with Mexico in recent years, ever since Texas had declared independence, and war now appeared imminent. For a naval surgeon, war might provide a theater for heroic action—and, like many men in their mid-twenties, Kane yearned to show his mettle.

The young man did not, however, aspire to sainthood. With his family, he regularly attended the Second Presbyterian Church. But by night he frequented disreputable "singing taverns," and even had a favorite called Drigo's. Wealthy and well educated, the scion of a powerful family, Kane would have been one of the most eligible bachelors in Pennsylvania even had he been ugly, morose, and obtuse. But he was accomplished, entertaining, and strikingly handsome, and he had not been home a month when he was writing to a male friend in Paris, "Do not forget [to send] my gossamer envelopes for the *pistolet d'amour*—for already I need their protecting influence."

Kane had enjoyed certain preliminary sexual intimacies with Helen Patterson, the sister of his old college roommate. She had put an end to this foolery, and later became a close friend—though not before Elisha wrote her a melodramatic, late-night letter insisting that he loved her, "and after what has passed [between us] why should I doubt but that you love me. . . . Do you not think, in recalling dear old times, that while you have yielded much, you have withheld more. . . . Do you not . . . reproach yourself sometimes in your heart of hearts for not having enjoyed less sparingly the bountiful cup of whose pleasures we barely sipped?"

At around this time, Kane began a more complete sexual relationship with a young woman named Julia Reed, one that would have far greater consequences. He probably met Julia at Drigo's. Certainly she came from farther down the social scale. And clearly, he took fewer precautions than he should have, because Julia Reed became pregnant.

Elisha did not love this young woman and did not intend to marry her. If the pregnancy became public knowledge, however, the scandal would ruin Julia Reed and damage the reputation of the Kane family. Elisha urged Julia to have the child and offer it up for adoption. With a close friend, John Taylor Jr., he exchanged letters about possibly installing the pregnant young woman in Virginia. On February 4, 1846, Taylor responded: "I think there

can be no doubt that our young Lady may find a pleasant place of temporary abode in Harrisburg, Port Royal, or in the country, at a point interme-
diate between these two. Four miles above me, there is a quiet, orderly and
for their station in life, a genteel family, who would take an unfortunate
young Lady."

When Julia Reed declined to leave Philadelphia, Elisha entrusted her to
a reputable physician, C.C. Van Wyck, and undertook to cover all medical
expenses. He prepared a document in which he undertook "to provide for
the said infant such sustenance and education as will best ensure its physical
and moral well being . . . [and to act in all other respects] as a kind and faithful parent or guardian should do." He agonized until Van Wyck wrote to
him: "Do not annoy or distress yourself about final results. You have done as
much as & more than could be asked of any individual in a like fix."

That Elisha Kane now confessed his situation to his father is possible but
not likely. The older man probably learned the truth from Elisha's eighteen-
year-old brother, Patterson. But that the attorney general found out about
Julia Reed is demonstrated by what happened next. In March 1846, John
K. Kane wrote to the secretary of the navy, George Bancroft. He requested
an appointment for his eldest son, and wondered whether Elisha's service
with the diplomatic mission to China could be counted toward the two-year
period required before an assistant surgeon was examined for promotion.
Bancroft replied that it could not. Instead, he offered Elisha an appointment
on the frigate *United States,* the flagship of a squadron about to sail for West
Africa to suppress the illegal slave trade.

Elisha had been yearning to transfer to the army in hopes of serving in
the looming war with Mexico. Border disputes stemming from the Texas
War of Independence of the previous decade and the increasing popularity
of Manifest Destiny—the doctrine that America had a god-given right to
expand from sea to shining sea—made conflict inevitable. That Kane did
not reject the navy's offer, resign his commission, and begin the process of
enlisting points clearly to the intervention of his father. For John K. Kane,
the spring of 1846 was no time for a scandal. President James Polk was

about to appoint him the district court judge of eastern Pennsylvania, an influential position from which he could not easily be removed—and in which, indeed, he would revel for the rest of his professional life.

In May 1846, when Congress declared war on Mexico and ambitious young men flocked to join the army—Philadelphia alone would produce thirty volunteer companies—Elisha Kane found himself embarking on an inconsequential voyage to West Africa. Although acutely aware that he had only himself to blame, Elisha felt "bitterly bitter" about this turn of events; yet he undertook to follow what his father had decreed to be the only acceptable course.

In Philadelphia, after a difficult labor, Julia Reed gave birth to a girl. Elisha learned the news—and received the final bill for medical expenses—while sailing off the coast of Africa. He left no record of his reaction. Julia may or may not have given up the child for adoption: no evidence exists either way. And she herself disappeared from the historical record without a trace.

7

Heart of Darkness

K ane's frigate, the *United States,* had been assigned to patrol the 1,200-mile "slave coast" of West Africa, which extended between Sierra Leone and Dahomey (now Benin). To the uninitiated, the itinerary sounded romantic—Cape Verde Islands, Principe Island, Monrovia, Accra—but the cruising proved hot and monotonous, and Elisha suffered, as usual, from seasickness. Naval regulations required Kane, as assistant surgeon, to inspect "the provisions, liquors, and water, which may be served out, and report the same to the commander, when unsound." He was also to "make known any want of care or cleanliness in the preparation of the food for the crew; or any instance of improper clothing, or personal neglect . . . in short, everything . . . conflicting against the comfort and health of the ship's company."

The young man battled boredom by honing his writing style in long letters home. In a July missive to his mother, Kane devoted seven pages to describing Porto Praya by moonlight, when "every ripple of its dark bay becomes a crescent spangle and its shoreline is haloed with the white glories of the surf. Its scanty palm trees cut against the sky, and whether they be palm trees or pitch forks, perform their only object in a black foreground which enables you to slur over the town to the soft shadows of the mountains which lie beyond it."

To a doctor friend in Philadelphia, Kane wrote more succinctly, and in a different mood entirely, that "of all the miserable blanks in one's existence the most miserable is an African cruise." On December 8, as a junior officer, Kane was compelled to attend the court martial of a seaman who had left a working gang at the customs house at Porto Praya. When the master-at-arms sent for him, according to documents Kane saved, the man refused to return. Captured and brought to one of the boats of the frigate, he tried to escape. This seaman was also charged with drawing a knife and stabbing a boatswain in his hand. Asked if he was guilty, the sailor "did plainly and explicitly answer 'guilty.'"

The court, "after due and proper deliberation, were of opinion that the offence of the prisoner should be punished by a number of lashes, not exceeding, nor less than, seventy two; to be inflicted upon the bare back of the prisoner, the said James Gorman, at such time and place as the commander of the squadron shall determine." Even a dozen lashes, administered to the bare back of a spread-eagled sailor, had been known to reduce powerful men to blubbering like children. Seventy-two lashes would be an emasculating, degrading procedure that, in the words of one eyewitness from this period, would turn a man's back into "a mangled piece of flesh, from which the blood ran in such quantities as to fill his shoes till they gushed over."

Compelled to watch this horror, Elisha Kane developed a loathing for naval regulations that would never leave him, and would later influence crucial decisions. His brother Thomas would trace this back to their grandfather Thomas Leiper, the Revolutionary War hero who "had all the aversion of my brother, Dr. Kane, to the infliction of unnecessary personal violence." Now, Kane felt sufficiently disturbed that he filed away sixteen pages of notes on the incident—though in his surviving letters home, he wrote not a word about the crime or its punishment.

Yet such were his immediate circumstances: brutal, bloody, and barbaric. In this context, the impact of affectionate letters from home can only be imagined. On December 24, 1846, a couple of weeks after he witnessed the flogging, his mother had written: "My dear Elisha: It is ten o'clock on Christmas night and I have my heart so full of you I feel as if scribbling to you would relieve me of some part of the burden." His mother reports that his father, working now as a district court judge, seldom leaves court before five o'clock in the afternoon, but that she has been "somewhat distracted in the above period, attending the opera, a ball and a musical fund concert." She relays news of uncles and aunts, and notes finally that "Tom is writing and Father thinks I must go and rest my weary limbs, so good night, dear Elisha, may all good angels guard your ways."

To this missive, Kane's cousin Lucy, age sixteen, added a few lines to "tell you how much everybody misses you and wishes for your return. We seemed quite lost without you this Christmas, and when the health of 'dear Elish' was drunk at dinner, we all wished you were with us, and that the two long years were over."

In yet another letter, alluding to his yearning for Mexico, his mother wrote that without him, home felt different: "We have no noisy Elish to bathe at all times of the day and sing the melodious song of 'Mexico so Low' or its rival 'Africa so gay.' . . . Nor have we even the Attorney General, but we have Judge Kane of the District Court seated quietly studying in the Library now his office, surrounded by bookcases filled with Law Books, while the former occupants of the shelves reside in the newly fitted book-cases in the study. At Aunt Eliza's habitation too, old Lapidea, there has been a change . . . [she] and Uncle George being now the sole inhabitants."

His sister, Bessie, wrote of studying French, practicing music, and taking dancing lessons, and concluded: "Do try and leave the hateful Africa. I wish we could banish the whole navy department in your place."

o   o   o

The settlement of Ouidah on the coast of Dahomey had been "discovered" by seafaring Portuguese in 1580. Early in the eighteenth century, they built a fortress and established themselves as slave traders. Local kings enriched themselves by cooperating. They learned Portuguese and intermingled with Portuguese-Brazilian families like the Sousas, whose descendants controlled the slave trade even after 1807, when it was supposedly abolished.

In 1846, while visiting Ouidah, Elisha Kane seized a chance to investigate that trade more thoroughly than most men engaged, as he was, in suppressing it. Three years before, while visiting Rio de Janeiro with the American legation, Kane had met a Brazilian slave trader, Francisco Felix de Sousa, who maintained headquarters at Ouidah. Now, one of de Sousa's sons—a man well advanced in years—entertained Kane and a couple of other officers at his palatial residence. Antonio de Sousa, Kane wrote, was "a harsh-visaged and somewhat stiffly deported personage with a sprinkling of the *militaire* leaking through his tropical attire. He was treated with evident respect, but at a glance would be set down for that which he was, a keen and knowing man of the world."

Kane hid his feelings and made "gradual advances into the good opinion of our hosts," never forgetting that "for the first time in my life I was surrounded by persons whose every interest was connected with the slave trade. That laughing Don Antonio who urged me so jovially to join him in [drinking Bordeaux] is the most blood-stained and anti-philanthropical scoundrel in Africa." Kane noted that "one gentleman opposite did not share fully in the general rejoicing. Here, thought I, is one man of sensibility and tact. He does not wish to show to American officers his participation in this hideous traffic. He even blushed—and I could not but feel a sort of sympathy for this one example of a slaver open to the error of his ways."

The more Kane learned about his host, the more appalled he became. During his fifty years in Ouidah, the visitor wrote, Antonio de Sousa had adopted "many of the vilest customs of the country. Within the walls of his present residence he had about 1000 wives—mere slave partners by whom . . . all the household operations were carried on. Not a man-slave but his own business agents were allowed within. In a word, it was a huge harem. In one chamber adjoining his own were at least 50 young girls of varied ages up to full womanhood. They were his *daughters*."

Intent on writing a book about all this, Kane took copious notes and drew sketches. On learning that de Sousa was about to send a caravan thirty miles into the interior, bringing jewelry and ornate furniture to a warlord who supplied slaves, Kane sought and received permission to travel with it. In the jungle, he discovered that "King Gezo" murdered men for the fun of it, kept a harem of young wives, and slept in an apartment paved with human skulls. More than half a century before Joseph Conrad wrote *Heart of Darkness,* Kane filled a notebook with details of Gezo's excesses. While appalled by conditions on board the vessels of slave traders, he could not help wondering whether the poor devils shipped out of the jungle, and so removed from Gezo's control, were not more fortunate than those left behind.

Back home in Philadelphia, Kane's letters from Africa caused discord and dissension. His brother Thomas, now a twenty-four-old lawyer, and the closest to Elisha not only in age but in temperament and talent, was already an outspoken abolitionist. He would soon become secretary of the Free Soil Central Committee of Pennsylvania, and would one day use his family home as a stop for the Underground Railroad, shuttling escaped slaves north to Canada.

Judge Kane, on the other hand, had allied himself irrevocably with southern Democrats and Presbyterians, who stood resolutely opposed to abolition. Before long, these differences would culminate in a family breach, when a new law required United States commissioners to return runaway slaves to southern territories under the Fugitive Slave Act. Having become a clerk to the district court in eastern Pennsylvania, and consequently a United States commissioner, Thomas would resign this latter post with a letter so fiercely denunciatory that his father the judge would charge him with contempt of court—a ruling that, had it not been overturned on appeal, would have sent the young man to jail.

But these events lay in the future. In 1846, ensconced as his father's law clerk and working out of an office in Philadelphia's Independence Hall, Thomas began developing communication skills his father had long since mastered—and which, soon enough, the young man would employ on behalf of his explorer-brother. Taking up the cause of the embattled Mormons, hundreds of whom were migrating westward from Illinois to escape religious persecution, Thomas flooded newspapers with unsigned accounts of injustice and hardship, and followed up with editorials calling for support. In December, he wrote to Mormon leader Brigham Young that it had been "next to impossible to do much for you before public opinion was corrected . . . [and so] it became incumbent on me to manufacture public opinion as soon as possible." His efforts proved "successful beyond my hopes."

From Philadelphia, Thomas urged Elisha to quit the navy, return home, resume his medical practice and start writing his travel book. He offered to support his brother materially through the transition, though he insisted: "You must marry.—Take any of the girls in town (which Judge Kane's son can) but marry you must." The time had come, he declared, "to begin the domestic duties, set on your own eggs and leave off promiscuous cock pigeoning." Judge Kane himself, now safely installed, reiterated this invitation in more gentlemanly fashion, informing Elisha that if he returned home, the whole family would do "all we can do to further your purposes to the utmost, means, action, influence,—all we have is yours."

Alone off the coast of Africa, Kane responded: "When I left you it was in such a state that I would have run to hell to escape a Paradise. . . . Circumstances were such that a short absence was essential. I was then advised upon a two-year cruise." In a draft letter to Thomas that probably he never sent, Kane added: "In two years I will be twenty eight. Am I to be in the Navy as a career or am I to make it subservient to a more solid [life] at home?" Ultimately, he "stopped oscillating" and decided "I am going to try my tug at home—if possible to retain the Navy as a potential reserve in case of failure but if I cannot do this . . . I am prepared to burn my bridge and resign."

He did not have to do so, however. After calling at Cape Verde, six of the frigate's crew had fallen ill with a tropical fever. As assistant surgeon, Kane spent two months caring for the sick men. Then, in February 1847, he himself came down with a severe case of "coast fever"—probably some form of malaria. For three weeks, he lay in a high fever. In March, the fleet surgeon, fearing for his life if he stayed in "this baleful climate," sent him home on a merchant ship. In a letter of reference, Dr. Thomas Dillard wrote, "I part with him with regret and shall miss him much." The senior doctor regretted losing "not only a useful and necessary assistant, but a valued and esteemed young friend."

On reaching Baltimore, about ninety miles from Philadelphia, Kane took a room at Barnum's Hotel. On April 6, 1847, far from fully recovered and not wanting to shock those who loved him, he wrote his father, asking that someone come to escort him the rest of the way home—either "yourself, Tom, or Pat." Affecting a lighthearted tone, he explained that he could "walk about passably" but "the legs are earthquaky, and the brain weak." He added: "I have a Robinson Crusoe beard, and—thanks to causes which I leave you to guess at—a Shaven Scalp. I fear then, being nervously inclined, to thrust upon you my shorn and unshorn visage."

He asked his father to tell no one outside the immediate family of his imminent arrival. "No kin's folk greetings—no Fuss. These things do not chime in with broken prospects and broken health." He was sick and depressed, but this time, at least, from across the seas, Elisha Kent Kane had managed to get home.

8

A MEXICAN ESCAPADE

The previous Christmas, Thomas had written encouraging Elisha to continue writing: "You must make the most of your time irremediably spent abroad, collecting materials; so as to be the writing Doctor of Philadelphia." Thomas envisaged a best-selling narrative "of slave ships, combats, cocoa nuts, Quashees, Mud Huts, Boarding parties, Fevers, Ivory, Palm Oil, etc., etc. cemented tighter by proper quantities of Blue Sea, Fire, Blood, and Tropical Sunshine."

Over the past several months, Thomas had sent model articles, clipped from newspapers and magazines, along with unsolicited editorial advice. Elisha dispatched several essays, and his brother astutely advocated a less ornate style: "Remember that your aim must be to prepare simple solid food, as you have always a profusion of confectionery on hand." Kane was at his best, according to Thomas, when he offered "a mixture of the touching and humorous," which often shone through in his "unguarded moments."

Looking back over his brother's travels, Thomas imagined a work containing eighty to a hundred pages on India, the same on the Philippines, and fifty each on China, Ceylon, Africa and Europe. Because illustrations would increase sales, Kane should "make a few more water colours if possible." Thomas assured his older brother: "Know your time is not thrown away as long as you can write. Your style is improving rapidly—and I can see that you want nothing but practice. You have more imagination & fancy than any of the family and have only to break your faculties into harness." In February, he elaborated: "Don't slant your paper. Fill note books of every kind with thoughts, hints, impressions, notes, facts, suppositions, whatever has at any time been in your brain."

In April 1847, when Kane moved back into the family home, he intended to complete this book project. He went to work gathering background material on the slave trade, some of it from government records, and filled twenty-eight foolscap-size pages that are now in the archives at the American Philosophical Society. To earn his living while he wrote, Kane leased an office with the intention of relaunching his medical practice.

Meanwhile, the Mexican-American War continued to rage. From the outset, young American men had heard the siren call. In Tennessee, 30,000 men had responded to a request for 3,000 volunteers. Yet late the previous December, when Thomas had expressed a desire to enlist, the Judge had written to Elisha: "Could you ever believe it! Your philanthropish-philosopher, anti-war, anti-capital-punishment brother . . . is rabid for a chance of shooting Mexicans, and would march, if I did not forbid it, as third lieut. of a company of rowdy volunteers." The Judge tried to secure a more senior, non-combatant position for his son, but Tom had not got beyond an interview at the White House in Washington, D.C.

Early in March, General Winfield Scott had landed 12,000 men on the beaches near Veracruz in eastern Mexico, then taken that port city. Now, Scott had begun the long push inland toward Mexico City, winning battle after bloody battle along the way. To a still-distant Elisha, the Judge had written: "The Army has gained glorious battles on the Rio Grande, Palo Alto and the Resaca de la Palma, covering themselves with glory and with blood, and whipping the Mexicans awfully; since which, they have marched to Monterey on the way to Mexico, and have taken the city after four days hard even desperate fighting."

Now, in late April of 1847, Elisha Kane got swept into the maelstrom. Several weeks after he arrived home from West Africa, still debilitated, he boarded a train for Washington, 130 miles away. Reasoning that, as a qualified doctor, he might yet see action in the war, he had solicited letters from the governor of Pennsylvania and others, and traveled now to secure a transfer to the army and immediate reassignment to Mexico. But he had not given himself time to recover, and he relapsed into feverish illness. He spent several weeks in bed in Washington, where his mother came and nursed him, and then several more convalescing at home.

By autumn, having regained his health, Kane felt restless. He had done some work on his travel book and, thinking that writing and teaching might prove a congenial mix, had applied to join the medical faculty at Girard College. He was only mildly disappointed when the one available position went to a more experienced physician.

Like countless other young men, Kane remained obsessed with the war in Mexico. This war, with the whole country behind it, represented their best chance to attain fame and glory, and to establish themselves as heroes. On October 23, at a gathering of the Wistar Party, the leading enclave of the American Philosophical Society (APS), held at his father's house, Kane gleaned from a fellow guest that President James Polk might be looking for a trustworthy courier to deliver a message to Mexico City. Kane slipped away and, without informing even his father, caught the night train to Washington.

The next morning, the young adventurer called on Secretary of State James Buchanan, Polk's right-hand man and an old friend of the Kane family, as well as a member of the APS. Buchanan outlined the situation. More than a month before, on September 13, General Scott had taken Mexico City. Since then, however, he had failed to communicate with the White House. The secretary and the president believed that General Scott was negotiating terms with the Mexicans, thereby exceeding his authority. They had sent him an order to cease and desist, but the general appeared to be ignoring it. Now, they wanted a messenger to reiterate the injunction.

Kane convinced Buchanan, who then persuaded Polk, that the president need look no further. Who better to carry a secret message through danger-ous territory than the well-traveled eldest son of a political ally? As a doctor, young Kane had a plausible alibi should he be intercepted: he had been sent to Mexico to report on hospitals and medical conditions. On November 5, 1847, Kane received the requisite special orders from the navy, along with official papers attesting to his cover story.

The following day, jubilant, he left for Mexico.

○   ○   ○

With the railroad system yet to be completed, Kane traveled west and south to New Orleans by train, riverboat, and stagecoach—a difficult journey of 1,500 miles. On his way to Pittsburgh, as if to demonstrate that he was still in his twenties, he climbed onto the cowcatcher of the locomotive. Soon afterward, he confessed to a friend: "Never had I such a twenty miles of one excluding, absorbing topic, how to hold on . . . I tore the heel from my boot, and smashed my thumb on the drag chain:—but I held on: and after it was all over, sneaked on to the cars, much relieved—a wiser and better man."

Kane would need a horse for his overland journey in Mexico, and in Louisville, Kentucky, he bought "a gallant gray"—a magnificent geld-ing that an army officer would later describe as the finest steed he ever saw in Mexico. From Kentucky, Kane also wrote his father, justify-ing his sudden departure: "I cannot help remembering our conversa-tions in which fickleness and instability were the attributed motives, and your fears that the community would think likewise." He insisted that he acted on "more direct and impulsive instigations of propriety. . . . Content yourself therefore with the fact that the Philadelphia Kane family is represented in the war." His tour of duty could be turned "to the Kane family advancement."

He would relay his official dispatches through home: "Whatever reaches you, purify it by the family filter and send it in its clear state to its instructed destination." Supremely conscious of the power of the printed word, he asked, unabashedly, that his father and brother Thomas "make extracts from my letters, work them up," and relay them to newspapers: "in a word puff me when you can."

On November 21, after a sixteen-day journey, Kane reached New Orleans. Almost immediately, he boarded the steamship *Fashion,* crammed to the gunwales with soldiers, civilians, army supplies, and cavalry horses, and departed for Veracruz. Weather forecasting remained an inexact art, and the ship sailed straight into the worst storm of the year—a "norther" that, in the Gulf of Mexico, brought waves twelve feet high and winds of 130 miles per hour (in contemporary terms, a Category Three hurricane or worse).

This tempest battered the *Fashion* so badly that her engines failed. As the ship heaved and bucked, Kane joined the soldiers in lightening her load by backing the army horses into the sea. He moved to sacrifice his own magnificent steed when officers stopped him. On the spot, Kane changed the horse's name from Tom to Relic. The gale continued and the ship took on water. Deckhands and volunteers went below and baled desperately, even using pots and kettles. The ship was foundering when, by an incredible stroke of luck, the storm swept her between two sets of reefs and into a sheltered bay—the only entrance to Veracruz Harbor. On January 1, 1848, after more than one month at sea, the *Fashion* docked safely, with no lives lost.

o o o

The Mexican adventure that ensued would prove so romantic, so much larger than life that, writing in 1857, Kane's first biographer, William Elder, feared readers would doubt his veracity. So, in addition to published newspaper articles, he amassed a collection of official letters and third-person testimonials that put the salient facts beyond dispute.

The day after he arrived in Veracruz, Elisha Kane mounted his horse and, with a few army officers, rode to the nearby Castle of Perote, an American stronghold in the southern Sierra Madre. Having ascertained that no regular soldiers would soon be traveling the 260 miles to Mexico City, he set out to overtake a renegade "spy company" hired to patrol the mountains.

Led by a tough hombre named Dominguez, formerly an officer with the Mexican army, this band of mercenaries comprised about 120 "skinners, bandits, and traitors."

Kane was determined to deliver his message, however, "in time for reputation or not at all," and by January 6 he had joined Dominguez and accomplished more than half his journey. Twenty-five miles east of Puebla, traversing a mountain pass near a town called Nopaluca and riding, of course, with the leaders, Kane rounded a bend and found himself face to face with about fifty Mexican regulars. These soldiers were traveling to Orizaba to reinforce a garrison in anticipation of an American attack. Among them were several junior officers, as well as a couple of captains and two generals: Anastasio Torrejon and Antonio Gaona.

Instantly, fighting erupted. Kane charged into the thick of the action, swinging his sword. He engaged a young major and his orderly in hand-to-hand combat. The orderly inflicted a flesh wound with his lance just as Kane, with a sword thrust to the chest, knocked the officer from his horse. Kane wheeled to parry another attack. But now the Mexican regulars, realizing they were badly outnumbered, dropped their weapons and threw their hands in the air.

A few soldiers had escaped, but four lay dead in the dirt and others were badly wounded. Kane watched, horrified, scarcely able to believe his eyes, as Dominguez and his lieutenants began slashing at the unarmed senior officers, refusing to accept their surrender—refusing to recognize the rules of civilized warfare. The young major he had wounded, who lay bleeding on the ground, called out to him while gesturing toward the unarmed generals, now bare-headed, fending off blows with their hands: "My father! Save my father!"

Kane needed no encouragement. Bent on preventing cold-blooded murder, he wheeled his horse into the melee and immediately found himself parrying an attack from some of his erstwhile allies. One lance struck him in the lower abdomen, and another caught Relic in the shoulder, driving the animal to the ground. Kane stumbled free and whipped out his pistol. By firing into the air, he drove the would-be murderers away from the Mexican officers. Then, glancing over at the wounded major, he realized that the young man was bleeding to death. Ignoring his own stomach wound, Kane hurried over and, using a table fork and a piece of packthread, extracted and tied off a slashed artery.

As tempers cooled, Kane learned that, while serving as governor of Puebla, General Gaona had once ordered Dominguez publicly whipped for robbery. Other members of the spy company had deserted the Mexican army and, if captured, would have been hanged as traitors. Hence the fury of their assault. Even so, at Kane's insistence, the mercenaries resumed their westward journey, now with forty-four prisoners in tow, the wounded among them jolting along in carts. Kane managed to get his horse onto its feet and to ride a few miles more, but then the steed went down for good, and the young American, after trying and failing to mount another animal, climbed into a cart with the wounded.

o   o   o

At Puebla, despite protests from Kane and the Mexican officers, the American colonel Thomas Childs ruled that the prisoners had been taken by Dominguez. General Gaona, reduced almost to tears by this, complained to a third American officer, Albert Brackett: "I respect the Americans. They are a brave and magnanimous people, but I have been captured by that man, who is a thief and a robber. My honor is gone."

General Gaona and his son, the wounded major, publicly proclaimed that they owed their lives to Elisha Kent Kane. With the Mexican War winding down—the Treaty of Guadalupe Hidalgo would be signed within one month—Childs put the general under house arrest and allowed him to return to his nearby estate.

The Gaonas were preparing a fiesta in Kane's honor when the young doctor fell deathly ill, a result of his wound. An American army surgeon and several Mexican doctors diagnosed "congestive typhus fever," clearly a result of infection. Kane lost consciousness, and Childs allowed the Gaonas to take him to their palatial home, where four physicians maintained an around-the-clock vigil. For twelve days, Kane lay in a coma, nursed around the clock by General Gaona's wife and daughters. A visiting American officer, W.W.H. Davis, learned of his condition while passing through Puebla and visited the Gaona hacienda: "We were ushered into the drawing room and there was presented as beautiful a picture as I ever witnessed in war time. Dr. Kane was lying on a cot; on one side sat Senora Gaona, an elegant-looking matron of forty; on the other her daughter, a beautiful girl of eighteen, watching over the sick man, with the same tenderness and care they would have given a son and brother. General Gaona, a distinguished-looking man, joined his wife and daughter in expressions of gratitude for the timely interposition of the invalid, at the risk of his own life that saved the life of husband and father."

While lying on that cot, Elisha scribbled a note to his parents and sent it off in care of the visitor. From Philadelphia, his mother responded: "After two days of the most torturing anxiety we were relieved by your letter of yesterday. What can we say or do to express our gratitude? First to our Heavenly Benefactor for sparing your life, and next to the noble, generous family of Gaona, who have under Providence been the means of preserving it. I feel how utterly inadequate words are to convey the feelings on this occasion, but the mother will sympathize with me, and comprehend at once what language cannot describe. Ask her to give some utterance to those around her of our heart-felt gratitude."

Subsequently, while still recuperating, but now at the home of the second general whose life he had saved, Kane wrote reassuringly: "I am twenty miles from Puebla, at the base of Popocatepetl—the rain falling, the wind howling, and some two thousand poor devils shivering under their tent poles. I am with General Torrejon [who had led the Mexican charge at the Battle of Buena Vista], snugly housed, warmly welcomed, and awaiting a call to supper."

On February 18, along with a military force of 2,000 men, Kane resumed his journey to Mexico City. General Gaona had offered him the choice of any of his horses to replace his Kentucky stallion, but Kane could not yet ride, so he traveled the remaining 160 miles in a rough cart. A second presidential emissary, arriving in the metropolis at the same time, rendered Kane's message redundant by informing General Scott that he had been relieved of his command.

In Mexico City, army surgeons examined Kane, saw the state of his lance wound, and declared him unfit for further duty. They ordered him home for treatment and sent him to Veracruz in a four-horse ambulance escorted by thirty dragoons. As he awaited a ship, the young doctor wrote to his father with the self-dramatizing romanticism that characterized his twenties: "I again return, a broken-down man. My hair would be gray, but that I have no hair. My hopes would be small, but that I have no hopes. Expect never to see me again, and my luck may prevent you from being disappointed. . . . Perhaps the fact of having saved six lives may make me a more important person in your eyes. It was a dear bargain, but I do not regret it."

o   o   o

Thanks to the tutelage of his father, Elisha Kane understood that to forge an enduring reputation—which was his ambition—he had to become known in his own time. And to accomplish that, he not only had to perform noble deeds, but to let the world know it—all without any unseemly clamoring after attention. At the same time, Kane remained idealistic and principled. From Mexico, while recovering from his near-fatal wound, he had sent home a letter describing events in the field and fiercely condemning the renegade spy company whose conduct had disgusted him. He instructed Thomas to "work up these facts and publish in the N.Y. Herald" and other newspapers: "I want for readers . . . a sort of excitement got up concerning this disgraceful corps."

In seeking publicity to build his reputation and advance his career, Kane was not unusual. According to his brother Thomas, a certain Sergeant William Wardhouse had written an account of his own heroics at the recent Battle of Opaluca, mentioning the names of other Americans who might secure its publication: "If he has thought he could try for a sword, he has written to the proper fellows of his Horse Company or other crony gang and has assured them that he will give them his first delegate vote after he returns home if they will be his friends enough to get up a subscription paper."

Tom assured Elisha that he had already been active, but indicated that he was dealing with newspapermen "who have had their regular business habits, and their regular habits of thought. I have neither been able to get any work out of them except between certain stated intervals devoted to eating, sleeping and resting, nor have I been able to take their opinions by storm." He had received no official notice of Kane's activities, "no extract from one, no dispatch, no newspaper, American or Spanish, nothing of the kind," and had only recently acquired a letter from Colonel Childs, "the first thing capable of being made the basis of a newspaperism."

Still, he had launched a publicity campaign by sending dispatches to the Philadelphia *Inquirer* and *The Pennsylvanian,* which duly produced headlines like "Gallant Conduct of Dr. Elisha K. Kane of the U.S. Navy" and "Romantic Incident of the War." The editor of the latter publication commented that "the remarkable adventure of our young friend Doctor Kane surpasses the wildest dreams of romance."

Inevitably, a few detractors wrote letters to the editor, driven to cynical disbelief by the theatricality of the stories—the exotic location, the chivalry, the two young officers, having met on the battlefield as enemies, ultimately joined together in friendship, and the beautiful senorita nursing the wounded hero back to health. All that was lacking was a marriage.

Even so, by mid-summer 1848, nudged along by the Judge, prominent Philadelphians were talking of recognizing their war hero with some public gesture. Kane himself, not yet fully recovered, did as he had done five years before: he withdrew to Lapidea, the country estate of his aunt Eliza and uncle George Leiper. There he outlined yet another book that he proposed to write, a sweeping history of the Mexican-American War that would run to forty chapters. He also accepted a commission to illustrate a book for a doctor friend, and the end result, *El Puchero: A Mixed Dish from Mexico* by

63

Richard McSherry, contains engravings that derive, almost certainly, from sketches he produced.

From Lapidea, Kane also wrote letters seeking compensation for the horse he had lost—money that eventually did materialize, though not in the amount justified by the magnificence of the animal. As well, he brought a formal charge against Dominguez and his mercenary band, insisting that they had threatened, robbed, and mistreated the prisoners. This campaign came to nothing, and Kane emerged disillusioned. He later declined to discuss the war, making an exception only to correct a detail about the emergency surgery he had performed on Major Gaona: "His wound was not in the groin; it was in the chest; and the artery was one of the intercostals."

According to biographer William Elder, who knew Kane and his family, "If he had lived a century after that experience [the skirmish at Nopaluca], he would not have been caught doing any more patriotism, unless it had first been warranted well principled, and its governing councils were somewhat more intent upon manly service to the country than the promotion of their own paltry interests."

As he regained his health, Kane felt the old familiar craving for engagement and activity. He sought two postings without success—one with the Philadelphia Navy Yard, another with a joint Army–Navy expedition to the Pacific coast to identify locations for naval stations. Eventually, disappointed at being rejected for this last post, and bent on furthering his naval career—he had not forgotten the Wilkes expedition—Kane accepted a routine assignment with a supply ship bound for the Mediterranean and South America.

Just before he sailed, however, early in 1849, he achieved a modicum of recognition. On February 8, at a gathering at Philosophical Hall organized by the American Philosophical Society and attended by scores of leading citizens, the young adventurer received a gold-sheathed ceremonial sword. A citation lauding his conduct in the service of his country had been signed by the attorney general of Pennsylvania (the Judge's successor) and the founding president of the American Medical Association, and noted in part, "Your casual encounter with the enemy in the Mexican campaign, as roman-

At Philosophical Hall, home to the American Philosophical Society,
Elisha Kane received a gold-sheathed ceremonial sword in recognition of
his "courage, conduct, and humanity" during the Mexican-American War.

tic as unexpected, was crowned, as an incidental exploit, with the distinction
due to gallantry, skill, and success, and was hallowed in the flush of victory
by the noblest humanity to the vanquished."

At the podium, accepting the magnificent sword that honored his "courage, conduct, and humanity," Kane said a gracious, heartfelt thanks. Yet
already he understood that local celebrity would never slake his thirst for
recognition. Already, aware that his time on earth would probably be short,
he was casting about for another opportunity to make his mark. As yet, however, Kane did not realize that, having achieved this victory to the south, in
tropical Mexico, his way forward lay in the opposite direction. Elisha Kent
Kane did not yet imagine that, for him, the path to glory rolled away to the
High Arctic.

9

RAISING THE CURTAIN

To judge from mythology, any transformative personal experience begins with a call to adventure, when the potential hero learns of some important quest or "high historical undertaking." In *The Hero with a Thousand Faces,* Joseph Campbell writes that "the call rings up the curtain, always, on a mystery of transfiguration—a rite, or moment, of spiritual passage, which, when complete, amounts to a dying and rebirth. The familiar horizon has been outgrown; the old concepts, ideals, and emotional patterns no longer fit; the time for the passing of a threshold is at hand."

For Elisha Kent Kane, the summons would come early in 1850.

The previous March, Kane had joined a naval vessel called the *Supply* as an assistant surgeon. Struggling as always with seasickness, he sailed to the Mediterranean and South America. He found the voyaging tedious and the brutality of shipboard discipline revolting. After seeing one man flogged three times and another receive fifty lashes—a beating reminiscent of the horror he had witnessed aboard the *United States*—he sought a transfer to the United States Coast Survey, which had been created to map harbors and coastlines.

Under the leadership of Alexander Dallas Bache—the nephew of George M. Dallas, Judge Kane's old friend—this department had become the leading proponent of "Humboldtean science" in America. At the turn of the century, the cosmopolitan German-born Alexander von Humboldt had established a new model for geographical studies. Humboldt spent five years exploring the interior of South America, taking meteorological readings and measurements while seeking global patterns and interconnections. In so doing, he forged a stellar reputation as a scientific truth-seeker who traveled to the far corners of the earth, risking his life while advancing the causes of both science and humanity.

By entering the Coast Survey, as David Chapin observed in *Exploring Other Worlds,* Kane not only became part of the Humboldtean process of gathering scientific data, but found a model of exploration worth emulating. Under Alexander Bache, men did much of their work outdoors, subordinating individual interests to the common good, and often sleeping in tents for weeks at a time. Assigned to the steamer *Walker,* Kane surveyed the southeast coast of the continent while proceeding to the Gulf of Mexico.

By January 1850, when he sailed into Charleston, South Carolina, Kane had begun following the search for Sir John Franklin, the British navigator who had disappeared while seeking the Northwest Passage. Five years before, with two well-equipped ships and 128 men, Franklin had sailed into the Arctic, confident he would solve the riddle of the Passage. Two years later, when he failed to emerge into the Pacific Ocean trailing clouds of glory, the British began sending out search expeditions by sea and land—in great numbers, and all without success.

In April 1849, Jane Franklin, wife of "the good Sir John," wrote to American president Zachary Taylor asking that the United States "join heart and mind in the enterprise of snatching the lost navigators from a dreary grave." This request might have accomplished nothing but for the involvement of New York shipping magnate Henry Grinnell, who perceived that the search for Franklin could be combined with a quest to test a scientific hypothesis that was attracting attention in American circles:

In 1845, British explorer Sir John Franklin (left) disappeared into the Arctic with two ships and 128 men. By 1849, New York shipping magnate Henry Grinnell had decided to sponsor an American rescue expedition.

that, at the top of the world, there existed an Open Polar Sea teeming with fish and mammals.

After exchanging letters with Lady Franklin, Grinnell had decided to sponsor an American search expedition. To keep expenses within reason, he needed the U.S. Navy to supply manpower and provisions—and so he told Jane Franklin. In December 1849, this persuasive woman wrote again to President Taylor. She stressed that the lost sailors, "whether clinging still to their ships or dispersed in various directions, have entered upon a fifth winter in those dark and dreary solitudes, with exhausted means of sustenance. . . . It is in the time, then, of their greatest peril, in the day of their extremest need, that I venture . . . to look to you again for some active efforts which may come in aid of those of my own country, and add to the means of search."

In January, Kane read that President Taylor had brought Lady Franklin's request to Congress and asked that the navy supply Grinnell's two vessels. As congressmen debated this request, Kane—who was still aboard the *Walker*—wrote a letter to the secretary of the navy, volunteering to serve with any Arctic search expedition that might be mounted. When he received no immediate reply, the young officer abandoned hope. He could not have known that Congress would approve the venture in May, largely because Henry Grinnell had arranged for two senators, his brother Joseph and his friend Henry Clay, to orchestrate congressional support.

On Sunday, May 12, while swimming in the Gulf of Mexico off Mobile, Alabama, Kane was called ashore to receive a surprising telegram. It was "one of those courteous little epistles from Washington," he would write, "which the electric telegraph has made so familiar to naval officers. It detached me from the Coast Survey, and ordered me 'to proceed forthwith to New York, for duty upon the Arctic Expedition.'"

o   o   o

Kane would complete the 1,300-mile journey in seven and a half days—at that time, no small feat of organization and endurance. He began by leaving Mobile on the first available stage coach to Montgomery. He then traveled by train and coach to Atlanta, and from there aboard two different trains to Augusta and Charleston. From that bustling port, he took a steamboat to Wilmington—a sixteen-hour trip. He then spent forty hours on three different trains, traveling through Richmond and Baltimore to his hometown of Philadelphia.

Several months before, to escape from the effects of industrialization, Judge Kane had moved the family several miles north of the city to an estate he called "Rensselaer," after his mother's family. Elisha's sister Bessie, then eighteen, wrote in her diary: "It is a large, handsome house, beautifully situated. I went with Tom to view the garden and the greenhouse and was perfectly delighted. A number of beautiful flowers left to perish in the garden were instantly appropriated to a bouquet, and I was almost wild with joy when I saw the variety of plants in the greenhouse. The house, too, was beautiful and so convenient."

Kane's mother furnished the home elegantly, filling the large drawing room with white-and-gold, cane-seated French settees and chairs, and the walls with rare paintings and gold-colored damask hangings. Between the long windows she placed two beautiful cabinets also brought from France. The mahogany dining table had been fashioned in England from a design by the Judge, who would declare that, at different times, five American presidents made use of it.

To Kane's sister, Bessie, who was visiting friends in New York, his mother wrote that she had been "sadly troubled by a telegraphic dispatch from Elisha. He is actually en route to Washington to receive orders for the North Pole. His letter of the day before was filled with the praises of his present position—but it is vain to grieve. Elisha cannot live without adventure."

To this, the Judge added paternal misgivings: "I cannot rejoice that he is going on this expedition; his motive is most praiseworthy, but I think the project a wild one, and I fear inadequacy in outfit. I wish most sincerely that Sir John Franklin was at home with his wife again, leading dog's lives together as they used to do,—or that Mr. Clayton had not been silly enough to write Lady F. his pretty letters of promises,—or that Gen. Taylor had not been such a sneak as to avoid the responsibility of carrying them out or urging Congress to do so. But it is as it is and we must make the best of it:—Oh! this Glory! when the cost is fairly counted up, it is no such great speculation after all."

At Rensselaer, on Sunday, May 19, after ten o'clock at night, the Kanes received a telegram from Elisha. The young officer would arrive in Philadelphia by train at three o'clock in the morning, and start for New York the next day. In the interim, he needed to accomplish much.

A few days later, on Tuesday, May 21, 1850, Jane Leiper Kane would write Bessie again, describing the chaos that had ensued: "I feel as if I had not yet waked from a hideous dream, and have been trying to shake off thought by house keeping bustle, but still a heavy weight oppresses me, and I feel as if Elisha had parted with us for an interminable period, perhaps forever." She would describe how, the previous Sunday night, she had gone off to get ready for bed, leaving Tom and the Judge chatting in the latter's office. Suddenly, "the dogs commenced such an uproar that Tom raised the window." There on the piazza below stood Mr. Field, a servant employed by their close friends (and relations) the Pattersons. "Come down," the man said. "I have a telegram from Elisha."

The family was summoned to Philadelphia: "Dear Aunt Patterson had made arrangements to receive us. Elisha would be in by the 3 o'clock (a.m.) train from Baltimore, and probably start for New York at nine. By this time, Godfrey (coachman) was roused; it was near two before we were deposited at your Aunt's. By half past, Elisha was with us, and by 4 o'clock the beds and sofas received our wearied bodies."

At six, Jane Leiper Kane and Helen Patterson arose and began organizing the work before them. As arranged, they woke Elisha, he took a bath, "and by seven we were all at the breakfast table." Two of the servants, Disco and Anthony, tackled Elisha's trunk, "throwing aside useless garments, replacing others, and raising a pile of soiled clothes absolutely startling. Your Aunt, however, is never conquered by difficulties; her women were ordered to come to a pause in the family wash, and concentrate their energies on Elisha's apparel, and they were ready in due time."

Judge Kane and three of Elisha's brothers—Patterson, John, and Willie, respectively twenty-three, seventeen, and twelve—"started off on missions after polar articles, and Godfrey came with the carriage, and I rode with Elisha (to be in his company) whilst he was on duty that required personal attendance. At noon Tom and a cab relieved Godfrey of the carriage, and by two Aunt's dining room received our entire family and Cousin Mary [Leiper]."

o   o   o

Shortly after noon, accompanied by his brother Tom, who was coming along to help, Elisha Kane boarded a train to New York, leaving his mother "anxiously thinking of all belonging to this annoying business; wondering if Elisha found the provisions for the voyage full and complete, whether he was able with Tom's assistance to supply his own deficiencies in New York, and [struggling against] a crowd of other equally disagreeable and saddening reflections."

As he traveled to New York on the final leg of his journey, Kane never doubted he would join one of two impressive ships. After all, the lost vessels of Sir John Franklin, the *Erebus* and the *Terror,* weighed 370 and 326 tons respectively, and could together accommodate more than 130 men. Nor was he alone in his expectations. Another officer who would sail with the expedition, Robert Randolph Carter, had just left the *Savannah,* a 1,726-ton ship with a complement of 480 men. This was the kind of vessel, surely, that would lead the United States' Grinnell Expedition in Search of Sir John Franklin.

But on Tuesday, May 21, when Kane reported at the Brooklyn Naval Yard, he discovered to his dismay that the Grinnell expedition comprised two vessels so small that only their masts showed above the edge of the wharf. The flagship *Advance* weighed only 144 tons, and the *Rescue* just ninety-one. Expected to carry a total of thirty-three men between them, these tiny "hermaphrodite brigs," with their square-rigged foremasts and schooner-rigged mainmasts were designed for maneuverability and speed, but lacked anything resembling naval trim. Half-stowed cargo cluttered their decks, and Kane felt he "could straddle from the main hatch to the bulwarks." The ships looked "more like a couple of coasting schooners than a national squadron bound for a distant and perilous sea."

Kane soon appreciated, however, that Henry Grinnell and expedition commander Edwin De Haven had worked hard to prepare the ships for Arctic service. The eighty-eight-foot-long *Advance,* on which Kane would sail as surgeon, had been doubly sheathed in thick oak planking and been reinforced from bow to stern with sheet-iron strips. Seven feet of solid timber filled the space behind the hull. The rudder could be hauled aboard, and the winch, capstan, and windlass "were of the best and newest construction." Kane also found the library well stocked, especially with books on polar exploration.

The navy-supplied equipment impressed him less. The antiquated stoves had been stowed deep in the hold, and the firearms, mostly ball-loading muskets, proved a "heterogeneous collection of obsolete old carbines, with the impracticable ball cartridges that accompanied them." Kane worried that the food supplies, while possibly adequate for the projected three-year voyage, would not prove varied enough to ward off scurvy.

With the "zealous aid" of Mr. Grinnell, who provided the funds, Kane spent several hours dashing around New York, purchasing thermometers, barometers, and magnetometers. These "would have been of use to me if they had found their way on board," he wrote later. From home he had brought along a few books, some coarse woolen clothing, and a magnificent buffalo-skin robe from "the snow drifts of Utah," a parting gift from his dearest brother. Later, Thomas would write, "I gave him the robe, which had been all winter the ornament of my office in old Independence Hall, with the feeling that it carried a blessing with it."

On the *Advance,* Kane would share a belowdecks cabin, smaller "than a penitentiary cell," with De Haven and the other two officers. This dank accommodation contained camp stools, lockers, and berths for four men, as well as a hinged table and a "dripping step-ladder that led directly from the wet deck above." Kane shielded his berth—"a right-angled excavation" six feet long, thirty-two inches wide, and less than three feet tall—with a few yards of India-rubber cloth.

Inside, on tiny shelves, he placed his books and a reading lamp. Then, using nails, hooks, and string, he suspended a few items along the wall: watch, thermometer, ink bottle, toothbrush, comb, and hairbrush. When, with all this accomplished, Kane "crawled in from the wet, and cold, and disorder of without, through a slit in the India-rubber cloth, to the very center of my complicated resources," he reveled in the comfort he had manufactured. And on May 22 at 1 p.m., the day after Elisha Kane reached New York, the *Advance* cut loose from the "asthmatic old steam-tug" that had towed it out of the Brooklyn Navy Yard and began sailing north.

10

An Arctic Baptism

No sooner had the *Advance* reached the rough open water off Sandy Hook, the barrier peninsula protecting Lower New York Bay, than Elisha Kane became seasick. As the ship plied north along the Atlantic coast, sailing past Nova Scotia, around Newfoundland, and into the Davis Strait, the young doctor remained so nauseous that his fellow officers feared for his health. When the expedition reached Greenland and put in at Disco Island, Edwin De Haven offered to send him home aboard an American whaling ship.

Kane declined in a manner that brooked no discussion. With that settled, and as he slowly recuperated, Kane became friends with De Haven, a fellow Philadelphian four years his senior. A no-nonsense man of action, De Haven had sailed with the Wilkes expedition (1838–43) and navigated the flagship *Vincennes* through hundreds of miles of Antarctic ice. In response to a request from Henry Grinnell, the Naval Observatory and Hydrographic Office had appointed him to lead this expedition. The oceanographer who ran that office, Matthew Fontaine Maury, had become the leading exponent of the theory that, at the top of the world, there lay an Open Polar Sea.

As the *Advance* sailed north, Kane perused Maury's analytical writings, wrestling with ideas that the theoretician would later incorporate in his 1855 classic, *The Physical Geography of the Sea*. After years of study, Maury had established that whales sometimes carried harpoons in their backs from the Bering Strait, on the west coast of North America, to Baffin Bay, on the east coast. Because these mammals cannot travel that great distance under ice, he deduced that "there is at times, at least, open water communication through the polar regions between the Atlantic and Pacific Oceans." And so he revived the theory that an Open Polar Sea lay beyond a northern ring of ice—an idea born in the sixteenth century, when English merchant Robert Thorne speculated that the Northwest Passage might flow across the pole.

The explorations of the seventeenth and eighteenth centuries had created skeptics while proving nothing. More recently, Russian sailors had found open-water *polynyas* to the north of Spitsbergen, at latitudes above 79 degrees. These sightings suggested an Open Polar Sea, and Maury hoped this expedition might test the hypothesis. In searching for Sir John Franklin, De Haven would sail west through Lancaster Sound and the Barrow Strait to the Wellington Channel. Then, he would use his own judgment—but, certainly, he should explore north rather than south. If he encountered pack ice in the Wellington Channel, he should try another route, and proceed north through either Jones or Smith Sound.

Edwin De Haven, a practical seaman, would follow his orders to the letter. But he experienced no excitement in reading Maury. The imaginative Kane, on the other hand, could hardly contain himself. In discussions with the commander, the doctor showed such a passion for the oceanographer's musings that, when he floated the idea of writing a book about the voyage, De Haven—who dreaded the thought of producing even an official report—welcomed the initiative.

Before sailing, Kane had assured his brother Thomas that he would keep a journal that he could subsequently develop into a book. And he kept that promise. Night after night, while others slept, Kane huddled in his berth and scratched away by lamplight, bent on producing "a history of the cruise under the form of a personal narrative."

o   o   o

By the time he reached Greenland, Kane had sailed past his first iceberg—a gigantic cube coated with snow that resembled "a great marble monolith, only awaiting the chisel to stand out . . . a floating Parthenon." He had watched his first school of whales tumbling like porpoises around the vessel—"great, crude, wallowing sea-hogs, snorting out fountains of white spray." And he had marveled at the continuous sunlight of northern latitudes in summer: "The words night and day begin to puzzle me, as I recognize the arbitrary character of the hour cycles that have borne these names."

In the Whalefish Islands off Greenland, Kane discovered his first Inuit-Danish settlement. He would record a first impression that, within the next few years, he would repudiate so completely that it would stand only as the starting point of a personal transformation. But late in June 1850, on rowing ashore to a village of forty people, Kane and his fellow Americans felt disgusted by the realities of an Arctic hunting culture—the slabs of drying seal meat spread over the rocks, the dogs smeared with oil and blubber, and even the bones—of seal, walrus, and whale—buried in nearby mosses.

These nomadic people spent their summers in deerskin tents, their winters in semi-subterranean huts—habitations superbly adapted to Arctic winters and virtually identical to those in which, a few years later, Kane himself would seek refuge and huddle for warmth among men, women, children, and dogs. But now, as an American newcomer to the north, Kane judged these dwellings to be filthy and overcrowded: "One poor family had escaped to their summer tent, pitched upon an adjacent rock that overlooked the sea. Within a little area of six feet by eight, I counted a father, mother, grandfather, and four children, a tea-kettle, a rude bow, two rifles, and a litter of puppies."

Kane joined a boat party that rowed to Lively, on the nearby island of Disco, to gather furs and information, wending through towering icebergs in an eddying current that swept along like a millrace. Lively comprised a "group of rude houses, mottling the sky with the comfortable smoke of their huge chimneys," dominated by an antique, gable-fronted house that belonged to the Danish inspector who presided over the area. This "accomplished and hospitable gentleman" not only helped Kane gather furs throughout the settlement, but "actually robbed himself to supply our wants." Here in Disco Harbor, as Kane well knew, whalers had seen the two ships of the Franklin expedition for the last time, attached to a massive iceberg.

In 1850, on June 29, the Grinnell expedition sailed northwest. Two days later, still in the Davis Strait, and after passing through what Kane described as "a crowd of noble icebergs," the two ships encountered a berg-dotted expanse of pack ice. Prevailing currents usually pushed this so-called "Middle Ice" to the west, opening a channel along the Greenland coast. Whalers would follow this laneway as far north as Melville Bay—little more than an indentation—and then swing westward, crossing Baffin Bay north of the Middle Ice, through the relatively ice-free North Water.

Occasionally, to save valuable summertime weeks, voyagers tried to cross Baffin Bay by threading their way through the Middle Ice. In 1819, Edward Parry had succeeded in this; fifteen years later, he wasted two months trying. Now, in July 1850, Elisha Kane described the "vast plane of undulating ice" as creating an unspeakable din of crackling, grinding, and splashing: "A great number of bergs, of shapes the most simple and most complicated, of colors blue, white, and earth-stained, were tangled in this floating field." One evening, while standing on deck, he counted 240 icebergs "of primary magnitude."

On July 6, Kane got a chance to scrawl a note to the person he loved most: "My dearest mother: I had given up all hope of writing to you from Upernavik, when, by a most bountiful accident, an Esquimaux kayak paddled out and gives a possible chance of sending to all of you my dear love and remembrance." The following day, while progressing slowly north along the Greenland coast, conservatively following the northern passage, De Haven spotted an open channel leading westward. He decided to try his luck. The two ships made good progress through most of the day, but late in the afternoon, as the expedition approached a distinctive peaked island called the Devil's Thumb, the channel or "lead" narrowed, then closed and trapped the vessels.

De Haven tried to force a passage. During the next several days, he ordered his men onto the floe to work away with crowbars, boathooks, ice anchors, and warping lines. But the warm days flowed away through one week and then another. Eventually, the endless sunshine would do its work. Meanwhile, Kane analyzed the ice pack and identified four varieties of ice. One was the "true material of the winter floe, varying in thickness from seven feet to as many inches." Another was "water-sodden" and seldom exceeded one foot in thickness. A third was honeycombed or cellular, and "so soft you could plunge a boathook through it"; and a fourth he judged as finely granulated as loaf sugar, yet tough as asphalt.

Kane also spotted his first polar bear, a creature nine feet long that, at a distance of half a mile, reminded him of "a colossal puss in boots." With several other musket-carrying men, he gave chase: "We were an absurd party of zealots, rushing pell-mell upon the floes with vastly more energy than discretion." One man broke through the ice, but after rescuing him, the others gave chase for three more hours. Finally, "repeated duckings in water at 30 degrees cooled down our enthusiasm. The bear, meantime, never varied his unconcerned walk. We saw him last in a labyrinth of hummock ice."

After three weeks, the ice pack began to break up. Late in the afternoon of July 28, the sailors spotted open water to the north and east. And at 9:30 p.m., they cast off, set the main sail, and "with feelings of joyous relief, began to bore the ice." The ships beat a retreat toward Melville Bay and, after ricocheting off a few floating hummocks, succeeded in tying fast to a heavy floe connected with land.

The Grinnell expedition had still to cross Melville Bay. Over the past three decades, 210 ships had been lost trying. According to Kane, attempted transits of this bay had contributed most of the catastrophes that "have made the statistics of the whalers so fearful. . . . It is rarely that a season goes by in which the passage is attempted without disaster." Twice in the night, all hands were called up on deck to use towlines and the winch-like capstan to warp the ship out of the path of looming icebergs. "Imagine a mass as large as the Parthenon bearing down upon you before a storm-wind!" While anchored in Melville Bay, with icebergs and hummock ridges cemented into an ice base ten feet thick, the entire coast lashed by an angry sea, Kane began to grasp the scale and "the stupendous results of ice action."

Standing on the deck of the *Advance,* he noticed that, while the surface ice drifted steadily south, several of the larger icebergs moved north, "crushing through the floes in the very eye of the breeze at a measured rate of a mile and a half an hour." This gave him the idea, entirely consistent with the teachings of Matthew Maury, that a great ocean undercurrent flowed northward, independent of prevailing winds, carrying with it any icebergs that protruded far enough downward into the water—an idea that, the next time he found himself in Melville Bay, Kane would use to save his ship.

11

THE BEECHEY GRAVES

By mid-August, the Americans understood that they would have to winter, as Kane put it, "somewhere in the scene of Arctic search." Having lost three weeks to the ice near the Devil's Thumb, and two more to Melville Bay, they had sailed west, entered the open North Water, and begun to make good time. Several weeks previously, at the Whalefish Islands, the Americans learned that a couple of British search ships had already visited Disco. Those vessels could draw on small steam engines for emergency use, and would now be far, far ahead. Kane and his companions had dreamed of enjoying the fellowship of the British searchers, "dividing between us the hazards of the way, and perhaps in the long winter holding with them the cheery intercourse of kindred sympathies. We waked now to the probabilities of passing the dark days alone."

But on August 19, as the *Advance* neared the entrance to Lancaster Sound, its sailing master spotted two British vessels following in the ship's wake. Within four hours, the larger of the two drew alongside. It proved to be the *Lady Franklin,* under the redoubtable Captain William Penny. He, too, had run into problems in Melville Bay. Before sailing on past the slower

Advance, he reported that Commodore Austin's four-vessel expedition was in the area, and also the provision ship *North Star.*

A couple of nights later, while sailing through Lancaster Sound, driving before a strong wind and taking water at every roll, the Americans overtook yet another British vessel. This small schooner, towing a launch and "fluttering over the waves like a crippled bird," proved to be the *Felix.* Kane watched as "an old fellow, with a cloak tossed over his night gear, appeared in the lee gangway, and saluted with a voice that rose above the winds." Two decades before, Sir John Ross had been shipwrecked and survived four winters in the Arctic. Now he roared joyfully, "You and I are ahead of them all!"

Ross came on deck, a vigorous, square-built man looking younger than his seventy-three years would suggest, and reported that Austin's four-boat squadron had taken refuge in various bays, and that Penny was lost in the gale. At thirty, Kane knew enough Arctic history to appreciate the encounter—to delight in meeting John Ross here, near Admiralty Inlet, where, seventeen years before, the old sea dog had contrived to escape an icy incarceration. Kane also marveled that, despite opposition and even ridicule, Ross had sailed in search of his old friend in "a flimsy cockle-shell, after contributing his purse and his influence."

During the next couple of weeks, while the ships remained within hailing distance, Kane would seek out old John Ross to solicit his opinions and hear his stories. Ross told Kane that he had talked with Franklin before the latter sailed. He had warned Sir John against "the caprice or even the routine of seasons" and urged him to ensure that he always had an escape route in case he got trapped in the ice. "It was thus I saved myself from the abandoned *Victory* by a previously constructed house for wintering, and a boat for temporary refuge."

Kane took these words to heart. One day, while being tested, he would act upon them with crucial effect. Given that the young surgeon had crossed a threshold of sorts simply by sailing on this Arctic expedition, John Ross takes on a mythical aspect, becoming a guide figure representing what Joseph Campbell calls "the benign, protecting power of destiny." On August 23, when Kane wrote a letter to his brother Thomas, roughing out an article about the voyage so far, he encouraged him to develop it: "Say something too in enthusiastic eulogy of old Sir John Ross—this veteran, dear Tom, has left upon me sentiments of admiration tinged with sadness."

Later, in the book he would write and publish about this first Arctic expedition, Kane would indicate the significance he attached to his meeting with Ross by quoting the veteran sailor at length, explaining: "I have given this extract from my journal because the tone and language . . . may be regarded as characteristic of this manly old seaman."

o   o   o

Within days of this encounter, having passed Cape Charles Yorke and Cape Crawford, the Americans enjoyed a third meeting, this one with the *Prince Albert,* which had been sent out by Lady Franklin under Captain Charles Forsyth. Kane observed that this topsail schooner, a ninety-ton pilot boat refitted for Arctic service, was poorly equipped for Arctic conditions, and resembled the American expedition in one respect: "They had to rough it: to use a Western phrase, they had no fancy fixings—nothing but what a hasty outfit and a limited purse could supply."

William Parker Snow, a civilian traveling with Forsyth at the behest of Jane Franklin, would portray Kane in a published account as a refined, well-traveled raconteur: "Of an exceedingly slim and apparently fragile form and make, and with features to all appearances far more suited to a genial clime, and to the comforts of a pleasant home, than to the roughness and hardships of an Arctic voyage, he [Kane] was yet a very old traveler by sea and land . . . a congeniality of sentiment and feeling brought us deep into personal conversation."

On August 25, having parted from the *Prince Albert* and fallen behind the *Rescue,* the *Advance* approached Cape Riley. From the deck, the Americans spotted two cairns, the larger marked with a flagstaff. They landed and, in the larger cairn, found a tin canister containing a note. Two days before, the British Captain Ommanney had called here with the *Assistance* and the *Intrepid,* both from Austin's squadron. He had discovered traces of a British encampment nearby, and noted that similar findings had been reported on nearby Beechey Island, at the entrance to the Wellington Channel.

Later, in his book, Kane would suggest that Ommanney had suppressed a significant aspect of his landing: "Our consort, the *Rescue,* as we afterward learned, had shared in this discovery, though the British commander's inscription in the cairn, as well as his official reports, might lead to a different conclusion. [The *Rescue*'s] Captain Griffin, in fact, landed with Captain Ommanney, and the traces were registered while the two officers were in company." To this theme—the exclusive nationalism of the imperial British—the proudly American Kane would return.

Now, he inspected Cape Riley, notebook in hand. He identified five distinct "remnants of habitation": four circular mounds of crumbled limestone, clearly designed as bases for tents, and a fifth such enclosure, larger and triangular in shape, whose entrance faced south toward Lancaster Sound. He also found large square stones arranged to serve as a fireplace and, on the beach, several pieces of pine wood that had once formed part of a boat. In Kane's view, the evidence was meager but conclusive: "All these speak of a land party from Franklin's squadron."

Next morning, the *Advance* sailed on toward Beechey Island, which "rode up in a lofty monumental block" of characteristic mountain limestone and which Kane insisted on identifying more precisely as a promontory or peninsula, because a low isthmus linked it to the much larger Devon Island. By August 27, five vessels under three commanders—William Penny, Sir John Ross, and Edwin De Haven—stood anchored within a quarter mile. Not far from Beechey, between Cape Spencer and Point Innes, Penny had discovered some additional traces of Franklin's expedition—tin canisters with the manufacturer's label, scraps of newspaper dated 1844, and two pieces of paper bearing the name of one of Franklin's officers. In his private, 161-page journal, Kane revealed his persistent belief that the lost expedition might yet be found: "Penny seemed to think that these [relics and their scattered situation] indicate a party in distress. Cast away and now perhaps on road to England via Cape Riley. Cannot agree with these [conclusions]. A migrating party they certainly are or were, but the ships may yet be in the land of the living."

After breakfast, Kane and De Haven took a boat ashore to investigate for themselves. Soon, along with Ross, Penny, and a couple of other officers, they were standing on the icy shore, discussing how best to cooperate in continuing the search. Penny sketched out a rough proposal: he would search to the west; Ross would cross Lancaster Sound to communicate with the *Prince Albert* and prevent her from sailing south unnecessarily; and the Americans, with whom he had already consulted, would proceed north through the Wellington Channel.

With this agreed, Ross left to return to the *Felix*. Kane was talking with Penny, who had speculated in print about the existence of an Open Polar Sea, when he looked up and saw a seaman hurrying across the rocks. The sailor shouted against the noise of the wind and the waves: "Graves, Captain Penny! Graves! Franklin's winter quarters!"

The officers hurried to meet the messenger, scrambling up the snowy slope to higher ground. After catching his breath and responding to questions as best he could, the seaman led the way along the ridge, and eventually to the crest of Beechey isthmus. Kane wrote: "Here, amid the sterile uniformity of snow and slate, were the head-boards of three graves, made after the old orthodox fashion of gravestones at home." The three mounds adjoining them formed a line facing Cape Riley, visible across a cove.

The headstones bore inscriptions declaring them sacred to the memories of three sailors: W. Braine of the *Erebus,* who died April 3, 1846, at age thirty-two; John Hartnell of the *Erebus,* no date specified, dead at age twenty-three; and John Torrington, "who departed this life January 1ˢᵗ, a.d. 1846, on board of H.M. ship *Terror,* aged 20 years." In describing this scene, Kane drew attention to the words "on board" and added, "Franklin's ships, then, had not been wrecked when he occupied the encampment at Beechey."

Drawn by James Hamilton after a sketch by Elisha Kane, and engraved by John Sartain, this is a romanticized representation of the gravesite of the first three sailors to die during the last expedition of Sir John Franklin. Kane was present at the discovery of the site, a galvanizing moment that inspired him to lead a search expedition.

The excitement of this discovery of graves would be felt down through the decades—indeed, for over a century. In the 1980s, a Canadian forensic scientist exhumed the three bodies, well preserved by the Arctic ice, for analysis. The resulting book, *Frozen in Time,* by Owen Beattie and John Geiger, argued that lead poisoning from canned food played a role in the demise of the Franklin expedition.

Now, on August 27, 1850, Elisha Kent Kane copied the inscriptions from the headboards and sketched the three graves against the desolate landscape. He then scoured the area, which abounded in fragmentary remains—part of a stocking, a worn mitten, shavings of wood, the remnants of a rough garden. A quarter mile from the graves, he came upon a neat pile of more than 600 preserved-meat cans. Emptied of food, these had been filled with limestone pebbles, "perhaps to serve as convenient ballast on boating expeditions."

Countless other indications, including bits and pieces of canvas, rope, sailcloth, and tarpaulins, as well as scrap paper, a small key, and odds and ends of brass work, testified that this was a winter resting place. Nobody turned up any written documents, however, nor even the vaguest hint about the intentions of the party. Kane judged this remarkable—"and for so able and practiced an Arctic commander as Sir John Franklin, an incomprehensible omission."

Others, given the benefit of hindsight and the accretion of evidence, have questioned whether Franklin was as competent as some of his contemporaries believed. In 1850, Elisha Kane noted only that it was impossible to stand on Beechey without forming an opinion about what had happened to the British explorer. Before offering his own, he reviewed the incontestable facts. During the winter of 1845–46, the *Terror* had wintered here. She kept some of her crew on board. Some men from the *Erebus* were also here. An organized party had taken astronomical observations, made sledges, and prepared gardens to battle scurvy.

Beyond this lay speculation. Kane inferred the health of the expedition to be generally satisfactory, as only three men had died out of nearly 130. He puzzled over the abandoned tin cans, "not very valuable, yet not worthless," and speculated that they might have been left if Franklin departed Beechey in a hurry—as a result, for example, of the ice breaking up unexpectedly.

The main question, of course, was where had Franklin gone? Kane judged that Franklin "had not, in the first instance, been able to prosecute his instructions for the Western search; and the examinations made so fully since by Captain Austin's officers have proved that he never reached Cape Walker, Banks' Land, Melville Island, Prince Regent Inlet, or any point of the sound considerably to the west or southwest."

In fact, though all the Arctic experts present at Beechey—including William Penny and Sir John Ross—shared this belief, Austin's officers in their four ships had proven nothing. In 1854, explorer John Rae would discover that Franklin had indeed sailed south and west from Beechey, making his way down Peel Sound before getting trapped in the ice.

But in 1850, Kane and his fellow searchers, entranced by the notion of an Open Polar Sea, never considered that Franklin might have sailed north up the Wellington Channel and then south again before he even put in at Beechey. Instead, Kane imagined that in the spring of 1846 Franklin had gazed out anxiously, waiting for the ice to open. The first lead to appear would almost certainly run northwest along the coast of Devon Island. Would Franklin wait until Lancaster Sound opened to the south, and then sail back to try the upper reaches of Baffin Bay? "Or would he press to the north through the open lead that lay before him?"

Anybody who knew Franklin's character, determination, and purpose, Kane insisted, would find the question easy to answer. "We, the searchers, were ourselves tempted, by the insidious openings to the north in Wellington Channel, to push on in the hope that some lucky chance might point us to an outlet beyond. Might not the same temptation have had its influence for Sir John Franklin? A careful and daring navigator, such as he was, would not wait for the lead to close."

12

LOCKED IN THE ICE

As September began, the *Advance* started across the mouth of the Wellington Channel so that, sheltered by Cornwallis Island, it could then travel north. Kane saw white whales, narwhals, and seals, as well as two polar bears. But he marveled most at the ice, which he called "tremendous, far ahead of anything" he had yet seen. He described upraised tables fourteen feet thick and hummocks forced skyward by pack ice, rising "in cones like crushed sugar, some of them forty feet high." One night, De Haven roused him from sleep at two o'clock to look at the ice—great blocks piled twenty feet and more above their heads, and immense, floating hummocks thirty feet high, some of them grazing the ship.

The advancing season brought colder temperatures. And the Americans, especially those from the south, felt the change. Their stoves, hurriedly stowed deep in the hold back in Brooklyn, remained inaccessible, buried beneath thousands of pounds of provisions, including coal. Nor did comparisons help. Before leaving Beechey, Kane had spent three days aboard the *Resolute,* the recently arrived flagship of the Austin expedition. From the British ships, according to Robert Randolph Carter, first officer of the *Rescue,* the young surgeon brought back "glowing accounts of their comforts. He actually had sheets to sleep in every night." Kane himself confessed to being dazzled by the preparedness of the *Resolute* for winter, and wrote that he "had to shake off a feeling almost of despondency when I saw how much better fitted they were to grapple with the grim enemy, Cold. Winter, if we may judge of it, by the clothing and warming appliances of the British squadron, must be something beyond our power to cope with; for, in comparison with them, we have nothing, absolutely nothing."

On September 4, Kane killed his first polar bear, shooting it from the bow of the *Advance* when the creature swam too near. With several other men, he managed to drag the carcass into a small boat and haul it aboard. The bear measured eight feet, nine inches, weighed 1,600 pounds, and would provide an immense amount of food. The enormity of the creature, its roundness and muscularity, put the men in mind of a small elephant.

During a storm one evening, while sitting quietly around their snug little table, the officers were startled by a crash. They rushed on deck to see that a massive chunk of ice was rushing down upon the ship, driven by a fierce wind. It hit the nearby *Rescue,* lifting her out of the water and snapping her cables, but then launched that ship through an area of young ice. The men of the *Advance,* which was warping desperately, managed to move their ship a few yards closer to shore—just enough that the great field of ice swept past, narrowly clearing the stern.

Soon, temperatures hovered around the freezing point, even during the day. The Americans still had no functioning stoves. At night, after drawing the India-rubber curtains of his berth and lighting his lamp, Kane could see his breath as he wrote in his journal, "This is not very cold, no doubt—not very cold to your forty-five minus men of Arctic winters; but to us poor devils from the zone of the liriodendrons and peaches, it is rather cool for the September month of water-melons."

On September 8, the men cut an opening in the field ice and dragged the *Advance* into the main flow of Lancaster Sound, where young ice mixed with icebergs that had washed south down the Wellington Channel. In the distance, Kane could see two of Austin's westward-bound ships, the *Resolute* and the *Pioneer*, trapped in the pack. But then, enviously, he watched those sailing vessels use steam power to break free and plow ahead into the wind. William Penny then overtook those two ships, leaving Kane to fret that except for Sir John Ross, who was traveling in the opposite direction, "we are now the last of all the searchers."

Stormy weather and pack ice swept the Americans beyond the Wellington Channel and past Cornwallis Island. Temperatures had sunk to well below freezing. Writing in the fireless cabin, Kane noted that both the water and the coffee had frozen solid. The navigation, at least, was exciting. In all his Arctic readings, he had never read of any such tumult: "We are literally running for our lives." Surrounded by moving icebergs large and small, the *Advance* drove westward under full sail, ignoring small bumps and making for the shelter of Griffith Island.

De Haven managed to find a sheltered area of comparatively open water. But soon afterward, he signaled the *Rescue* to cast off and make for home. He had hoped to sail north up the Wellington Channel. But his orders stipulated that he should try to avoid being trapped in the ice over the winter, and should instead "make his escape, and return to New York in the fall."

The Americans regretted leaving their fellow searchers. About fifty miles from the British ships, however—"as complete a separation as an entire continent"—they encountered thickening ice. One evening as he sat writing in his berth, rubbing his stiffened limbs to warm them and listening to the crunch, crunch, crunch of the sailing ship as it pushed through the ice, Kane heard the sound become intermittent, and then subside altogether. "Down came the captain: 'Doctor, the ice has caught us. We are frozen up.'"

Kane donned furs and went up on deck. Wind filled the sails, but without effect. In the gathering darkness, he could see nothing but ice, ice, and more ice, no matter where he looked. The American ships had ground to a halt in the middle of the mouth of the Wellington Channel. There they sat, helpless, frozen into a vast, icy waste.

o   o   o

On the afternoon of September 16, a cloud lifted as Kane stood on deck. Looking east toward Devon Island, roughly thirty miles away, he realized that he was gazing at coastline he had never seen before. In the distance, he recognized Beechey, the isthmus of the graves, and realized that the ship stood just off Cape Bowden. Locked within a field of ice, the American ships had begun drifting north. This movement continued, the *Advance* crunching and creaking in the ever-thickening ice. One afternoon, the ice banks rose to the bulwarks as two giant ice tables collided. But then the ice subsided. The drift continued, and soon the *Advance* lay beyond Cape Bowden, the most northerly charted landmark—twenty miles beyond, twenty-five, thirty. No longer could Kane make out even the high bluffs of Barlow's Inlet.

One afternoon during a gale, while writing in the cabin, Kane felt a rumbling sensation so strange that he dashed up on deck. He watched as an expanse of ice around the ship, already bristling with hummocks, suddenly exploded under the pressure of a still greater ice field driven before the wind, cracking every which way and throwing up tables of ice. For a while, great chunks towered above the bulwarks, but then they toppled over and left the *Advance* floating in a mass of shards.

The ice refroze; the northward drift resumed. Day after day, the ice carried the ships farther into uncharted territory. Kane helped De Haven name the geographical features: here was the Maury Channel, there Griffin Inlet. On September 22, just above 75 degrees and gazing still farther north, the doctor discerned a large body of unknown land and suggested naming it "Grinnell Land," after the expedition's sponsor.

Later, when Kane wrote his book about this expedition, he challenged the legitimacy of the latest maps out of London, which gave this territory a different name (Albert Land), based on a subsequent sighting by British navigators. Admitting that the controversy "is perhaps of little moment," yet he devoted 3,000 words, or more than ten printed pages, to making his case, arguing that while a mere sighting no longer conferred ownership, "the comity of explorers . . . holds it for law every where that he who first sees

This superb pencil sketch, entitled The Rescue in her "ice dock," *is believed to be one of the few surviving drawings of hundreds done by Elisha Kane.*

and first announces shall also give the name." Kane eventually carried the day, and British maps began using "Grinnell Peninsula."

Now came another partial breakup. Tables of ice "piled themselves in angry confusion against our sides," rearing up above the ship and lifting the *Advance* eighteen inches out of the water. In the dark and cold, all hands worked with picks and crowbars to chop away the most threatening fragments, some of which rose five feet above the deck. Kane observed that, during one fourteen-minute stretch of crashing and banging, the ship moved eighty feet. When the tumult ended, the *Advance* sat cradled by several tables of ice, one end eighteen inches higher than the other. The *Rescue* sat nearby, both ships surrounded by hummocks that looked like the "snow-covered barriers of street rioters."

Early on October 1, feeling so securely wedged that no further movement would be possible, the men began "breaking hold" to retrieve the buried stoves. Two weeks before, the officers had managed to reach a Cornelius lard lamp that not only brightened the cabin, but raised its temperature to

44 degrees Fahrenheit. Still, with the dark nights growing longer and the cold deepening, the crew went to work with a will. By forming a line and passing the coal in buckets, they emptied five tons of the black fuel onto the ice and laid hands on the stoves.

Around ten o'clock in the morning, a large crack appeared in the field, running east and west to the horizon. Shortly after noon, the wind shifted, the ice tables began moving, and another great crack appeared, this one running north and south. Within minutes, the entire ice field began breaking up, and all hands, including officers, went desperately to work to reclaim everything that had been piled on the ice. By the time darkness fell, although exhausted, they had retrieved everything but a couple of tons of coal.

At midnight on October 6, with yet another storm raging and the *Advance* again adrift, Kane wrote wryly: "An odd cruise, this. The American expedition fast in a lump of ice about as big as Washington Square, and driving, like the shanty on a raft, before a howling gale." Next morning, when he went on deck, he found the ship twenty miles south of its previous position. The pack ice had begun carrying the Americans back the way they had come.

The ship's position remained so precarious, so liable to sudden and violent change, that the men did not get the stoves working until October 19. By that time, on at least one occasion, when the lamp died out during the night, the cabin temperature dropped to 16 degrees Fahrenheit. Kane tramped the deck to keep warm, but also, despite the cold, successfully hunted seal by practicing "the Esquimaux tactics of much patience and complete immobility"—all of which prompted him to marvel at the adaptability of the human body.

The Americans erected tentlike shelters on the decks of both the *Advance* and the *Rescue*. They removed bulkheads, set up stoves at both ends of each tent, and allowed officers and men to live together. On the *Advance,* Kane fitted a series of canvas gutters around the cabin hatchways. These caught the water that condensed near the ceiling, and kept water from dripping onto the floor.

As the southward drift continued, Kane gave lectures on scientific topics. Also, according to Robert Randolph Carter, the "little doc" emerged as the best chess player in the company. And when, late in October, carried along by the pack ice, the *Advance* emerged from the Wellington Channel, Kane led a party ashore toward Beechey isthmus, where John Ross was thought to be wintering. After trekking five miles through rough hummocks, alternatively climbing, falling, and slipping into pools of water, he arrived at a black lane of open water that forced him to turn back.

Now the ice pack carried the two ships east through Lancaster Sound, back toward Baffin Bay, at about five miles a day. In the worsening cold, dried apples and peaches froze solid in their barrels. Men would chop them out with heavy axes and thaw the lumps near a stove. They used saws to cut blocks of brown sugar, and chisels and mallets to get butter and lard. Kane noted that, at 30 degrees below zero, pork and beef hardened into a mosaic that would repel a simple axe and yield only to crowbar and pickaxe.

On November 9, the sun did not rise above the horizon. The Arctic night had begun. Given the cold, the darkness, and the monotonous diet, Kane studied "the bleached faces" of his mess-mates and feared for their health. He instituted a regimen of compulsory exercise, forcing even the officers out onto the ice field in temperatures of 50 below zero, leading them in running, hummock-sliding, and games of tag, leapfrog, and football—anything to ward off scurvy.

13

AFTER EIGHTY-SIX DAYS

By the end of November, the *Rescue* had been so badly battered that, if the ice were to break up and release her, she would probably sink. De Haven brought her sixteen men aboard the already crowded *Advance*. Now thirty-three men inhabited a space Kane described as smaller than his father's library. They lived among damp furs, soiled woolens, cast-off boots, and sick companions, in a space heated by three stoves and a cooking galley and lit by three bear-fat lamps "burning with the constancy of a vestal shrine."

Kane convinced De Haven to increase rations and insisted on airing the cabin more frequently. Through December, despite his efforts, he watched the health of the crew deteriorate. Eight men suffered from swollen gums, the first sign of scurvy, and Kane diagnosed one case of pneumonia. On Christmas Day, after a special dinner and a glass of cognac—prescribed "to protect the mess from indigestion"—all hands participated in a footrace. Kane was appalled to see the strongest man aboard collapse in a faint. On New Year's Day, 1851, the men ate plum pudding and wine, but Kane reported that "there was no joy in our merriment: we were weary of the night."

Around midnight one night in mid-January, cracking ice threatened both vessels. From one o'clock until six-thirty, all hands remained on deck wearing shoulder harnesses, ready with sledges and rubber boats to abandon ship. That emergency passed, but the continuing threats took a toll. By the end of February, twenty of the twenty-five crewmen and all eight of the officers had the ulcerated gums, joint pains, and swollen limbs that denoted scurvy.

Kane felt weak, had trouble carrying a musket, and could scarcely limp around on deck. Old wounds opened up, among them the lance wound he had suffered in Mexico, and "even old bruises and sprains, received at barely remembered periods, came to us like dreams." Still, Kane remained upright and relatively healthy, probably because the frigid environment protected him against viruses that, in warmer climes, and especially in tropical heat, tended to reactivate the lurking streptococci of rheumatic fever.

Meanwhile, even De Haven, a man of strong constitution, took to his bunk with scurvy so serious that the doctor thought he would die. Years later, Kane would elaborate in a snippet of transcribed conversation that not only captures his cadences, but describes a situation absent from any other written record. Asked about the "soul's power over the body," Kane flatly declared: "The soul can lift the body out of its boots, sir. When our captain was dying—I say dying, I have seen scurvy enough to know—every old sore in his body was a running ulcer. I never saw a case so bad that either lived or died. There was trouble aboard—there might be mutiny. So soon as the breath was out of his body we might be at each other's throats. I felt that he owed even the repose of dying to the service. I went down to his bunk and shouted in his ear, 'Mutiny, captain! Mutiny!' He shook off the cadaveric stupor: 'Set me up,' said he, 'and order those fellows before me.' He heard the complaint, ordered punishment, and from that hour convalesced. Keep that man awake with danger, and he wouldn't die of anything till his duty was done."

o   o   o

In writing about Arctic expeditions, explorers usually relayed little about the effects of their absence on those they had left behind. In this regard, Elisha Kane proved no exception. But on January 26, 1851, acting on false reassurances, Jane Leiper Kane wrote a letter to Elisha: "At last word has come from Mr. Grinnell that we can communicate to you. What a fearful separation it has been, dear Elisha, that in seven long months we could not even hold communication by the pen. It was a false imagining of your mother that would have found consolation in breathing forth her fears to you. I find I cannot put them into words, I have only one absorbing thought, your little vessel blocked in by icebergs, and the oppressing doubt that you never be extricated to gladden my eyes again. I cannot as your father brighten the picture and fancy you in possession of sure tidings of Sir John Franklin, or creeping out at Behring Straits as Mr. Grinnell imagines. I can only bow in meek submission, ejaculating prayers for your deliverance to Him who has marked out this dangerous path for you."

Nor would Kane write much about the psychological effects of isolation and extended darkness, the debilitated state of mind brought on by a months-long hunkering-down in the wintertime Arctic, and which the Spanish, more familiar with exploring at the opposite end of the earth, would call *loco antardida*. But, like most of his fellow travelers, he suffered from depression.

On January 29, when, for the first time in eighty-six days, the sun was to rise above the horizon at midday, the entire crew gathered on deck to celebrate the moment with three cheers—everyone except Kane, who felt "in no mood to join this sallow-visaged party." Instead of remaining with his companions, he shouldered his musket and strode out across the ice to a solitary spot a mile away, thinking morosely of family and home. As the transformative moment approached, he climbed a hummock and, in the distance, saw his fellow voyagers formed into a line on the ice.

On the horizon, a crimson blush slowly brightened to incandescent white, and finally the sun appeared. Kane "looked at him thankfully with a great globus in my throat." Then came the three cheers from the ship, and Kane fired his musket at a tiny star-target he fixed to a hummock, speculating that many years would pass before another American rifle "signalizes in the winter of Baffin's Bay the conjunction of sunrise, noonday, and sunset."

Over the next days and weeks, as hours of daylight increased and hunting improved, the men grew healthier—though now they battled snow blindness, the result of sunlight glancing off the white snow. The best protection, Kane wrote, came not from the goggles or colored lenses they had brought with them, but from Inuit technology: a stick of hard wood with a slit that admitted a narrow pencil of light.

Early in March, De Haven began to repair the damaged *Rescue* by digging an eight-foot-deep trench around the ship, leaving the keel in eighteen inches of ice. This novel dry dock enabled work crews to rebuild the stern post and install a new bowsprit. On April 22, to the jubilation of the whole expedition, the men of the *Rescue* returned to their own vessel.

One month later, when land became visible for the first time in ninety-nine days, Kane confirmed with sightings what he already knew: the pack ice had carried the two ships through Baffin Bay almost to the narrows of the Davis Strait. Finally, on June 5, spring breakup announced its arrival with a loud cracking. The ice field, which had entrapped the expedition for eight months and twenty-four days, and had transported the American ships more than a thousand miles, suddenly began undulating violently, "as if our ice were a carpet shaken by Titans." As he stood watching the ice rising, falling and bending as it transmitted an advancing wave, Kane felt almost seasick.

Three days later, near the western shore of the Davis Strait, the *Advance* and the *Rescue* floated free. Desperate for fresh food and rest, the Americans made for the Whalefish Islands, threading their way through a labyrinth of ice pans and bergs. The *Advance* reached Disco on June 17. The men stuffed themselves with eider, codfish, and seal, drank copious amounts of beer, and "danced with the natives, teaching them the polka." Incredibly, after just five days, and with Kane finding time to sketch the "more fantastical" icebergs, the Americans again sailed north to renew the search for Franklin.

o   o   o

De Haven sought to cross Baffin Bay and re-enter Lancaster Sound, but for two months the Middle Ice proved impenetrable—not just to the Americans, but to a British ship that joined them in warping, tracking, and boring. The *Prince Albert,* Lady Franklin's schooner, had returned to the Arctic under Captain William Kennedy. During the three weeks when it lay nearby, Kane became good friends with Kennedy's first officer, Joseph-René Bellot, a French volunteer and a favorite of Lady Franklin.

Kane would describe how, while tramping across the ice with Bellot and two others, he spotted a small polar bear. He and Bellot tried to circle around a large iceberg and drive the creature toward their companions. "We got within about one hundred and twenty yards of him before he galloped off. M. Bellot, in his excitement, tumbled down twice, and fired once." Bellot would also write of the friendship, observing of Kane that "there is no subject of our conversation on which I do not receive useful information from him." One afternoon in early August, while approaching the *Advance,* Bellot slipped into a crevasse. He might have drowned if Kane had not jumped off the ship and pulled him out.

Now, in August 1851, the *Prince Albert* abandoned attempts to forge a passage through the Middle Ice. She found an open lead trending south and, on the thirteenth, sailed that way to seek an alternative route. Six days later, bowing to the impenetrability of the ice pack, and also to the reality that the scurvy-ridden crew might not survive a second winter in these regions, the Americans turned around and sailed for home.

The final leg of the voyage lasted almost six weeks. But long before September 30, 1851, when the *Advance* sailed into New York Harbor, Elisha Kent Kane knew he had found his life's work. Despite its hardships and deprivations, the sixteen-month expedition had whetted his appetite. He would return to the High Arctic. He would return to seek survivors of the lost Franklin expedition, and to discover what lay at the top of the world—almost certainly an Open Polar Sea.

14

DEATH IN THE FAMILY

Back home in Philadelphia, acting to fulfill a cherished ambition, while insisting on the scientific seriousness of his purpose, Elisha Kent Kane began writing a book intended for a broad general audience: a narrative of the Grinnell expedition. Drawing on his detailed journals, he made slow progress at first because he proved such an eloquent speaker that he received many invitations to lecture about his Arctic adventure. These included a series of three lectures to be delivered at the Smithsonian Institution in Washington, D.C. In the first, on December 29, 1851, he told the story of the Grinnell expedition, highlighting the eight-month drift in pack ice. In the third, he described the hazards of Arctic exploration—icebergs, darkness, scurvy, cold—and such meteorological phenomena as auroras, refraction, and ice blinks, or mirages.

Kane viewed his second talk, which he delivered on New Year's Eve, as pivotal. In it, he discussed the lost expedition of Sir John Franklin, arguing that the missing mariners had sailed north through the Wellington Channel and become trapped behind an ice barrier in an Open Polar Sea. By now, Kane had assimilated the existing literature that explored this hypothesis.

The notion of an Open Polar Sea had become popular among English and French geographers in the mid-eighteenth century. By 1818, the self-educated John Cleves Symmes, a retired American army captain based in St. Louis, had begun elaborating it. He proposed a theory of Holes in the Poles, and insisted that the earth was hollow. Traveling Ohio and Kentucky by horse and wagon, Symmes had advocated that explorers sail both north and south beyond the barriers of ice.

In the 1820s, Jeremiah Reynolds, editor of the *Wilmington Spectator,* took up the cause. Reynolds not only led a sailing expedition south, but wrote an 1835 bestseller about it called *The Voyage of the United States Frigate Potomac.* Reynolds also inspired *The Narrative of Arthur Gordon Pym* by Edgar Allan Poe, which drew on the idea, and built support for the United States Exploring Expedition in which Edwin De Haven had sailed under Charles Wilkes.

At the Smithsonian, Kane argued that Franklin and his men had sailed north up the Wellington Channel and penetrated the ice barrier to the Open Polar Sea, but then got trapped. There, he suggested, "unable to leave their hunting ground and cross the frozen Sahara which intervened between them and the world from which they are shut out," they subsisted on plentiful animal life. Despite stormy weather, Kane drew capacity crowds to his lectures—a series that, according to the *National Intelligencer,* proved "one of the most interesting courses ever to be delivered at the Institution."

As January unfolded, Kane spoke in New York and Baltimore, where at the Maryland Institute he twice addressed audiences of more than 2,000. His uncle George Gray Leiper, an ex-Congressman and judge then sojourning in Baltimore, wrote: "He has made a decided hit here. . . . His lectures are very interesting, and were listened to with great attention and silence. When he mounts the rostrum he looks more like a boy of seventeen" than one who has traveled the desert sands and spent months trapped in the Arctic ice, only to float, when released, "in company with stupendous icebergs which made the gravest tremble for their personal safety." On May 7, 1852, back in Philadelphia, Kane entertained the American Philosophical Society—where his father, a member since 1825, now served as vice-president—by speaking and exhibiting specimens of vegetable matter he had collected during the long ice drift that marked his latest adventure.

To Henry Grinnell, who had agreed to finance a second expedition, Kane mentioned that he had been corresponding with Jane Franklin. The previous year, he had sent her his argument that some members of the lost expedition remained alive in an Open Polar Sea. She responded that his letter had given her great comfort and satisfaction: "We are longing for the appearance of your book. It will I am sure be one of the most graphic, most touching and most elegant histories of arctic adventure, if I may judge by the few specimens I have seen of your able pen." More recently, Lady Franklin had indicated that she was "delighted to hear of the enthusiasm your lectures have everywhere created, and not at all surprised that it should have been so."

Kane assured her that he would resume the search for the missing Sir John, either serving under the veteran William Penny as part of a multi-vessel undertaking, or else commanding a smaller sortie of his own. But he politely rejected her suggestion that, accompanied by her own small vessel, the *Isabel,* he sail the *Advance* up the Pacific coast of North America and past the Bering Strait. He did not believe that her husband would be found in that distant region.

Kane proposed instead to sail through Baffin Bay to the North Water, as he had done with De Haven. He would then proceed still farther north into Smith Sound. In 1846, as he well knew, a renowned Russian explorer, Baron Friedrich von Wrangel, had argued before the Royal Geographical Society that the best way to reach the North Pole was to probe Smith Sound using dogs and sledges. Just four months before, in August 1852, British captain Edward Inglefield had penetrated that sound to 78 degrees, 28 minutes—eighty miles farther north than any previous explorer. Before being driven south by a gale, the British captain had seen nothing ahead but open water. Had Inglefield been gazing at an entrance to the Open Polar Sea? Kane felt certain that he had.

But to prove it, this junior naval officer required financial backing. Originally, he envisioned a squadron comprising Grinnell's two sailing ships, a stout navy steamer, and a crew of fifty men. Congress had so far proven reluctant to approve any such expensive undertaking. Fortunately for Kane, John Pendleton Kennedy had recently become secretary of the navy. A lawyer and ex-Congressman, this cultivated southerner had a keen interest in science, and had helped Samuel Morse build the first telegraph line between Washington and Baltimore. As the author of three notable novels about early life in America, Kennedy also enjoyed a literary reputation, one burnished by his having acted as a patron to Edgar Allan Poe.

In mid-November 1852, Kennedy listened as Kane spoke passionately of his projected expedition. Impressed by the vision and commitment of the younger man, he offered to place him on "special duty," guaranteeing him a higher rate of pay, and promised also that the navy would provide both crewmen and provisions. Kennedy was a close friend of the American banker George Peabody, with whom he had served in the American army during the War of 1812. And before long the philanthropist Peabody, who lived in London, and so knew all about the lost Franklin expedition, had stepped forward with a contribution of $10,000.

o   o   o

Earlier in 1852, while writing and lecturing mainly about his first Arctic expedition, and gathering support for a second, Elisha Kane had worked so hard that he made himself sick again. He tried a radical diet that worsened his condition, and finally a medical friend, fearing "an attack of apoplexy, paralysis or some other form of cerebral explosion," convinced him to resume eating normally.

During this time, his father and his brother Thomas applied themselves to extracting and editing a readable book from his journals. "The introduction is in progress," Tom wrote, "and will not fail you. Perhaps we can do a good deal without you, for as I look into the volumes after the first, I am surprised to see how little I would be content to change, and how large a portion can best keep the journal form. *It is intensely interesting.*"

In July, regarding the second half of the opus, Tom wrote: "Father is satisfied with me that it will be best very much cut down. You have picked many of the plums out of it for the rest of your cake, and the interest will be apt to pall after you have escaped the Pack and seem to be Homeward Bound." And in October, the Judge himself observed: "Reading over the book carefully so far, I think it is 2/3 finished, & very good. The writing of the rest may occupy six busy weeks, counting in the revisal."

During the spring of the year, as Elisha recovered his health, his brother Willie, who turned fourteen in April, developed a lingering illness. Probably it was meningitis, although Asiatic cholera had killed more than a thousand Philadelphians two years before, and in the 1840s the poorer sections of the city had endured epidemics of smallpox, typhus, tuberculosis, and scarlet fever. Elisha adored his youngest brother, and over the years had not only corresponded with the boy, but kept his letters.

"Dear Elisha," Willie had written at age five or six. "I go to the public school but am in the lowest division and expect to be promoted next week. We have got a new teacher to our division who is as croop as anything. I was put on the hour line for letting some pencils drop out of my pockets and they forgot to call out my name after school and I went to Mr. Wood and told him about it and he excused me." At age seven, Willie warned that he would not write as frequently as he had done lately "till you write to me how you escaped from the Indians and the shark. Good bye. Your affectionate brother, W.L. Kane." A third letter, written in block letters, asks plaintively: "Dear Elisha, Oh when will you come home?"

Now, while absent from home and treating his own questionable health with a "water cure" then in vogue, Elisha received alarming news from his brother Thomas, who wrote: "I wish I could reply to your dear left-handed but right-hearted letter as it deserves; but the truth is that our thought has

After the death of Kane's brother Willie, the family could not bear to remain at Rensselaer, the house in which the boy died. They built a new home and, in Willie's memory, called it Fern Rock. The house has long since been demolished, but Fern Rock is now the name of a neighbourhood in North Philadelphia.

all been engrossed by Willie, while we have no desireable news to communicate about him. . . . But, dear Elish, I must tell you: Willie is no better. And to say this now, after so much time has been consumed, is almost to say that he is worse."

Elisha returned home and, as a medical man, insisted on tending the boy.

All through the summer of 1852, he and his mother frequently took Willie outside for picnic teas, heading to a giant boulder surrounded by ferns—"Willie's Fern Rock." Late in August, when despite his best efforts the boy died, Elisha plunged into a depression. Indeed, the death of Willie shook the family so profoundly that they left Rensselaer and moved back to the city. Jane Leiper Kane wrote to Elisha that "if we could only see him as he is, a glorified being, in the bosom of his Savior, our grief would be subdued." But she could not, nor could she bear to return to the home where the boy had died. Finally, the family would sell Rensselaer and build another home nearby—a place they called Fern Rock.

15

THE SPIRIT RAPPER

In mid-November 1852, still haunted by Willie's untimely death, but with just six months remaining in which to complete his book and prepare his next Arctic expedition, Elisha Kent Kane resumed a fierce lecturing schedule. But suddenly, even as he did so, he found himself swamped by an unexpected challenge. It arrived like a rogue wave at sea—a giant wall of water that, washing over him, changed his life irrevocably.

The crisis had been foreshadowed by a mundane coincidence. A couple of years before, from Greenland, Kane had sent an evocative description of the Arctic to his brother Thomas, who had undertaken to serve as his unofficial publicist. Tom forwarded Elisha's missive to Horace Greeley, editor of the prestigious *New York Tribune* and an ally in both his anti-slavery and pro-Mormon campaigns. The newspaper carried the letter on June 8, 1850—in the same issue, and on the same page, as an article promoting two young spiritualists, Margaret and Kate Fox.

Greeley sent a copy of the page to Tom, and thanked him for the letter from Elisha: "Nothing I have read from the Arctic regions for years pictured them so freshly [or proved] . . . so interesting." In that same communication, the newspaper editor mentioned the Spiritualist craze sweeping

America, and the bizarre "spirit rapping" engendered in the presence of the Fox sisters, who had begun attracting attention near Rochester in upstate New York: "I am sure it cannot be accounted for by merely human agency. It is a puzzle which you will some day be interested to investigate. A mere fraud could not live so long and spread so widely."

Rochester is located in the so-called "burned-over district," where, during the Second Great Awakening of the early 1800s, the fires of evangelical revival blazed brightly. The area was settled by Quakers and other radical Protestants who believed in direct communication with their god; in the 1820s and '30s, it gave rise to both William Miller, whose teachings spawned Seventh-Day Adventism, and Joseph Smith, who received an angelic revelation that led to the founding of the Mormon church.

In the 1850s, Greeley was not alone in his approbation of the Fox sisters. Their séances attracted men like James Fenimore Cooper, author of *The Last of the Mohicans;* William Cullen Bryant, poet and editor of the *New York Evening Post;* and Nathaniel Parker Willis, editor of the *Home Journal.* Willis described the young women as "considerably prettier than average," and added that he found it "difficult to reconcile their appearance with the fact that they have been worked upon for two years by the phenomena of unexplained visitations."

Others had proven harder to charm. After one demonstration, James Gordon Bennett huffed in the *New York Herald,* "For two shillings our citizens can go and see an open and professed ventriloquist, who will make more unearthly noises, imitate knocking, bell ringing, cork drawing, pigs squealing, and do a hundred other things more wonderful than the ventriloquists of the Rochester knockings, who have so successfully and ludicrously humbugged these twelve great philosophers."

As a man of science, Elisha Kane leaned toward this latter perspective. Still, in mid-November 1852, having learned that one of the famous Fox sisters was conducting séances at Webb's Union Hotel, located on Arch Street in central Philadelphia, he took a break from his book, strolled over to the hotel from the family's city house in Girard Avenue, and knocked at what he believed to be the correct door. A respectable, middle-aged woman answered. Behind her, Kane could see a demure young woman sitting at a table near a window, immersed in a French grammar. Surprised by the gentility of the scene, Kane said: "I beg your pardon. I have made some mistake. Can you direct me to the room where the 'spirit manifestations' are shown?"

The older woman assured him that he had come to the right place. She introduced herself as Mrs. Fox, ushered him into a parlor, and collected five dollars for a private séance. She disappeared for a moment, then returned with the young woman he had noticed in the window. Mrs. Fox introduced her daughter, Maggie—at nineteen years of age, easily the most famous Spiritualist medium in America.

By this time, with four years of experience, Maggie had perfected the art of the séance. Petitioners, having been enjoined to behave respectfully, would be invited to ask questions of departed spirits. If those spirits felt cooperative, they would respond by making a "rapping" sound; occasionally, they would use five knocks to "call for the alphabet," and then laboriously spell words out.

That morning in November 1852, Kane asked polite questions about Sir John Franklin and his late brother, Willie, and listened while the spirits rapped out cogent responses. He did not figure out how Maggie did her trick; but he knew that somehow she was perpetuating a hoax—as, years later, she herself would publicly confess.

Despite this perception, or perhaps because of it, Kane felt intensely attracted to the spirit rapper. Again and again, newspaper reports had described the Fox sisters as remarkably pretty. But later, puzzling over his feelings in a letter to Maggie, Kane would challenge this, writing that he knew several young women as pretty as she was, but that they inspired in him nothing like the same attraction: "One of the very first things that drew me towards you," he would write, "was your ladylike manner and deportment. . . . very gentle and quiet, and modest, and retiring, as a lady's should be."

But that accounts for only half the attraction. In subsequent letters, Kane would refer repeatedly to Maggie's deceitfulness. For example, he would write: "Is it any wonder that I long to look—only to look—at that dear little deceitful mouth of yours." Clearly, he was smitten with Maggie's dual nature—so demure, yet so deceptive. He became enthralled the instant he perceived that this angelic creature was consciously and deliberately perpetuating a devilish hoax, and that she had been doing this successfully enough, over the past four years, to forge a national reputation and earn a handsome living.

That first morning, Kane left without revealing his feelings. But, unusually, he returned next day to request a second séance. This time, Kane studied Maggie with what she felt to be disquieting intensity. And he managed to speak to her briefly in private, long enough to inquire about her studious side. Like Horace Greeley before him, Kane suggested that Maggie should be in school: "This is no life for you!"

So began an intense courtship—a passionate wooing conducted partly through notes and letters that, having survived, reflect the tumultuous emotions of a lover caught in an emotional maelstrom. Such stories make painful reading, and this one would emerge after Kane's death in excruciating detail. His love letters would be published, together with bridging material, in a book entitled *The Love-Life of Doctor Kane*—a work that, while generally faithful to well-documented truth, also contains exaggerations.

This much is certain: at age thirty-two, Elisha Kent Kane fell in love. The patrician Philadelphian fell in love with a young woman so wildly inappropriate that, when he wasn't dreaming of her, he was agonizing over whether he could free himself from her web of enchantment; and if he could not, whether, despite the scandal such an outcome would precipitate, he could find some way to marry her.

o   o   o

In the mid-nineteenth century, aristocratic Philadelphians shared many characteristics and attitudes with upper-middle-class visitors from England, who judged them most congenial—intelligent, refined, and hospitable. The

Englishman William Chambers, writing in 1852, cited their "pleasant evening parties, their love of literature, their happy blend of the industrial habits of the north with the social usages of the south." An American contemporary, Charles Godfrey Leland, offered an insider's perspective: "The lines of demarcation in [Philadelphia] society were as strongly drawn as in Europe, or more so, with the enormous difference, however, that there was not the slightest perceptible shade of difference in the intellects, culture, or character of people on either side of the line. . . . Very trifling points of difference, not perceptible to the outsider, made the whole difference between the exclusive and the excluded."

And yet, some differences proved perceptible enough. During the previous century, only property owners could vote or hold office—which meant one man in fifty. In the 1770s, 10 percent of Philadelphians owned 89 percent of all property, and fewer than 20 percent owned their homes. Since then, those numbers had become slightly more egalitarian. But by the 1840s, only 477 Philadelphians had fortunes exceeding $50,000, the sum necessary to keep a carriage, according to Leland, and these constituted the "money aristocracy." This upper class remained theoretically open to those who proved their worth. But in 1834, when the wealthy Pierce Butler married the celebrated British actress and writer Fanny Kemble, who came from a prominent theater family, upper-crust Philadelphians frowned upon the union: actresses were regarded as "loose women." The marriage came to grief mainly over opposing views of slavery, and ended in divorce in 1849.

This was the social context in which, in late 1852 and early 1853, Elisha Kane courted Maggie Fox. Every couple of days, he brought flowers, and once he arrived with *Undine* by Friedrich de la Motte, which tells the story of a water nymph who, by marrying an itinerant knight, gains an immortal soul. Kane also wrote Maggie instructional love poems, including one of four stanzas that depicted a laughing girl who was happy before she began practicing a "deceitful art."

By now, Kane knew that, along with her younger sister Kate, Maggie had launched the Spiritualist craze almost by accident. Born on October 7, 1833,

The Fox Sisters in the early 1850s: left to right, Maggie, Kate, and Leah. As by far the oldest sister, Leah orchestrated an elaborate hoax that launched a Spiritualist craze and made celebrities of the younger "spirit rappers."

in Prince Edward County, Upper Canada, on the north shore of Lake Ontario, she moved across the lake with her family in 1848, to an isolated farmhouse in Hydesville, New York. Here, she and Kate discovered that by snapping their double-jointed toes like fingers, they could produce a sharp rapping sound and project it around a room. The girls pretended that these noises were produced by departed spirits, and used the "rappings" to frighten their parents and credulous neighbors. Before they knew it, they had tricked so many adults that they feared to confess the truth.

Their much older sister, Leah, a single mother in her thirties, arrived from Rochester to investigate. This no-nonsense woman took the girls aside and quickly ascertained what they were doing. Sensing an opportunity, instead of revealing the truth, Leah told the girls to keep their secret. She applied herself to publicizing the rappings as a legitimate mystery, and before long had her sisters entertaining the wealthy and well-respected of New York City—people like Horace Greeley.

Now, early in 1853, Elisha Kane escorted Maggie around Philadelphia in the family carriage. At first, he would bring Mrs. Fox as chaperone, but later he brought others, like the collusive wife of his friend Robert Patterson. At times, these chaperones rode in separate carriages. Kane knew that his family would oppose any liaison with Maggie Fox—especially his rigid, uncompromising father, who had already suggested that he marry a certain wealthy young woman. The Judge, Kane knew, would regard his marriage to a "spirit rapper" as damaging to the family name. And he strongly suspected that, rather than countenance any such union, the Judge might disinherit his eldest son—just as he had once been prepared to jail Kane's brother on principle.

Elisha Kane remained vulnerable to this possibility, as he had yet to achieve financial independence. But the dilemma only stoked his passion. Again and again, Kane had demonstrated that he loved nothing better than a daunting challenge—be it a volcano in the Philippines, an awkward monument in Egypt, or a contingent of Mexican regulars in the Sierra Madre. The insane difficulty of winning Maggie Fox made the inducement irresistible. Possibly, Kane's passion derived from an unconscious need to assert his independence—not only against his powerful father, but against the elevated expectations of aristocratic Philadelphia. And the theatricality of the endeavor increased its appeal.

In any case, thinking with the clarity typical of besotted lovers, Kane reasoned that if he could convince Maggie to abandon spirit rapping, he could educate her into respectability. Six decades before George Bernard Shaw would write *Pygmalion,* drawing on Greek mythology to dramatize the story of a professor transforming a working-class girl into a middle-class paragon, Kane set out to do precisely that in real life.

During the two months that began in mid-January 1853, while shunting between cities along the eastern seaboard, lecturing to raise funds, Kane not only visited Maggie every chance he got, but sent her more than twenty letters. These missives, most of them undated, reveal the ambivalence, insecurities, and vacillations typical of those passionately in love: "Why do you not write to me? Have you forgotten your friend? . . . Oh, dear Maggie, when I think of you in your humble calling, and of myself with my toiling vanities and cares, I only feel that I am about to leave you; and feeling this, how very, very, very much I love you. I am a fool for this, yet I know that you have some good reason for not writing. Send me a lock of your hair; for unless it comes I will not come to see you."

At the same time, Kane agonized over Maggie's "spirit rapping." Since blossoming in 1850, when in New York City alone it could claim 40,000 adherents, Spiritualism had come increasingly under attack as fraudulent. Kane perceived that the movement was losing any vestige of respectability, and that this threatened their relationship. In trying to awaken Maggie to this danger, he sometimes revealed an entrenched sense of social superiority, the eventual eradication of which would require nothing less than a life-and-death struggle in the most extreme climate known to man. Then he would write: "When I think of you, dear darling, wasting your time and youth and conscience for a few paltry dollars, and think of the crowds who come nightly to hear of the wild stories of the frozen north, I sometimes feel that we are not so far removed after all. My brain and your body are each the sources of attraction, and I confess that there is not so much difference."

Around this time, Kane also confided: "I miss you when I look over my crowded table, with its books and papers. I miss you when I mount my horse for one of my wild rides. I miss you when listening to the empty fashion nonsense of my fashionable friends, who think themselves so much better than yourself. What is it that I miss in Maggie Fox, that I cannot find in them? I'll tell you. It is not beauty, for they are as beautiful as you. It is not kind words or demonstrations, for they go further than you. But it is in that strange mixture of child and woman, of simplicity and cunning, of passionate impulse and extreme self-control, that has made you a curious study. Maggie, you are very pretty, very childlike, very deceitful, but to me as *readable* as my grandmother's Bible."

Kane saw himself as a man of facts and stern purposes: "My life is only commencing as far as regards the weary road ahead of me, and, if Providence prolongs it, I will leave after me a name and a success. But with all this, I am a weak man and a fool; weak, that I should be caught in the midst of my grave purposes by the gilded dust of a butterfly's wing; and a fool because, while thus caught, I smear my fingers with the perishable color."

Again and again, he insisted that Maggie deserved better than a life of charlatanism. The feisty young spirit rapper, intellectually no match for the cerebral Kane, fought back by playfully calling him "preacher." After all, while incessantly criticizing, he kept urging her to abandon the only adult life she had known—not to mention her friends and relations and a profession, admittedly controversial, that had transported her from a dreary farmhouse in upstate New York to first-class hotels and the drawing rooms of the rich and powerful. Among her supporters, Maggie could still count not only Horace Greeley, editor of the most influential paper of the day, but Nathaniel Pitcher Tallmadge, a former governor of Wisconsin, and Waddy Thompson, an ex–brigadier general who had served several terms as a Congressman.

At different times, both parties tried to break off the relationship. At one point, Kane wrote: "Maggie, darling, don't care for me any more. I love you too well to wish it, and you know that I really am sold to different destinies; for just as you have your wearisome round of daily money-making, I have my own sad vanities to pursue. I am as devoted to my calling as you, poor child, can be to yours. Remember then, as a sort of dream, that Doctor Kane of the Arctic Seas loved Maggie Fox of the Spirit Rappings." Shortly after sending such a missive, and like many a baffled lover before and since, Kane would be imploring his darling to write: "Dear, dear Maggie. Have you ceased to care for me? Me whose devotion you now can see, and of whose true, steadfast love every fibre of your heart can assure you! . . . Do you want me to cease my attentions? Say so, dear Maggie, and even if it kills me I will not annoy you; God knows I love you too much to give you pain or trouble."

After one rift, initiated at the insistence of Mrs. Fox, Maggie repented and wrote Kane regretting her "very tiresome life" and asking his advice and counsel. He told her to stick to her good resolutions and promised to help her escape a life "worse than tedious, it is sinful."

One evening not long after this exchange, Kane lingered in the parlor after Mrs. Fox had left. According to *Love-Life,* which drew on subsequent interviews, he again spoke to Maggie of her ambiguous calling and insisted that she was fit for better things—indeed, for "the highest destiny of a woman," by which, as a man of his times, he could only mean marriage and motherhood. He asked whether she would be willing to abandon her present life and devote herself to acquiring an education that would fit her to live in an entirely different sphere. This would mean making a sacred promise, he warned—one that would bind her heart and soul. But if she would undertake to do this, she would eventually be transformed. She would become worthy of one whose existence would be devoted to her. "And when you are thus changed, Maggie," Kane said, "I shall be proud to make you my wife."

Maggie reported this contingent proposal to her mother, who expressed misgivings. Kane would soon sail away to the Arctic, and who knew for how long? How would Maggie fare in his absence, especially if she ceased spirit rapping, as he insisted she must? Also, why this demand for secrecy? If the doctor was going to marry her daughter, why couldn't they proclaim it to the world? Like many another young woman, Maggie Fox overruled her mother. To Kane, she said yes. Afterward, accompanied by Robert Patterson and his wife, the explorer drove her out to his family's country estate, the vacant Rensselaer, and showed her around. Returning to the carriage, he drew her attention to Mrs. Patterson's engagement ring, a diamond set in black enamel. The next day, when suddenly he produced three rings and asked her to choose among them, Maggie chose the one most like Mrs. Patterson's.

And with that, a forbidden courtship became a secret engagement.

16

The Open Polar Sea

By December 14, 1852, Kane had been able to stand before the American Geographical Society and lay out a detailed itinerary for the second Grinnell expedition. Speaking to an audience of geographers and scientists in the chapel at Columbia University, the articulate, charismatic naval officer sought support for a voyage of exploration with a dual purpose: first, to retrieve any survivors from the lost expedition of Sir John Franklin, which had disappeared in 1845; second, to discover the Open Polar Sea, a temperate basin that, he believed, encircled the North Pole.

In this well-crafted lecture, which ran to 5,000 words, Kane drew on his sixteen months in the Arctic while reviewing the evidence favoring the existence of the hypothetical ice-free sea, or *polynya*. Presenting himself as an adventurous, scientific-minded doctor in the Humboldtean tradition, Kane suggested that this open sea, which almost certainly teemed with fish and mammals, lay beyond a barricading circle of ice and measured roughly 6,000 miles in circumference and 2,000 in "rude diameter."

In describing this annulus, this "ring surrounding an area of open water," he reviewed the testimony of northern explorers, starting in the sixteenth century, with men like Henry Hudson and Martin Frobisher, and culminating with Edward Inglefield, who had recently penetrated Smith Sound to establish a new "farthest north" in the western hemisphere. Before being driven back by a gale, Inglefield had seen nothing ahead but open water. Had the British naval officer chanced upon an entrance to a great Mediterranean that drained the northern slopes of three continents? Kane believed that he had.

What's more, he believed that the Franklin expedition, traces of which he had seen in the Arctic, might well have entered that polar basin by an alternative route—sailing north up the Wellington Channel—and been trapped behind the circumpolar barricade. After all, had not the massive, years-long search orchestrated by Lady Franklin generated "complete proofs" that her husband had gotten lost neither to east nor west? In seeking tangible support, Kane argued further that because he would be searching for Franklin, his projected expedition transcended geographical concerns and curiosity: "The question of access to the Arctic pole—the penetration to this open sea—is now brought again before us, not as . . . a curious problem for scientific inquiry, but as an object claiming philanthropic effort, and appealing thus to the sympathies of the whole civilized world—the rescue of Sir John Franklin and his followers."

Kane argued that several expeditions had shown the Wellington Channel "to be a tortuous estuary," and he doubted that a current search led by Sir Edward Belcher would succeed: "The chances are against their reaching the open sea." He concluded by outlining and seeking support for his alternative approach. From shipping magnate Henry Grinnell—formerly president of the Geographical Society, now a vice-president, and currently beaming in the audience—Kane had acquired the use of the sturdy brigantine *Advance*. In the spring of 1853, he would sail north to Greenland and Smith Sound, then proceed up that waterway as the weather turned cold, "forcing our vessel to the utmost navigable point."

Establishing a base camp on terra firma, he could expect to find animals to sustain hunting travelers and to secure the assistance of "Esquimaux," whose settlements almost certainly extended far north. During the ensuing winter, with the brig frozen in ice, he would dispatch dogs and sledges north to lay depots of provisions along the Greenland coast. Come spring, bent on finding survivors from the Franklin expedition, he would take sledges and small boats and make for the Open Polar Sea: "Once there, if such a reward awaits us, we launch our little boats, and, bidding God speed us, embark upon its waters."

That December night in New York, the eloquent Kane gave a bravura performance. When he had finished, the American Geographical Society voted to thank the secretary of the navy for his generosity, and to set up a five-person committee to work with him, as well as the Coast Survey and the Smithsonian Institution. Elisha Kent Kane had acquired all the official backing he would need to make his expedition a reality.

He still lacked sufficient funds, however, and so, on the lecture circuit, he maintained a furious pace. In Baltimore, he drew an audience of 3,000 to the Maryland Institute. According to the *Baltimore Sun,* "The gallant speaker was often interrupted by loud applause." Kane gave yet another talk at the Smithsonian Institution in Washington, then conducted several lectures in New England, where he was feted by the mayor of Boston.

The young adventurer proved a popular speaker. On February 17, for example, a Boston newspaper reported that "a highly intelligent audience . . . listened with profound attention and with tokens of delight to one of the most interesting lectures we have heard for a long time." After providing some context, the article described Dr. Kane: "He is a small man, slightly made, full of energy, intelligence, and enthusiasm, and with an organiza-tion which makes one think of Damascus steel. His manner is modest and winning, and his agreeable voice, choice language, and gentlemanly deport-ment would give interest to the most commonplace topic." Kane spoke not of the commonplace, however, but "of the fatality which has attended explorers in the Arctic regions," as well as the first Grinnell expedition. At a second lecture, he would discuss the probable fate of Sir John Franklin: "He cannot fail of a crowded house."

The lecturer sent a clipping of this report to Maggie Fox, observing: "How disgusting is this life, to be discussed by the papers! I need not be so proud, Maggie, for I am no better than the 'rappers.'" Despite this disavowal, he thrived on the attention—and managed to raise $1,400 for the cause. Yet even with the contributions of scientific bodies like the Smithsonian Institution, the National Observatory, and the American Philosophical Society, and of individuals like Grinnell, Peabody, and Kennedy, who worked through the United States Navy, Kane would need every penny.

During the early months of 1853, the explorer worked hard to secure congressional aid. He commuted between Philadelphia, New York, and Washington and called on any senator who would see him. To Kennedy, he wrote that the struggle was exhausting him: "I have not averaged more than three hours' sleep a night since I left." In early April, he sent a rapid series of telegrams: "Things look black"; "Still seeing senators"; "A bare ghost of a chance." But he reported the clincher by letter: "The result of a hard week's work is—a sacrifice of time, money and influence!"

Through all this, and while simultaneously working on his book, which he had promised to deliver before he sailed, Kane maintained a voluminous correspondence. He wrote steadily to his closest American allies, John Pendleton Kennedy and Henry Grinnell, and frequently to scientists Spencer F. Baird, Alexander Dallas Bache, and Matthew Fontaine Maury. He also exchanged letters with Arctic explorers in the U.K., among them Edward Parry, John Richardson, James Clark Ross, and Edward Sabine. And he responded weekly to letters from Lady Franklin, who was orchestrating the search for her husband.

Early in 1853, Kane read that Edward Inglefield, who had sailed into Smith Sound the previous year, would soon undertake another voyage to those environs in a steam-powered vessel. Despite disclaimers from Lady Franklin, he suspected that Inglefield intended to race him into the sound with a view to discovering Franklin and the Open Polar Sea. Early in March, he wrote to Grinnell that the only way to compete "with the screw-steamer of Inglefield is by an early presence in Melville Bay, which may enable us to enter the North Water with the whaling-fleet by the June passage."

That same week, a government shakeup resulted in the departure of John P. Kennedy as secretary of the navy. The newly appointed James C. Dobbin would provide nothing like the same support. And on April 10, despite having had a long talk with President Franklin Pierce, Kane left the White House with nothing but good wishes. A few days later, still worried about acquiring enough provisions for a three-year voyage, as well as instruments and apparatus, Kane traveled to New York to assemble a crew and supervise the stowing of cargo.

The previous November, while still hoping to lead two ships into the Arctic, Kane had written in care of Lady Franklin to his French friend Joseph-René Bellot, inviting him to join the expedition and offering "the nautical command of one sailing party while afloat, and Second only to myself in the general direction of our operations." Late in January, when he finally received the letter, Bellot respectfully declined Kane's "kind and considerate offer" in a reply that demonstrated both his charming sensitivity and his superb command of English: "I must at once say do not wait for me, and the best reason I can give is that I do myself intend trying to get our government to send an expedition either by way of Spitzbergen or by Bering Straits. And how gratifying it would be for both of us to meet there again, and warmly shake hands in the frozen wilderness. Notwithstanding this, I can assure you, dear and excellent friend, nothing would be more highly flattering to me than this compliment paid to my endeavours in the noble cause we both embarked in. I might very well expect kind demonstrations from the English people, as gratitude alone induces them to it, but it falls short as an honor paid to me of your own much valued appreciation of my good will and devotedness. Depend upon it, I feel more than I can say for your recollection of bygone days."

Through early 1853, Kane battled a recurring fever. In mid-April, soon after he reached New York, his low-grade illness exploded into a devastating attack of rheumatic fever. Henry Grinnell and his wife moved the stricken explorer into their palatial home on Bond Street. William Morton, the steward who had sailed with Kane on the first expedition and signed on for the second, voluntarily assumed the duties of a sick nurse and moved with him.

Preparations had reached a critical stage. Kane paid close attention to securing special food supplies, including pemmican, meat biscuits, and pickled cabbage (as protection against scurvy). He also ordered rubber and canvas tents, five boats (one a metallic lifeboat), and half a dozen sledges, some of which he designed himself. He had also assembled most of the crew—but not all. While confined to his bed, Kane looked to his trusted friend Cornelius Grinnell, eldest son of the expedition's primary sponsor, to add a couple more men. Grinnell went to the waterfront and hired two robust seamen—assistance that would prove a mixed blessing.

By mid-May, Kane had recovered sufficiently that he could visit the *Advance* daily, though he felt so sore in the morning that, before he could get out of bed, Morton had to massage his limbs for an hour. To Kennedy, he wrote, "After a cruel attack of inflammatory rheumatism, and three weeks of complete helplessness on beam-ends, I find myself ready to start."

With his departure imminent, Kane realized he would be unable to finish his book. "I fear that there will not be a readable book," he wrote, "unless that dear working father does the didactic and Tom the attractive." But Tom, now thirty-one, had recently married and moved to western Pennsylvania, where he was practicing law and assisting the Underground Railroad in transporting escaped slaves to Canada. Fortunately, Elisha's father, the formidable but highly literate judge, agreed to prepare the last chapter from the explorer's notes, and then to see the book through the press.

17

Constancy & Change

Almost incredibly, while writing, lobbying, organizing his expedition, and shunting between Philadelphia, Washington, and New York, Kane kept up his passionate relationship with Maggie Fox. Even illness could not silence him: "Maggie, I am sick—sick at the hotel—sick with hard work, and with nobody to nurse or care for me. You saw how wretchedly I looked when in New York; I am far worse now, and without any chance of resting. Is it any wonder, then, that I long to be with you, to have again the lazy days and sit by your side talking nonsense?"

As regards his engagement, Kane recognized the need for continued secrecy, though at times he felt moved to tell the world. While having lunch at a quiet country inn, for example, Kane introduced Maggie to the innkeeper as "the future Mrs. Kane." According to *Love-Life,* he also drove her to Laurel Hill Cemetery and showed her the family vault his father was building: "Here, Margaret, will be your last resting place." Not long afterward, in a moment of near-madness, Kane wrote Maggie that "I should much like to present you to my father." Soon enough, he thought better of that.

Around this time, almost certainly, the explorer and the spirit rapper became physically intimate. Not surprisingly, documentation is lacking.

And only in later letters do we find Kane asking if he can visit Maggie at 10:30 p.m., and imploring her not to say no. At one point, the explorer writes, "I have rode in this cold wind nearly eighteen miles; but this afternoon shall see me in your company." To which Maggie responds with a playful double entendre: "I am delighted, dear friend, to know that I will have the pleasure of your company this evening. But I fear you will be too much fatigued to ride—will you not?"

Mrs. Fox remained uneasy. Again and again, Kane took her aside for a long, reassuring talk. He tried repeatedly to explain that secrecy was necessary because his family was not normal. And that, while society at large, probably even high society, could be made to accept a spirit rapper as a respectable marriage partner, his own parents would never countenance such a liaison—not for their eldest son. His father would disinherit him first. And anybody who thought otherwise did not know Judge Kane. To gain acceptance into the Kane family, Maggie would have to distance herself from spirit rapping. This she could do during the explorer's absence by attending a finishing school—an undertaking for which he would pay all costs. Not only that, but Mrs. Fox could help him choose the school. With this last gesture, Kane won her to uneasy neutrality, although she responded that, with regard to the school, she "should prefer to leave it [to you] to make the selection."

Maggie's sister Leah proved more problematic than Mrs. Fox. She had controlled the spirit-rapping enterprise from the outset, deploying Maggie and Kate with a sharp eye to commercial possibilities. Thanks to this family business, Leah Brown, recently remarried, was living more grandly than ever before—and she cared not a fig for anyone's good opinion. Adamantly opposed to Maggie's withdrawal from Spiritualism, she became the explorer's worst enemy. Kane called her "the Tigress." In New York, he was driven to smuggling notes to Maggie though her sister Kate, or else through Cornelius Grinnell, who would turn up at the "promiscuous circles" open to several persons at once.

By this means, Kane let Maggie review his correspondence with Lady Franklin. Indeed, he told his brother Patterson that he communicated with

The 1850s home of Mrs. Susanna Turner is today a private residence.
When he left for the Arctic in 1853, Elisha Kane installed Maggie Fox in
this house west of Philadelphia, not far from Lapidea and Leiper House.

Maggie mainly for the sake of that tragic woman, who was keenly interested in what the spirits might reveal about her lost husband. Around this
time, Kane wrote Maggie of the duplicity of her profession: "I believe the
only thing I ever was afraid of was, *this confounded thing being found out.*"

At one point, when Maggie informed Kane that the wife of American
president Franklin Pierce had requested a séance, he implored her: "Don't
rap for Mrs. Pierce. Remember your promise to me." He realized that if
Maggie's chicanery became public knowledge, anyone who had been
duped—like the president's wife—would be outraged. And that would put
Maggie beyond the pale. Even so, after his fiancée went ahead and rapped
for Mrs. Pierce, Kane figuratively threw up his hands and inquired, "Tell
me how Mrs. Pierce got on!"

Other letters, some smuggled past Leah while Kane and Maggie were
living in New York, concerned locating an appropriate school. Among his

well-connected friends, while making inquiries, the explorer presented himself as a disinterested party acting altruistically to assist a young woman. But few of them were fooled—especially when, with Maggie and Mrs. Fox, Kane traveled to New Haven, Connecticut. There, he visited and rejected two schools: one used a dangerous burning fluid and the other offered only a stuffy upper room.

Finally, Kane acted on a suggestion from his favorite aunt, Eliza Leiper, who lived with his uncle George at Lapidea, eighteen miles west of Philadelphia, near the house in which his mother had spent her summers growing up. She suggested installing Maggie with the family of a respectable woman named Susanna Turner, who rented a home nearby in an area called "Crookville," after a property owner named Crook.

On April 4, 1853, Aunt Eliza wrote: "I have just returned from town and am very tired, but will write a few lines and give you the information you desired. Mrs. Turner was here this afternoon and says she will receive the young lady as one of her family, afford her the opportunity of improvement, give music lessons and make her as comfortable as their limited means will allow them. The compensation is ten dollars per week. My opinion is decidedly in favour of this situation. I know Mrs. Turner's family unexceptionable, mother and daughters well informed, tastes cultivated, cheerful dispositions and religious." Later, she added that Mrs. Turner had a daughter trained in music, French, and deportment. Maggie would be the sole boarder, and would have a room and piano to herself: "There, dear Maggie," Kane wrote, "you will be a lady; your own mistress, and a person regarded with respect by the whole house."

With others, and especially those closest to him, Kane walked an emotional tightrope. He kept the truth of his love for Maggie Fox, and above all the secret of their engagement, even from his brothers and Cornelius Grinnell. They believed not that he had promised to marry the young woman, but that he had taken her as his mistress. And, in accordance with the unwritten code among gentleman rogues, they stood prepared to assist him, to relay his correspondence, and quell any rumors.

Given his highly developed sense of honor, Kane agonized over his own duplicity. But from where he stood, passionately in love with Maggie Fox, he could see no other way forward. Ultimately, his fears would prove well founded. But now, with little time to think, he raced from one duty to another.

On April 11, from Washington, he wrote to his cousin Mary Leiper, now married and living in Baltimore, that he wished to retrieve a flattering portrait of himself that he had left with her. Wishing to leave it with Maggie Fox, he wrote: "My dear Mary: The cousin of old memories will call tomorrow to bid you good bye and take away his last youthful phiz. Excuse this abrupt reclamation of a miniature but I will replace it by another which, while you can keep in your heart what I was—will keep in your eyes what I am now."

Two days later, on April 13, Kane became a Freemason, joining a far-flung fraternity whose members, among them Sir John Franklin, attested to believing in a supreme being. A century before, in 1755, Philadelphia masons had dedicated the first Masonic building in America. Kane received all three degrees of brotherhood in Franklin Lodge No. 134. Probably he joined in emulation of his father, who had served as lodge master in 1825. The night before he sailed for the Arctic, Kane would be feted by Masons belonging to the Grand Lodge of New York. He would thank them with characteristic eloquence, accepting their accolades as the representative of a cause "which perhaps may claim to associate Christian charity with American enterprise—the attempt to save a gallant officer and his fellows from a dreadful death, without inquiring whether he or they and ourselves are citizens of the same or of another race, or clime, or nation. . . . Brothers, we are called in our day, perhaps, to make Masonry what it should be—not a sectarian society, to garb, or rank, or enroll men, to separate them from their fellows, but a bond to unite the good and true in a common union for the common defence and welfare of all who are good and true men."

Meanwhile, in May 1853, the furiously busy explorer commissioned a visiting Italian artist, Joseph Fagnini, to paint a portrait of his fiancée. Maggie gave her final sitting in New York on Thursday, May 26. The following day, along with Mrs. Fox, Kane escorted her to Philadelphia, and there said a painful goodbye. Back in New York, where he was busy supervising final preparations, he wrote to Maggie that he felt "oppressed with the unreal vagueness of a dream. Oh, my Maggie, think of me—always think of me—with respect . . . lean on me, me, hope in me, bear with me—*trust me!*"

The following night, Friday, he called on Mrs. Fox, who told him that she had left Maggie at Mrs. Turner's house, weeping and disconsolate. On Saturday morning, with three days to go before he sailed, Kane rushed back to Philadelphia, then hurried on to the house in the country. From New York, he had brought a canary as a present. But in his harried state, he had somehow misplaced the caged bird, probably at a coach house.

At Mrs. Turner's home, Kane and Maggie said yet another tearful goodbye. Back in Philadelphia, he advertised for the lost canary, and on May 30, the night before he sailed, he wrote Maggie announcing the recovery of "our little bird," which he promised to send by messenger: "Guard and cherish the little wanderer thus returned to the fold. Make it an evidence of my thoughtful attention to your every wish. An emblem, too, dear darling, of my own return, when, after a dreary flight, I come back to nestle in your bosom."

Clearly, he never imagined that the canary might one day be perceived as more symbolic of his fiancée, who would be confined in his absence to a gilded cage. But after counseling Maggie to live a life of purity and goodness, Kane concluded: "Thus live, dear Maggie, until God brings me back to you—and then, meeting my eye with the proud consciousness of virtue, we will resign ourselves to a passion sanctioned by love and marriage. Golden fields shall spread before us their summer harvest, silver lakes mirror your very breath. Let us live for each other—Farewell!"

The following day, when Elisha Kent Kane sailed north out of New York, he blithely assumed that, during his absence, time would stand still—that when he returned from the Arctic, he would take up with Maggie Fox where he left off. He forgot that, even if Maggie remained constant, the people around her would move forward—and not necessarily to a gentler, more accommodating place.

{ II }

TRIAL BY WINTER

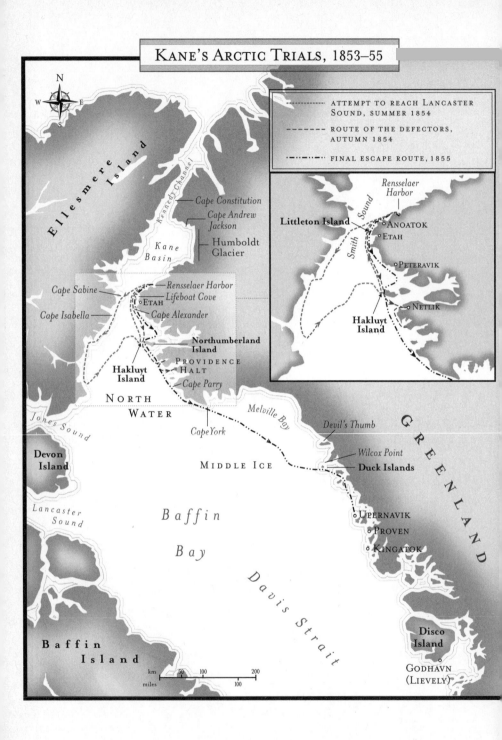

KANE'S ARCTIC TRIALS, 1853–55

N
W · E
S

········· ATTEMPT TO REACH LANCASTER
SOUND, SUMMER 1854

－－－－－－ ROUTE OF THE DEFECTORS,
AUTUMN 1854

－··－··－ FINAL ESCAPE ROUTE, 1855

Ellesmere Island

Kennedy Channel

Cape Constitution

Cape Andrew
Jackson

Humboldt
Glacier

Kane
Basin

Cape Sabine
Cape Isabella

Rensselaer Harbor
Lifeboat Cove
ETAH
Cape Alexander

Northumberland
Island

PROVIDENCE
HALT

Hakluyt
Island

Cape Parry

NORTH
WATER

Melville Bay

Cape York

Devon
Island

Jones Sound

Lancaster
Sound

MIDDLE ICE

Baffin

Bay

Devil's Thumb

GREENLAND

Wilcox Point
Duck Islands

UPERNAVIK
PROVEN
KINGATOK

Davis Strait

Baffin
Island

Disco
Island

GODHAVN
(LIEVELY)

km 50 100   200
miles   100

Rensselaer
Harbor

Littleton Island

Smith Sound

ANOATOK
ETAH

PETERAVIK

NETLIK

Hakluyt
Island

18

DEFYING THE ICE

Nineteenth-century exploration, though it paid homage to the precision and exactitude of science, can best be understood as a conceptual art in which the idea creates the meaning. Arctic explorers who sought the Northwest Passage did not just "discover" islands, straits, and bays that the Inuit had already visited; they elaborated and refined the concept of the Passage—the notion that a navigable channel extended across North America from the Atlantic Ocean to the Pacific. That governing idea not only provided a yardstick, a way of measuring who contributed what, but also gave symbolic meaning to the entire enterprise.

With the second expedition of Elisha Kent Kane, the geographical focus shifted from the Northwest Passage to the Open Polar Sea and the North Pole. But the more profound activity, the creation of meaning where none had existed, remained unchanged. That wresting of significance from nothingness, an archetype of the universal human challenge, explains the enduring attraction of the northern explorers: they fought nothingness and won. To Kane, scientific discovery and geographical exploration mattered immensely, but no more than honor, morality, and the regard of posterity.

Judged in this context, Elisha Kent Kane emerges as an artist of enormous accomplishment. He recorded his experience, trials, and achievements, primarily in language, but also in vivid sketches and drawings. Ultimately, he would create an exploration classic: an illustrated, two-volume narrative of man confronting nature at its most extreme. He would build this monumental work, *Arctic Explorations,* out of the journals and logbooks he kept throughout the voyage.

Because the surviving record remains incomplete, recent discoveries notwithstanding, it is important to note that sometimes the absence of documentary evidence can reveal a significant truth. For example, if we know that a man was in London, England, at ten o'clock one night and in Toronto, Canada, at ten the next morning, we do not need a ticket stub or a name on a passenger manifest to know that he flew overnight from London to Toronto. And if he says otherwise, he is lying. While researching *Lady Franklin's Revenge,* I found documentary evidence revealing that in the 1830s, Jane Franklin became friendly with a missionary named Rudolf Lieder. Her journals and letters showed the two becoming increasingly intimate—and then, suddenly, as the relationship reached a crescendo of intensity, poof! Lieder disappeared without a trace.

Before this period and afterward, the documentary record is exhaustive, sometimes overwhelming. Yet not a single letter, not a single reference, remains in the archive at the Scott Polar Research Institute from the months when Jane Franklin traveled around the Mediterranean with Lieder. Did she suddenly stop writing? The notion is ludicrous. Obviously, the archival record has been scoured. Any letter or notebook page alluding to Lieder has been removed. Not only that, but the sudden, absolute dearth of documentary evidence tells us that somebody had something to hide.

As it was with Jane Franklin and Rudolf Lieder in the 1830s, so it is during this next period with Elisha Kane and Maggie Fox. The journals and records from Kane's second Arctic expedition, even those newly discovered, contain no mention of Maggie Fox—not a single reference. Given what happened before Kane sailed, and in the light also of what happened after-

Maggie Fox, age nineteen, finished sitting for this portrait (left) by Joseph Fagnini on May 26, 1853. Five days later, when Kane sailed out of New York, he took this painting with him. The engraving of the explorer (right), which looks to be based on a flipped version of a photograph by Matthew Brady, graces the first volume of Arctic Explorations. *Kane was thirty-three when he sailed.*

ward, this seems incomprehensible—unless one realizes that the record has been scrubbed clean.

Several of Kane's letters exist only as transcriptions in someone else's hand. From these, almost certainly, references to Maggie Fox have been expunged. More tellingly, the absence of any reference to Maggie in his Arctic journals suggests not that Kane forgot the woman he loved—much less that he did not love her—but that he kept a separate journal in which poured out his deepest feelings. When, at certain low moments during the Arctic sojourn now beginning, Kane would address dark thoughts to family members, the informed reader will understand that, in another journal, he was writing to Maggie Fox—and that, for reasons which will become clear, that record has ceased to exist.

But none of this crossed the explorer's mind when, on May 31, 1853, cheered by flag-waving crowds lining the wharves, encouraged by marching bands, and accompanied by steamers and small boats, Elisha Kent Kane sailed out of New York Harbor in the *Advance*. On the opening page of his logbook, he described the scene: "The wharves were crowded and as the steam-tug which held our little craft in tow passed slowly along the shipping, salutes, bell ringings, and huzzas came to us in one continuous clamour. The steamer *Union* followed as an escort—from her decks came the yelling 'three times three' of some eight hundred mouths—and the tug—well-named the *Titan*—was filled with sympathizing friends." This send-off, he added, proved welcome: "To men bound for the Arctic region, sailors with undigested shore habitudes, officers with heads full of home thoughts and disrupted associations, this big response came very cheeringly."

Almost immediately, Kane moved into a more personal mode, introducing the subjective element that distinguishes his work: "I had lived for the past two years as, I suppose, all men live—with much to regret and something to cherish. I had followed one preponderating motive directly connected with my better nature; but had marred it by a host of interludes uncomfortable to recall. On the very eve of a consummation to much care and effort, these strange episodes which accompany our one great act bound me to the shore and filled me with sweet and bitter memories." At this point, rather oddly, he shows his self-consciousness as a writer by alluding to himself in the third person: "Kane had to put his heel down and crush feelings which he does not wish here to bring back as mingled with the bridge stink and hurrahs came home hard the pressing farewells of Father, and Tom, and Pat, and John, and those too dear friends, God bless them!"

Three years before, almost to the week, Kane had sailed out of New York as a mere surgeon aboard the first American expedition in search of Sir John Franklin. Now he was "in command of an expedition as efficient, and which came with it even more of public sympathy." With Kane went sixteen men— a motley crew, more romantic than experienced, that included a Danish carpenter, Christian Ohlsen; a German astronomer, August Sonntag; and a French cook, Pierre Schubert, who had worked at Delmonico's in New York, one of Kane's favorite restaurants. Among his thirteen fellow Americans

*William Godfrey, the
bane of the expedition.*

were a recently qualified twenty-two-year-old physician, Isaac Hayes; an
executive officer, Henry Brooks, who in the U.S. Navy held the humble
rank of boatswain, or bosun; and a swaggering harbor boatman, William
Godfrey, who had emerged from the rugged East Side of New York.

The idealistic Kane, who detested the authoritarianism and brutality of
the conventional navy, dispensed with the complicated rules that usually
governed ships in favor of three simple regulations, which he announced
before departure. They stipulated absolute subordination to the officer in
command or his delegate; abstinence from all intoxicating liquors, except
when dispensed by special order; and the "habitual disuse" of profane language. With these three rules in place, he reasoned, what could go wrong?

When the captain boarded the *Advance,* according to junior officer Henry
Goodfellow, a friend of the Kane family, "instead of the former restlessness
and intense vitality, he had the subdued look of a broken-down invalid."
Clearly, he had not fully recovered either from his latest bout of rheumatic
fever or from his leave-taking of Maggie Fox. Then, a few hours out of New

York, the brig encountered rough seas and Kane got wretchedly seasick. Six days out, in his logbook he wrote, "Sea Sick!!!!" And the following day, he ends his entry: "Very Sea Sick!!"

In an early letter home, he confessed that a spell of vomiting had almost prevented him from taking routine observations with his sextant. But illness aside, as he informed his sister, he was settling all too comfortably into command: "Soon—disgustingly soon for our better natures—we learn to take to ourselves the perquisites of accident—and this trade of authority sits so easily upon me that I feel as if to be toadied to was a natural and inevitable province of my peculiar self. The best piece at table—the best places on deck—the smile at a bad joke—the affected comprehension of a good one—the deference to an absurd idea—the jump at a request or suggestion—all these—which would kill dear Tom—I take as naturally as the filling of a Burgomaster's pipe—smoking, puffing, pausing, and casting away, just as it suits or does not suit I myself."

The anti-elitist in Kane fought against "this 'Big Injin' feeling" and fretted about embracing "the necessary despotism of authority," but the first-time captain need not have worried: this expedition would eradicate any ingrained tendencies toward snobbishness and complacency. Now, according to Goodfellow, Kane grew "fond, on fine afternoons when the sun shone out, of reclining on a large tarpaulin-covered box on the quarterdeck, where wrapped in a buffalo-robe, he would write his journal or watch the working of the ship and seem to forget his exhausted frame."

After two weeks and more of rough sailing, the *Advance* reached St. John's in Newfoundland, still a proud British colony. Feted as heroes because they were searching for Franklin, Kane and his men stayed long enough to take on provisions and cooking utensils. In his journal, Kane wrote: "There was a strong feeling in this little town towards our expedition. The brig was crowded with citizens from morning to night and a public dinner was on the tapes when I wrote begging its non prosecution. Officers and men were lionized and I am ashamed to say that few underwent the ordeal of hospitality unscathed. Two men, John Blake & William Godfrey, were not only

sailor drunk but sailor outrageous—the rest I kept sober by excluding contact with the shore."

This is the first mention of trouble with these two men, and as yet, clearly,
Kane anticipated no escalation. Having described how the governor of the
island, G. Kerr Hamilton, visited the brig—"Mrs. Hamilton had to be hoisted
over the side"—he reported the generous gift of eight Newfoundland sled
dogs (later reduced, in his book, to six), and half a dozen barrels of seal flippers with which to feed them.

The St. John's Lodge of Freemasons held a reception to honor Kane, an
event he described privately with characteristic irreverence: "Our fellow
craftsmen, our brethren of the Masonic order, gave me a collation and a
flag [a pennant he pledged to fly in the Arctic]. An address was read by the
grand something and a reply made by the grand humbug. We were escorted
to our boats, the regimental band in full blast, and on the highest rock of
the headland the governor had stationed his own bands—and crowds of
citizens. Music and loud hurrahs accompanied us out to sea." And also the
sounds of a fiddler playing "Yankee Doodle." Just before leaving, Kane took
aboard a young Irishman, Thomas Hickey, to serve as second steward or
cabin boy—an action for which he would have reason to be thankful.

As the *Advance* sailed north along the coast of Greenland, slowed by a
lack of wind, Kane grew stronger. In a letter to his father, he described how
he had saved precious time by not waiting to anchor outside small trading
settlements, but by forging ahead in an open whaleboat. He had managed
to secure all necessary furs (reindeer, seal, and bear), as well as moccasins,
sledges, harnesses, and a great many working dogs. He rejoiced especially
in these last: "He (the dog) is the camel of these snow-deserts; and no Arab
could part with him more grudgingly than do these Esquimaux."

Toward the end of June, at the coastal port of Fiskernaes, Kane inquired
about adding an Inuit hunter to his crew. The local superintendent recommended Hans Christian Hendrik, a nineteen-year-old expert with kayak
and javelin. Kane remained dubious until this chubby young man, "as stolid
and unimpressible as any of our Indians," demonstrated his skill by spearing

a bird on the wing. Kane not only agreed to pay Hans a modest wage, and to leave his mother two barrels of bread and fifty-two pounds of salt pork, but "became munificent in his eyes when I added the gift of a rifle and a new kayak."

Years later, Hendrik would corroborate this account in a first-person narrative published as *Memoirs of Hans Hendrik, the Arctic Traveller.* He wrote the manuscript "in tolerably plain and intelligible Greenlandish," according to first translator Henry Rink, and explained that he decided to join up when he learned that Kane would pay him well. His father, assistant to the three priests in the community, had died the previous year, and by volunteering Hendrik hoped to help his mother. She begged him not to go, he reports: "But I replied, 'If no mischief happen me, I shall return, and I shall earn money for you.'"

On July 10, with young Hendrik aboard, the *Advance* reached Sukkertoppen, or Sugarloaf, where an isolated peak soars 3,000 feet above the sea. The Danish settlement at its base, which he judged the most "picturesque" of those in Greenland, moved him to reveal something of the artistic sensibility that made him unique among Arctic explorers. In his published book, he writes: "It was after twelve at night when we came into port; and the peculiar light of the Arctic summer at this hour,—which reminds one

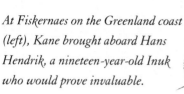

*At Fiskernaes on the Greenland coast
(left), Kane brought aboard Hans
Hendrik, a nineteen-year-old Inuk
who would prove invaluable.*

of the effect of an eclipse, so unlike our orthodox twilight,—bathed every
thing in gray but the northern background—an Alpine chain standing out
against a blazing crimson sky."

In his journal, we discover the artist at work. Kane settled on the word
"picturesque" after scratching out the less precise "attractive." And, after
suggesting that the settlement "embodied the very spirit of desolation," he
had penned a wordier first draft of his published description: "It was after
twelve at night as we entered port, but night no longer brought darkness.
The peculiar light of the arctic midnight summer which reminds me of
the effect of the eclipse—so unlike it is to orthodox twilight—bathed every
thing in neutral gray, but the northern background—a glorious alpine
chain—stood out against a crimson mackerel sky—and the moon in a feeble crescent seemed to be melting away before the daylight." The editorial
improvement is palpable.

One week beyond Sukkertoppen, still farther north in Proven, Kane
learned from men he had met during his first Arctic voyage that British
captain Edward Inglefield had visited two weeks before. He concluded,
plausibly enough, that the Englishman, who enjoyed the advantage of a
steam engine that could free him from pack ice, had taken a significant
lead in their unacknowledged race to the Polar Sea, the discovery of which

would immortalize its finder. According to his journal, "the probabilities of the steamer being already well on her way to the north [had] prevented my gratifying my intentions of stopping at Disco," where he would have left letters for home. Duty, however, "pointed to an opposite course. I am therefore hurrying on under heavy press of sail."

Kane worried that Inglefield would explore Smith Sound before he got there, so he raced onward. Later, he downplayed this, insisting that he believed the heavy ice would force his competitor to consume so much coal that he did "not fear much his anticipation of my discoveries in Smith Sound." In fact, Inglefield would not even enter those waters, having been dispatched westward to the Wellington Channel to communicate with the search squadron led by Edward Belcher.

By July 20, wasting no time, Kane had reached Upernavik, the last outpost of Western civilization. To his father, he wrote that he could "see 216 icebergs floating in a sea as dead and oily as the Lake of Tiberius. Yet I cannot warm my thoughts to talk about them." Based on his knowledge of the ice, he anticipated a safe and easy passage: "Say to Mother to have no fears on Arctic account. I am not entirely well, but as well as I would be at home, and so trusting in the Great Dispenser of good and ill that I am willing to meet like a man the worst that can happen to one secure of right, and approving heart and soul, of that in which he is engaged."

At Upernavik, Kane acquired twenty more dogs, bringing the total to over fifty. Also, he brought aboard Carl Petersen, a thirty-eight-year-old Dane who had lived most of his life in Greenland. As an interpreter and dog-handler, he had sailed with William Penny—and, indeed, been present at Beechey isthmus, like Kane himself, at the discovery of the three graves of the Franklin expedition. "It was quite a regular piece of diplomacy to obtain him," Kane wrote to Cornelius Grinnell, "as he had refused Inglefield, and settled himself down to a quiet winter with his wife. But he is now fast, and upon terms which considering his great Arctic experience, I consider moderate."

Later, Petersen would write that soon after he boarded the *Advance* he began having second thoughts. He admired the vessel's sturdy construction, notably the heavy deck beams, three-fold sheathing, and protective iron bars. But he judged the food supplies inadequate; these included "salted victuals and some dried meat in tin boxes," but none of the boiled provisions that British ships carried.

This, of course, was precisely why Kane had tried so hard to gain support in Washington. Having acquired 20,000 pounds of pemmican, as well as considerable quantities of meat biscuit, pickled cabbage, salt beef, dried fruits and vegetables, and a very moderate supply of liquors, he would write: "I can hardly claim to be provident, either by impulse or education. Yet, for some of the deficiencies of our outfit I ought not, perhaps, to hold myself responsible. Our stock of fresh meats was too small, and we had no preserved vegetables; but my personal means were limited; and I could not press more severely than a strict necessity exacted upon the unquestioning liberality of my friends."

Carl Petersen also viewed the crew as inexperienced, ill-disciplined, and incompetent. Why, fewer than half the men had been to sea! Again, Kane had anticipated him. Originally, he had envisaged a well-financed, four-vessel expedition manned by the American navy. In this hope, he had been thwarted. Despite the limited resources at his command, he had resolved to go forward.

Petersen, on boarding the *Advance,* "felt as if a presentiment whispered to me that this ship never would return and that my experience, perhaps, might prove useful to these daring but unskilled Americans." His was the negativity of the born critic. Even so, he would contribute as both hunter and tinsmith, and the final judgment of cabin boy Thomas Hickey that "except as an interpreter, [Petersen] was of very little service to the expedition" is unduly harsh.

The *Advance* had been sailing for almost two months when it reached the southern headland of Melville Bay, a crescent-shaped indentation extending along the coast, south to north, for 150 miles. Here, Kane weighed his options. Directly to the west, in the heart of the vastly larger Baffin Bay, lay the Middle Ice—a floating mass of ice fields dotted with giant icebergs, scores of them larger than the *Advance*.

Whalers had long since determined that in mid-summer the Middle Ice drifted westward, opening a channel along the Greenland coast. From the southern headland, called Wilcox Point, ships could usually proceed northward through what Kane called "a labyrinth of floes." But if ice conditions made sailing impossible, they could still progress by "tracking"—sending men with drag ropes to trudge along the ice belt, a solid platform permanently attached to the shore.

Later in summer, as continual sunshine melted the ice pack, the northward channel would become clogged with ice, and tracking along the shelf became dangerous. The Middle Ice itself remained, almost always, ominously impenetrable, although a few sailing ships had managed to traverse it. When they did get through, as Kane well knew, they reached the mouth of Smith Sound quickly, saving valuable time.

On July 27, 1853, as the morning sun cleared a heavy ice fog, Kane found the *Advance* standing a few miles offshore between Wilcox Point and a landmark island called the Devil's Thumb. Peering through his glass at the coast, Kane perceived that the ice belt was breaking up and decaying, a portent of difficult conditions. The season looked unusually advanced.

The captain faced a crucial decision. Should he continue to hug the coast and follow the safe but slow route to Smith Sound? Or should he attempt to navigate the treacherous Middle Ice, which had destroyed scores of whaling vessels but could shorten the voyage by days or even weeks? To the west, the floating pack ice seemed relatively loose, and a current was driving floes and icebergs northward. A channel opened up, promising a way through the Middle Ice. Carl Petersen, attached to the expedition without formal position, argued that the inshore track provided the only safe route.

But Kane believed that Edward Inglefield remained nearby, and that he was making for the open North Water beyond the Middle Ice, which led directly to Smith Sound. Without acknowledging this factor, but citing only observed conditions, the captain decided to "bid defiance to the ice." He would sail northwest "until arrested by the pack, and endeavor to double Melville Bay by an outside passage."

In *Arctic Explorations,* Kane would make light of the ensuing difficulties. Ultimately, thanks to his observational and analytical skills, as well as a bit of luck, he would surmount them. First, however, he faced setbacks. After several hours of clear sailing, the westward channel narrowed dramatically, and floating fields of ice began buffeting the *Advance.* Kane would acknowledge that "we drove into a couple of icebergs, [which] carried away our jib-boom, and destroyed one of our quarter boats." According to Petersen, inexperience and momentary confusion at the wheel led to a head-on collision with a massive iceberg—one that almost caused the ship to founder. The quick-thinking Christian Ohlsen saved the vessel by grabbing the wheel, and only the figurehead was split open.

The next morning, still surrounded by floes and towering bergs, some of them reaching a couple of hundred feet into the air, Kane redeemed himself by noticing a curious fact. While the floes and ice fields drifted south, carried by the wind and the prevailing current, the largest icebergs bashed northward. These monster bergs, he deduced, extended so deeply and broadly into the water that they tapped into a different current—one strong enough to drive them north regardless of surface conditions.

Kane realized that his best hope of escaping the smashing ice lay in attaching the *Advance* to a monster iceberg and treating it like a draft horse. He sent two men out in a boat with a mallet, a chisel, and an ice anchor. After a long struggle, they managed to plant the anchor and attach a towline. One of the two men, the powerful William Godfrey, would write later that they had no sooner scrambled back on board before the brig "began to bound forward like a wild horse."

To reduce the bucking effect, Kane shortened the towline and nestled the *Advance* beneath an overhanging projection of the iceberg, which towered over the main mast. Before long, he wrote in his journal, the men were "startled by a set of loud cracking sounds above us; and small fragments of ice not larger than a walnut began to dot the water like the first drops of a summer shower." With ice lumps the size of hen's eggs rattling down on their heads, and one sailor knocked flat onto his back, the men paid out the towline as quickly as possible, allowing the iceberg to shoot ahead.

The ship was still within fifty yards of the berg when the overhanging mass, which must have weighed at least fifty tons, broke off and fell into the sea, "crashing like near artillery," as Kane put it, and landing at the very spot where the *Advance* had been situated. The sailors cut the towline, sacrificing some 700 yards of it, but extricated the brig. After another five hours of hard heaving, they managed to attach the ship to another iceberg, lower and safer, and so resume their journey northward.

The following day, Kane changed icebergs again, eventually attaching the ship to a moving breakwater "of gigantic proportions: it keeps its course steadily toward the north, while the loose ice drifts by on each side, leaving a wake of black water for a mile behind us." On August 1, at around 10 p.m., with the Greenland coast—"a blank wall of glacier"—too close for comfort, and a channel opening to the northeast, Kane detached the brig from the iceberg. At that moment, he and his men "were favored with a gorgeous spectacle which hardly any excitement of peril could have made us overlook. The midnight sun came out over the northern crest of the great berg, our late 'fast friend,' kindling variously-colored fires on every part of its surface, and making the ice around us one great resplendency of gem work, blazing carbuncles, and rubies and molten gold."

All through the next day, with the *Advance* pitching and rolling, Kane "seldom left the top gallant yard," but remained in the crow's nest with James McGary, a veteran whaler, swaying and tottering high above deck while guiding the *Advance* through one narrow lead after another. In his journal, he found time to write only: "Ah! This Melville Bay! What a region of grand displays of fearful encounters and of tedious delays." Finally, around midnight on August 3, having emerged at last from the notorious Middle Ice of Baffin Bay, Kane wrote in his journal: "Devoutly thankful! This great bay with its labyrinths of icebergs is now behind us. The North Water, my highway to Smith's Sound, is fairly ahead."

19

THE BELLY OF THE WHALE

On August 6, 1853, the *Advance* passed between Capes Alexander and Isabella, the mighty headlands that mark the entrance to Smith Sound. Kane described an array of steep, forbidding cliffs ranging in height from 1,200 to 1,500 feet. These capes, he wrote, displaying his strong sense of mythology, "have been until now the Arctic pillars of Hercules; and they look down on us as if they challenged our right to pass." In mythology, according to Joseph Campbell, such a gateway marks a transition into "the belly of the whale" or a sphere of rebirth. The hero, he writes, "is swallowed into the unknown, and would appear to have died."

From the perspective of the civilized world, Kane certainly disappeared. Having passed between the pillars, he proposed to force the brig as far north as possible, whatever the risks. But now, displaying both the caution and foresight he had learned from old John Ross, he led a party ashore at Littleton Island near the Greenland coast. In an obscure cove, to guard against future emergencies, he buried a metallic lifeboat stocked with food, blankets, and other supplies. He covered it with sod, moss, and heavy rocks, drenching the top layer into a frozen mass to resist marauding polar bears.

In his private journal, reflecting on his decision to keep pushing forward,

Kane wrote: "It cannot be recklessness, this pervading sentiment of mine, at least I hope it is not, for I weigh carefully every consideration that may affect the interests of those under my command. Nevertheless as far as individual feeling goes, I believe I would start for the north on an iceberg. The Home folks would call this north but it is not north enough for me."

During the next few days, crewmen warped the brig along as the weather worsened and the several dozen dogs howled and complained and fought over anything that resembled food. Kane declared the unruly, thieving, wild-beast pack "worse than a street of Constantinople emptied upon our decks." Late in the afternoon of August 20, with the *Advance* sheltering against the moving ice behind an isolated rock, a heavy gale turned into the worst storm yet—what Kane called "a perfect hurricane."

That evening, while holding onto the deck railing in the blowing rain, he realized that he had never seen such wildly driving ice. Still, he felt secure enough, "with three good hawsers out ahead, and all things snug on board." He went below to get warm and dry, and had just crawled into his bunk when he heard a sharp twang. He knew right away that the smallest hawser, the six-inch chain, had snapped. The two larger moorings continued to hold.

But as he pulled on his clothes to investigate, Kane heard a second sonorous twang. The whale line had given way, and only "our noble ten-inch manilla still held on." McGary rushed down the ladder: "Captain Kane, she won't hold much longer. It's blowing the devil himself."

When Kane reached the deck, the heavy Manila cable was still proving its excellence, and the crew sang its praises—though too soon. "We could hear its deep Eolian chant," Kane wrote, "swelling through all the rattle of the running-gear and the moaning of the shrouds. It was the death-song. The strands gave way, with the noise of a shotted gun; and, in the smoke that followed their recoil, we were dragged out by the wild ice, at its mercy."

The men managed to steady the ship. For hours, they battled to keep it within the narrow, ice-clogged channel that ran north between the rocky shore and the driving ice field that rose to the west like a wall. Directly ahead, the channel narrowed into a maelstrom of grinding ice tables. All hands gathered on deck to watch in silence. At seven in the morning, with the churning masses of ice directly ahead, threatening to pulverize the *Advance* like corn in a gristmill, Kane dropped the heaviest anchor—to no avail. There was no withstanding the ice torrent that followed, and the men had time only to attach a buoy to the anchor chain before releasing it.

Driven again before the gale, the ship scraped along against a wall of pack ice forty feet high. One tumbling ice table rose above the gunwales and came crashing over the bulwarks, depositing half a ton of ice on deck. Ahead, there floated half a dozen icebergs, which were apparently unavoidable. But as the ship drew nearer, scraping and thumping along the pack-ice wall, Kane perceived that open water separated the icebergs from the floe.

As the *Advance* entered this passage, the icebergs, including two that soared high above the mast, came bearing down upon the brig, threatening to crush it. Just then, almost incredibly, a low, water-washed iceberg came driving up from behind, obviously swept along by some deeper current. As before, in the Middle Ice, Kane ordered an anchor planted in its face, with a whale line attached. Once again, the stratagem worked: "Our noble tow-horse, whiter than the pale horse that seemed to be pursuing us, hauled us bravely on; the spray dashing over his windward flanks, and his forehead ploughing up the lesser ice as if in scorn."

The channel narrowed to forty feet, but the *Advance* passed through—with so little room to spare that the portside whaleboat would have been crushed had the men not removed it from the davits. The brig ended up in the lee of an iceberg in an open channel. The worst was over. The gale would continue to blow; the *Advance* would get nipped and driven up and down an inclined plane of ice as if by some giant steam screw. And the men would face further testing, especially the four who almost got swept away on a floe and barely managed to scramble back aboard. But the northward voyage had survived its fiercest challenge—at least from the natural world.

o   o   o

With the temperature dropping and new ice forming, Kane continued north, mainly by tracking and warping. This last exercise, which involved planting a "warp anchor" and winching the ship forward by turning a capstan, proved especially arduous. But Kane had resolved to winter farther north than any other explorer. And, having reached a latitude well above 78 degrees, he knew that only the celebrated Edward Parry had managed to get nearer the North Pole—not by sailing, but by sledging from Spitsbergen in 1827. Feeling some vindication, Kane wrote in his logbook: "I am fervently thankful that we are now ahead of our predecessors, standing by positive observation where no one has stood before. With our exacting spirit of uncharitableness, no matter how inevitable the obstacle, failure meant disgrace. We are safe at least from that." In his published book, he rendered it more concisely: "There are those with whom, no matter how insuperable the obstacle, failure involves disgrace; we are safe at least from their censure."

But now a challenge arose—not from the extreme environment, but from the world of men. And the individual who embodied it was William Godfrey, the rough-and-ready New York boatman. The fretful Carl Petersen had been muttering to anyone who would listen that Kane had ventured too far north and should retreat for the winter. But it was Godfrey who loudly voiced this opinion, prompting Kane, who had no intention of retreating an inch, to call the men together to explain his rationale.

Godfrey had proven troublesome since early in the voyage. In *Arctic Explorations,* Kane would recall that he had "a couple of men on board whose former history I would give something to know—bad fellows both of them, but daring, energetic, and strong. They gave me trouble before we reached the coast of Greenland." He was referring to Godfrey and John Blake, the other late-hired tough, whose real surname was Hussey.

On July 5, according to the ship's log, Kane confined these two belowdecks for "insubordination and disrespectful language to Mr. Brooks [the first officer]." A few days later, several crew members complained that

Kane called this illustration The Nip Off Cape Cornelius Grinnell. *It shows that the ice conditions he encountered in August 1853 were far harsher than those that exist today in those same latitudes, where far larger vessels sail freely in open water.*

Godfrey was drunk and carousing in the seamen's mess. While confined belowdecks, he had discovered and stolen some alcohol. Two of Kane's best officers, Ohlsen and McGary, recommended putting Godfrey aboard a nearby whaler bound for home.

Yet Kane, reluctant to lose a strong, capable crew member, opted for a man-to-man talk with the miscreant. From Upernavik, he wrote to Cornelius Grinnell, who had hired the man: "Bill the pockmarked boatman, in conjunction with a certain John, insulted, by what sailors call 'Jaw,' a couple of the deck officers; whereupon I tied them, hand and foot, covered them up with warm buffalo robes, and nailed them under the booby hatch. After four days of darkness and bread and water, they asked to be relieved; promised to be good boys, and have been since two of our best men."

Not one month later, in the North Water, the swaggering Godfrey attacked an officer, the twenty-one-year-old sailing master John Wall Wilson, who was supervising a crew using whaleboats to tow the becalmed *Advance*. Thomas Hickey would write that Godfrey, "becoming disgusted with the exercise of rowing, gave an exhibition of talents as a pugilist. He made an assault upon Mr. Wilson, but was arrested before much blood was spilt."

Under naval regulations, the man would have been flogged until blood ran down his back. Shunning such measures, Kane had the incident investigated and "the result now on file decided me to confine Godfrey to the booby hatch on bread and water." Two days later, he allowed the prisoner a full ration of meat. And the day after that, when a gale arose and he needed all hands on deck, Kane released the man to active duty.

Later, in a book-length "counternarrative" prepared with the help of a ghostwriter, Godfrey would make no mention of these or subsequent incidents. He would argue instead that he was too much the proud, individualistic American to tolerate the rules and regulations of shipboard life—that "my early training, feelings of independence and sense of equality did not qualify me for the station in which I had thoughtlessly placed myself."

On August 26, while giving Godfrey the benefit of every doubt, Kane wrote in his journal that one crewman, "an excellent member of the party, volunteered an expression of opinion this morning in favor of returning to the south and giving up the attempt to winter." He reflected that it was unjust for a commander to expect his subordinates to share his commitment, as he "receives, if successful, too large a share of the credit." He called his officers together at once, he wrote, "in full formal council, and listened to their views in full."

Except for first officer Henry Brooks, who sided with Kane, all others favored returning southward to winter. Kane reiterated the importance of securing a position far enough north to expedite sledge journeys in search of Franklin. He explained that such a position could only be attained by continuing northward, and announced his intention of warping toward a visible headland. At the nearest possible shelter to that point, he would put the brig into winter harbor. The men, he wrote, received this decision "in a manner that was most gratifying, and entered zealously upon the hard and cheerless duty it involved"—with all officers and the captain himself taking a turn at the capstan.

In his counternarrative, Godfrey writes that this consultation occurred after Petersen and Wilson had scouted unsuccessfully for a sheltered wintering spot, and he notes that it involved not just officers but all the crewmen. But then he adds that the more experienced seamen "had sense enough to know that they were expected to coincide in opinion with the officers." So they hesitated to express themselves. As a courageous greenhorn, however, Godfrey declared that he could see no use in proceeding any further. "As for Captain Franklin, no doubt he is safe in heaven, if he was as brave a commander and as good a man as the books and newspapers represent him."

He writes that, after expounding on this theme, he assessed other motives for continuing the voyage and found none that could have much influence on the subordinate members of the expedition: "Granting that it would be a glorious achievement to plant the American flag on the pivot of the earth's axis, we who handle the ropes would seldom be mentioned in connection with that achievement." He concluded that "the wisest course would be to turn the head of the *Advance* southward, and either to steer homeward, or to take another route by the way of Lancaster Sound, where we may possibly be able to make some progress."

These arguments, expressed with an eloquence far beyond Godfrey, benefited from hindsight. The semi-literate boatman also declared that his freely expressed opinions "seemed to give some offense to the officers," and although he received only a little browbeating, some of them regarded his "inconsiderate speech . . . as a sly demonstration of mutiny."

But here he gets caught in a contradiction. In portraying himself as the misunderstood common man—an individual "not prepared, at all points, to fill a station in which humility and submissiveness were the most desireable and indispensable qualifications"—Godfrey insists that he has offended "the aristocracy of the brig" by expressing his opinions, and that the officers disliked him for this reason. In truth, all but one of the officers agreed with him—or at least with the thrust of his argument. They, too, urged Kane to retreat southward. Why would they dislike him for articulating their own views?

If they disliked Godfrey, they must have had other reasons. The contradiction reveals how, with his ghostwriter, Godfrey would twist the truth when it suited him. That Kane sought to persuade his men through consultation, rather than ruling by decree, shows how deeply he believed in the democratic process. And that he continued to press northward in the face of near-unanimous opposition demonstrates that he would override that process when necessary—that he could be as bloody-minded as his quest demanded.

20

SCIENCE & SPECULATION

On September 10, 1853, with the temperature standing at 14 degrees Fahrenheit and the young ice surrounding the brig thick enough to support men and sledges, Elisha Kane began settling in for the winter at a latitude of about 78 degrees, 40 minutes. He had warped the *Advance* into a sheltered cove he named Rensselaer Harbor, after his family's country estate: "It was secure against the moving ice, lofty headlands walled it in beautifully to seaward . . . yet it was open to the meridian sunlight, and guarded from winds, eddies, and drifts."

Kane assigned men to build a storehouse on a nearby island, which he named Butler Island. He had salmon, trout, and salt codfish placed in barrels, and also some pickled cabbage, and steaks strung on lines "like a countrywoman's dried apples." With Sonntag, the astronomer, he situated the observatory on a rocky islet he called Fern Rock—"a little spot that I long to see again." One building housed surveying instruments, including a transit and a theodolite; an adjoining wooden shelter, constructed to admit air but not wind, contained thermometers, barometers, and magnetic instruments.

The climatic information Kane collected here, which he carefully preserved, must surely be regarded as invaluable to any contemporary scientist studying climate change in the High Arctic. Not long ago, a study in the journal *Current Biology* indicated that the ice in northeast Greenland is melting an average of 14.6 days earlier than in the mid-1990s. But Kane provides a more distant touchstone. His two-volume *Arctic Explorations* includes eighteen indices running to an extraordinary 168 pages, incorporating tables of data like the mean daily temperatures of the surface water, and even a foldout chart graphing the "mean monthly isothermal lines of Baffin Bay."

Now, in the autumn of 1853, the commander assigned Ohlsen and Petersen to construct a shed-like superstructure over the deck, using planks he had brought for this purpose. He designed it to combine "the utmost ventilation, room, dryness, warmth, general accommodation, comfort,—in a word, all the appliances of health." Kane also prescribed a room between decks for the cooking stove. To mark the transformation from voyaging to sojourning, he reverted from the nautical system of measuring time to the twelve-hour civilian cycle.

Kane constructed a kennel on Butler Island, but the dogs refused to use it, preferring to sleep on bare snow within range of human voices. He found it "strange that this dog-distinguishing trait of affection for man should show itself in an animal so imperfectly reclaimed from a savage state that he can hardly be caught when wanted!" Others found this trait less endearing, with William Godfrey, for example, complaining of the howling of the "perverse brutes."

The captain spent hours learning to drive a dog team, practicing until his arms ached. The typical eighteen-foot whip, he noted, had a sixteen-inch handle—a short lever to throw out such a length of seal hide. But the dogs would respond only to this lash, and "you must be able not only to hit any particular dog out of a team of twelve, but to accompany the feat also with a resounding crack." Then you had to retrieve the lash, which was apt to get tangled among dogs and lines, or else wrap itself around a chunk of ice and "drag you head over heels into the snow." With practice, he learned that six dogs made a powerful team, while four could whirl him around near the brig.

Kane also addressed a continuing problem. For the past four months, almost since leaving New York, the men had been sharing their quarters with large numbers of rats. As September ended, the captain decided to fumigate the vessel. With fellow doctor Isaac Hayes, he prepared the "vilest imaginable mixture" of brimstone, burnt leather, cayenne, tobacco, and arsenic. He poured this "diabolical concoction" over the blazing coals of four fires. In his journal, he wrote: "All hands thus excluded slept under buffalo robes on deck—this with the thermometer at but ten degrees above zero was no fancy camping. We made a frolic of it and passed a comfortable night."

However, the rats survived. Thus, Kane decided to take more lethal measures. Having blocked up all cracks and crevices, he produced great quantities of carbonic-acid gas by burning charcoal in three stoves. During this exercise, the French cook, Pierre Schubert—a zealous professional, Kane wrote in his journal, not lacking in "bull-headed intrepidity"—slipped below to season a soup; he did not, as Godfrey would later have it, descend "to dress a slice of ham for the captain's dinner."

Emerging from the galley, Schubert began to wobble, clearly overcome by gas. Morton rushed down the ladder and managed to haul the unconscious cook onto the deck before he, too, collapsed. Kane went down to open the hatches. He smelled burning wood. He checked the forecastle and found it smoky but free of flames. Then he felt the gas affecting him. His lantern went out as he reached the bulkhead door and discovered a three-foot circle of the deck ablaze.

Holding his breath, Kane made it to the foot of the ladder before collapsing, overcome by gas. Henry Brooks arrived and managed to haul him to the surface. The captain recovered, reported what he had seen, and, with four men, established a relay system, passing buckets of water from the brig's emergency fire hole. Within ten minutes they had extinguished the blaze, which had originated in the remains of a barrel of charcoal behind a wall ten feet from the stoves.

Schubert remained in bed for a day and, alluding to a French balladeer, Kane observed: "I can hear him chanting his Beranger through the blankets

In Midnight in September, *we see the* Advance *in Rensselaer Harbor, with crewmen fixing the brigantine into position. By the tenth of the month, with the temperature dropping to 14 degrees Fahrenheit, the men would be walking on ice that surrounded the vessel.*

in his bunk, happy over his holiday, happy to be happy at every thing." The captain, who had inhaled still more carbonic acid, suffered for two days from palpitations and vertigo. The experiment had killed twenty-eight rats. Others survived and multiplied, but as Godfrey observed, rightly this time, the science-minded Kane was "not sufficiently satisfied with the results of his charcoal experiment to give it a second try."

o　o　o

Late in August, before warping the *Advance* into position, Kane had taken seven men and, leaving the trusted Ohlsen in command of the brig, set out on an exploratory mission. He needed to see what lay beyond the northern edge of the bay. At first, the party sailed along the coast in the lightest of the whaleboats, the *Forlorn Hope,* bashing through the young ice still forming between the ice belt and the pack.

But within twenty-four hours they encountered a wall of ice sixteen feet high. They hauled the boat up onto this elevated ice belt, which Kane found overhung by cliffs, scattered with giant blocks of ice, and interrupted by gorges and chasms. Yet he surmised that, later in the season, it might serve as a north-south highway. After stowing the whaleboat beneath a large hummock, the men ventured north, bedding down nightly with pemmican and hot tea.

After reaching a small bay, they found their way blocked by a glacier. They crossed it with difficulty, using ropes and frequently lying at full length upon the ice. On the far side, conditions proved so rough that they had to unload the sledge and, for three miles, carry their supplies on their backs—including the heavy theodolite. Kane ascertained that the coastal cliffs stood at a mean elevation of 1,300 feet. And he determined that, in five days of grueling work, he had traveled just forty miles from the brig.

He decided to leave the sledge and walk on, carrying nothing but instruments, pemmican, and one buffalo robe per man. Traveling this way, almost Inuit-style, the men covered twenty-four miles in a day. On September 5, they arrived at a large bay and "a roaring and tumultuous river . . . the largest yet known in North Greenland." Kane named it the Mary Minturn River, after the sister-in-law of Henry Grinnell.

The trekkers forded the river in the morning, taking "plunge-baths as often as we trusted our weight on the ice-capped stones above the surface." The next day, seven miles beyond the river, Kane left four of his men to recuperate. With three volunteers, carrying only his Fraunhofer pocket sextant, a walking pole, and three days' allowance of pemmican, he walked sixteen miles across the ice to the northeastern headland of the bay. He named this headland Cape William Makepeace Thackeray, after a favorite author best known for *Vanity Fair.*

About ten miles beyond this cape, and before heading back to the ship, Kane climbed one last headland. He put his telescope to his eye: "I shall never forget the sight, when, after a hard day's walk, I looked out from an altitude of eleven hundred feet upon an expanse extending beyond the eightieth parallel of latitude." In his published book, he would describe how the western shore of Smith Sound, a land mass now known as Ellesmere Island, disappeared to the north; how, in the far distance, a stream of icebergs increased in numbers as they receded; and how, beyond these, the way seemed less obstructed. Without fully realizing it, Kane had glimpsed his first major discovery: "To my right, a rolling primary country led on to a low dusky wall-like ridge, which I afterward recognized as the Great Glacier of Humboldt."

On September 20, bent on using a series of sledging expeditions to reach the Open Polar Sea, Kane dispatched a seven-man party to place a cache of provisions along the route he intended to travel by dogsled. The seven hauled a total of 1,200 pounds of provisions, including 800 of pemmican, with which to establish the first of three depots. To lead this scouting party, Kane chose second officer James McGary, the reliable ex-whaler.

McGary set out with six men dragging a thirteen-foot sledge called the *Faith*. A gift of the British Admiralty, it usually required eight or nine men. Besides 1,200 pounds of provisions, the *Faith* carried an India-rubber boat, a canvas tent, and seven buffalo robes and mackinaw blankets. In his book, Kane would note that he soon learned to reduce traveling gear, increasing both comfort and efficiency as he discarded supposed necessities: "Step by step, as long as our Arctic service continued, we went on reducing our sledging outfit, until at last we came to the Esquimaux ultimatum of simplicity,—raw meat and a fur bag."

Kane had already sent three men to scout the Greenland interior. They had traveled ninety miles beyond the coast and returned to report seeing an endless vista of ice, a few reindeer, numerous hares and rabbits, and no ptarmigan. Ultimately, the captain wrote, they had reached "a glacier, four hundred feet high, and extending to the north and west as far as the eye could see. This magnificent body of interior ice formed on its summit a complete plateau—a *mer de glace*," or sea of ice.

The captain had yet to grasp the magnitude of the Greenland ice sheet, which spawns the glaciers and giant icebergs of Melville Bay. But as Edmund Blair Bolles would write in *The Ice Finders,* except for a few travelers to Antarctica and a handful of Inuit, Kane's three scouts had stood looking out over "more ice than anybody on earth had ever seen."

Early in October, when the depot party under McGary had been absent two weeks, Kane began to worry that their supplies would be running low. On October 10, with one other man, the brawny John Blake, he took a light sledge and four of the best Newfoundland dogs and headed out onto the ice to find the missing men. The temperature stood at 4 degrees above zero Fahrenheit.

For five days, despite deepening cold and dangerous fissures in the ice, the travelers averaged twenty miles a day. Three times, the two hindmost dogs skidded into open water at the bottom of a crevasse. Then, while trying to clear the widest chasm yet, all four dogs and the sledge slipped into the water. Kane cut the lines immediately, and with Blake managed to save both sledge and dogs. But now, with the temperature hovering below zero, the wet men risked freezing to death.

Men and dogs started at a run for the solid ice belt along the shore, and as Kane later reported, "by the time we had gained it we were steaming like a couple of Nootka Sound vapor-baths." By alternately exposing the tent and their furs to the air, and beating the ice out of both, the men dried their bedding enough to allow for sleep. The dogs shared the tent with them, providing warmth as well as fragrance, prompting Kane to observe: "What perfumes of nature are lost at home upon our ungrateful senses!"

On the morning of October 15, about a hundred miles from the brig, Kane perceived a dark object moving strangely against the white snow in the distance. Gradually, it resolved itself into a broken line—the returning sledge party! All seven men remained healthy, though they had eaten almost all their food, and some were suffering from frostbitten toes and fingers.

o   o   o

In *Arctic Explorations,* Kane would describe the McGary-led sortie in an appendix prepared from field notes by Amos Bonsall, a reasonably literate Pennsylvania farmer. The recalcitrant William Godfrey, who participated in the outing, would describe it in his counternarrative. After slogging north for five days, the party left a first cache of pemmican, bread, and alcohol just beyond Cape Thackeray. Three days farther north, they placed a second cache of beef and pemmican.

Then, fifteen days out, nearing a latitude of 80 degrees, the party came face to face with a glacier so massive it halted their progress along the Greenland coast. Beyond an open crack sixty yards wide, Bonsall wrote, and running east and west for miles, the men could discern nothing but "an almost impenetrable mass of bergs . . . nothing but high icebergs with narrow passages between them choked up by hummocks and squeezed ice." To Kane, it sounded like an ice barrier encircling an Open Polar Sea.

The men tracked westward along the base of the glacier, and on October 10, still unable to cross, placed a third and final cache on a recognizable island. In a natural excavation among the cliffs, they buried the remaining 800 pounds of food, including 670 pounds of pemmican and forty of meat biscuit. Over this they piled heavy rocks, then smaller rocks, and finally sand and water to create an impenetrable mass. Kane explained that they did this to guard against polar bears, noting that the Inuit to the south had warned him of their extraordinary strength.

In his counternarrative, Godfrey highlights the hardship of the trek. He complains that the men were used like draft animals. He describes how, at 40 or 50 degrees below zero, a man could spend two or three hours heating a pot of coffee. He recounts how a sledge broke through some recently formed ice, so that bedding got saturated and men had to sleep in wet blankets. He remembers his comrades cursing and swearing and "damning all arctic expeditions, and all who ever took a part in contriving them." Godfrey vividly evokes the effects of extended exposure to extreme cold. Inured by his iron constitution, he describes temporary fits of madness that resembled intoxication, with men singing scraps of old songs, gesticulating violently, and uttering wild exclamations: "There was something haggard and ghastly in their mirth."

Yet Godfrey reveals his limitations by scarcely mentioning the mighty glacier that forced the party westward. With the help of a ghostwriter, the muscular ex-boatman could describe the pain of snowblindness, or how

In the Humboldt Glacier, which extends along the Greenland coast for sixty miles at a height of 300 feet, Elisha Kane had discovered the largest glacier in the northern hemisphere. He named it after the legendary geographer Alexander von Humboldt, and his vivid descriptions fostered the scientific concept of the Ice Age.

icicles formed on beards and mustaches, and even how the cold could reduce men to a lunatic condition. But he lacked the sensibility and imagination to grasp that he had come face to face with the greatest glacier on the planet earth.

Kane, who had seen the glacier only at a distance, described the icy wall as roaring with avalanches, and observed that it "constantly threw off its discharging bergs breaking up the ice for miles around." Having interrogated McGary and Bonsall, he related how, in the middle of their first night at the foot of the glacier, the men awoke to a sudden cracking and a jolting sensation. In pitch darkness and intense cold, they packed up their tent and furs, lashed them onto the sledge, and beat a retreat from a teetering ice platform that had seemed rock solid.

Bonsall would later reveal that, even before the men left the brig, Kane had expressed curiosity about the glacier. The captain would not get a close look at it, and so apprehend its magnitude and significance, until the following spring. And yet, on hearing a detailed description, Kane thought of Alexander von Humboldt, widely acknowledged to be the father of modern geography. Early in 1853, while putting together his crew, and seeking specifically a qualified astronomer, Kane had sought the help of that eminent scientist, now living in Berlin at age eighty-three.

Kane had probably written to him in French, because on March 3, 1853, Humboldt replied in that language with an effusively apologetic letter. He was in despair, he wrote, at having to respond negatively to the genial confidence with which Kane had honored him. He had tried hard, with the assistance of a friend, to locate a suitably qualified astronomer, but time had proven too short.

Humboldt apologized: *J'aurais été si heureux de prouver a Votre Gouvernement combien je suis devoué de coeur et d'âme a l'Amérique, que je regarde comme une seconde patrie.* [I would have been so pleased to show your government how deeply I am devoted, heart and soul, to America, which I regard as a second homeland.] *Un vieillard antédiluvien, voyageur comme Vous, Monsieur, fait des voeux les plus ardens pour le succès de la noble enterprise dans laquelle vous vous trouvez courageusement engagé.* [An antediluvian figure, a traveler like yourself, Sir, yearns ardently for the success of the noble enterprise on which you find yourself courageously engaged.]

In the High Arctic, faced with naming a spectacular discovery, Elisha Kane had responded by giving it a name wholly appropriate: the Great Glacier of Humboldt.

21

DECADES BEFORE SHACKLETON

Elisha Kent Kane could not know it, but six decades would elapse before any explorer faced a series of trials comparable to those that loomed before him. Those later challenges would arise not here in the Arctic but at the opposite ends of the earth, in Antarctica. Early in 1915, sixty-two years after Kane's trek, Sir Ernest Shackleton would find himself just outside the Antarctic Circle, locked in the ice with twenty-seven men.

After ten months of privation and freezing-cold misery, Shackleton would abandon his ship the *Endurance* and lead his men in a desperate flight for survival, man-hauling sledges and sailing hundreds of miles in a small, open boat. Along the way, the British commander would contend with the despair of some men, the rebellion of others. He would make mistakes, some of them grievous, and lose three men who, while not under his direct command, belonged to his expedition. Ultimately, Shackleton would inscribe an adventure at the bottom of the world that would bear more than passing resemblance to the one now beginning at the top.

As the Arctic winter took hold, bringing round-the-clock darkness and temperatures that hovered around 25 degrees below zero, Kane and his men found their clothes barely adequate. Except at Spitsbergen, which is warmed by ocean currents, no Europeans had ever wintered this far north. Kane arranged fires and ventilation fixtures to keep the mean temperature belowdecks at 65 degrees.

With twenty men and fifty dogs on board, he sought to avert sickness with good hygiene, and kept the crew busy scrubbing decks and bulkheads. Bent on avoiding scurvy, he mustered the men for health inspection every Sunday after prayers, then checked and cleaned the living quarters. Running low on meat, he relied on cabbage, and then raw potatoes and lime juice. Even so, men began showing symptoms of scurvy—sore joints, swollen gums, and patchy discolorations on the skin.

In November, Kane's "wretched rheumatism" incapacitated him for a while. Still, driving himself to collect biological and geological specimens, he found he could walk thirty miles a day without feeling any heart pains. He went on short journeys for hunting and reconnaissance, and found several deserted places where "Esquimaux" had built and abandoned huts. During the voyage north, Kane had written of the Inuit several times in his journal. He reported, for example, that nearly thirty years before, a smallpox epidemic had "desolated the coast" around Upernavik. "During this pestilence, among the natives," he wrote, "instances of appalling suffering occurred. An aged woman was pointed out to me who alone was spared after the destroying angel had glutted himself upon everyone around her."

And, in a note immediately following this observation, but clearly added later, Kane sought to set the record straight: "These Esquimaux to the north of the Melville Bay glaciers were described by Sir John Ross [after his first voyage, begun in 1818]—and since by the occasional visits of the whaling and discovery ships. The name applied to them of Arctic Highlanders is in the highest degree absurd. By the very nature of their life they are a coast people deriving support from the sea—and by the well known laws of Polar Climate a mountain life is an impossibility."

Now, having as yet discovered no Inuit in the vicinity, Kane kept his men active with outdoor sporting events, and indoors with card games, chess, and readings. He organized a "fox-chase" around the deck and offered a

Guernsey shirt to the sailor who avoided his fellows the longest—a shirt won by William Godfrey. Despite his best efforts, however, even Hans Hendrik, the native Greenlander, suffered from the darkness and cold.

"Except upon the islands of Spitzbergen," Kane wrote in his journal, "which possessed the advantages of an ocean (insular) climate, we are the first Christians who have ever wintered in so high a latitude. Our rivals in this melancholy procedure were Russian sailors—men inured to hardship and cold—and I confess that the terrible failures of the early Dutch, who had perished year after year without a living comrade to record their fate— came to me sometimes with unpleasant recollections. The darkness has yet ninety days to run before it lightens up even to our present doubtful day of an hour—and the entire absence of the sun will be four months and twenty days—or 140 days." As for the cold, Kane added: "The mean temperatures of October and September show . . . greater cold than the same months during our last voyage—and Parry's Melville Island experience [in 1819], heretofore the lowest mean annual temperature upon record, is higher than our own for the same months."

In mid-November, Hans Hendrik declared that he could no longer tolerate such a confined and miserable existence. He bundled up his clothes, took his rifle, and prepared to leave. Later, in his published memoir, Hendrik would write: "Never had I seen the dark season like this. To be sure it was awful. I thought we should have no daylight any more. I was seized with fright, and fell a weeping. I never in my life saw such darkness at noon time. As the darkness continued for three months, I really believed we should have no daylight more."

Hendrik decided to remain after talking with Kane. The commander ascertained that the young man yearned after "one of the softer sex at Fiskernaes," and noted that "he looked as wretched as any lover of a milder clime." Kane gave him a dose of salts and a key promotion: "He has now all the dignity of a henchman. He harnesses my dogs, builds my traps, and walks with me on my ice-tramps; and, except hunting, is excused all other duty. He is really attached to me, and as happy as a fat man ought to be."

Kane's culturally sensitive response to Hendrik, who had difficulty adjusting to a shipboard existence, led Godfrey to feel so jealous that he referred to the youth as "the captain's pet Eskimo."

Also in November, as emerges only in his journal, Kane tried an experiment in democracy. With a self-satisfaction that would later be exploded, he describes how he called a mass meeting "to devise ways and means of passing the winter in a manner conducive to harmony & happiness. . . . It was a new experiment—this Democratic way of throwing upon subordinates a legislation independent of their commander—and I know that many of my naval friends would regard it as subversive of all discipline. I don't care if it only give me a healthy happy and efficient crew and discipline may go to the devil. It is an artificial word at best."

At first blush, Kane wrote: "The thing worked well—as it has worked before—and I hope will work often in times to come. The meeting was duly organized. I called Brooks to the chair and the different gentlemen with Mr. Goodfellow as secretary went regularly to work and proposed, debated and carried a lot of measures—into which all will enter with spirit as they are fruits of their own work." As a result, he reported, the men would publish a newspaper with himself as editor. There would be a masquerade fancy ball, a school in which Sonntag would teach the rudiments of navigation, and daily exercises with the sledges, football, and fox-trap examinings. "We are to have an oration on our darkest day—the midnight of our long arctic winter—the climax of heavy gloom, and Dr. Hayes was elected to deliver the address." Kane himself narrowly escaped election to this honor, although Dr. Hayes was his candidate.

"After much fun," Kane wrote, "and a glass of whisky and water, we adjourned at 11 p.m." In his private journal, though again not in his published book, he added: "All this could not, I believe, take place with any other people than Americans. The bare idea in an English ship would be preposterous. But we are brought up to have a will and to recognize its sovereignty."

Later, as an approach to Arctic exploration, Kane would find his faith in "one man, one vote" sorely tested. But now he launched a short-lived newspaper called *The Ice-Blink*. In mid-December, he led the ship in celebrating the birthday of Henry Grinnell. And on Christmas Day, besides holding a "best dinner" and reading Christ's Sermon on the Mount to all hands, Kane sponsored a fancy-dress ball at which, according to young Thomas Hickey, "all the fashionable people of the brig were present, dressed in every variety of costume." Hickey added that Godfrey, "who had always a liking for something strong, tapped a keg of alcohol which Dr. Kane had put aside for preserving specimens of Natural History. Partaking rather freely of this delightful beverage, he was discovered, and compelled to exchange his ball jewels for a pair of iron bracelets."

In mid-December, the men had lost the last vestiges of midday twilight. Often, the darkness was so deep that they could not see to count their fingers, and except for a vague skyline glimmer over the hills to the south, Kane could find "nothing to tell us that this arctic world of ours has a sun." According to Godfrey, the sky itself "could not be seen without a thrill of horror, so repulsively unnatural was its appearance. The arctic heavens, after the disappearance of the sun, resemble a vast arch or dome of granite . . . . When the moon is visible, the sky glistens with a faint metallic luster, like the interior of the dome of a German church lined with lead." He insisted that a man's very soul felt "suffocated by the oppressive gloom, the horrid silence, the changeless appearance of surrounding objects."

In January, as temperatures dropped to 50 and then 60 degrees below zero, the dogs reacted strangely. They showed signs of a canine scurvy, probably the result of a vitamin deficiency. Kane speculated that the disease had a mental or psychological aspect, and that "the absence of light contributed as much as the extreme cold" and lack of nutrition.

He worked desperately to save his Newfoundland dogs. He had them nursed like babies—"tended, fed, cleansed, caressed, and *doctored,* to the infinite discomfort of all hands." But what began as epilepsy quickly evolved into "a true lunacy." The dogs barked frenziedly at nothing, walked back and forth incessantly, lay for hours in moody silence, then suddenly started howling and running up and down as if pursued. Some dogs died within days, while others lasted a few weeks. Most often, they died of lockjaw within thirty-six hours of the first attack. Before the sun returned, more than forty dogs had died, leaving only seven to haul sleds.

o   o   o

Late in 1853, during the initial skirmishing with the cold and dark, Kane had established a routine. All hands would rise at seven-thirty. They would conduct ablutions on deck, open hatches and doors to air their quarters, and return below for a breakfast of hard tack, pork, stewed apples, raw potato, tea, and coffee. Smokers would enjoy a pipe until nine, and then every man would go to his station—Ohlsen to his carpenter's bench, Brooks to his canvas-cutting, McGary to sewing, Whipple to making shoes, Bonsall to tinkering, Baker to skinning birds. Hayes copied logs, Sonntag took readings, and Kane wrote, sketched, and drew maps.

At noon, the captain would conduct an inspection and issue any special orders. Then he would exercise and train the dogs—his own "peculiar recreation." Afternoons were highlighted by a small "dinner" of pickled cabbage, dried peaches, and raw potato. The men would then nap, exercise, and amuse themselves until six o'clock supper, a meal the captain described as resembling breakfast and dinner, "only a little more scant." The officers would report to Kane, and he would sign off on the log, the weather, and the temperatures before turning to his journal. Evenings might include reading books or magazines, or playing games of cards or chess.

The routine proved less happy than it might have because of the shocking cold. Early in January 1854, Kane writes in his journal, "A doubt arose in my mind as to the sufficiency of our stock of coal. Upon gauging the stock on hand I found a decided deficiency. I make here no comment as to the cause of this other than to say that the executive officer overstepped his allowance and blindly reported to me a consumption just one half of that which actually entered the stoves. . . . Our stock required at best economy and effort to eke it comfortably out, but with the precautions which I had adopted, it would have been ample. By a blind but not willful mismanagement we are now reduced to but six and a half tons. I am thankful that the idea of regularly gauging the hold has been pointed out in time [to ameliorate] this alarming deficiency."

While the mean outdoor temperature hovered around 40 degrees below zero, Kane had to limit fuel use to three buckets of coal per day. The men had to chop ice to make drinking water. The lamp oil ran out, so Kane had to write by muddy candles made of cork and cotton and floating in saucers. Only Morton and Schubert escaped scurvy, and judging from the pale, haggard faces of his shipmates, Kane concluded "that an Arctic night and an Arctic day age a man more rapidly than a year anywhere else in all this weary world." In his journal, on January 19 he wrote: "Poor Brooks hardly able to walk with scurvy. His leg is very much drawn up. My own gums begin to bleed and the cases generally seem to be at a stand. The sleeplessness—a more trying symptom—continues. Much of this to be attributed to the darkness. Our thermometers record a minimum of –52."

In these conditions, Kane cannot help thinking of the dogs. On January 20, he writes: "This morning at five o'clock—for I am so afflicted with the insomnia of this eternal night that I rise at any hour between midnight and noon—I went up on deck. It was dark and . . . the cold not permitting even a swinging lamp, not a glimmer came to me through the ice-crusted window panes. While cudgeling my brains as to the best method of steering clear of the frozen fear—my two surviving Newfoundland dogs put their cold noses against my hand and instantly commenced exuberant antics of satisfaction. It then occurred to me how very dreary and forlorn it must be to these poor dogs, at temperatures of +10 indoors and –50 without, living in darkness only broken by an accidental light and with nothing either of instinct or sensation to tell them of the passing hours or of the lost daylight. No wonder that the poor devils made much of one."

A few days later, also in his private journal, Kane records two versions of an incident in which he was "forced to shoot a dog that had become ferocious." Because of the cold, he was keeping all the dogs belowdecks, although "nothing but the extreme necessity of saving the animals for our sledge travel would have led me to inflict them on our company." One of the men, John Blake, who was also known as William Huzza and Charles de Forrest, threatened to shoot one of the dogs.

This Blake "was a thorough reprobate," Kane wrote, "a good worker and a seaman but ferocious and insubordinate. He had been tried for his life for the late mutiny and murder on board the ———— and had repeatedly threatened our crew. John had had many warnings for previous ill conduct; on the present occasion he behaved with open insolence and insubordination. Fearing his example upon Godfrey . . . I arrested him [John] at once, and binding him, placed him in solitary confinement. The dog which he had threatened to shoot, I shot myself."

Kane continues: "John, George Whipple and William Godfrey are three men—thank god the only three—who trouble me. The shipment of these men was a grave mistake. Of all services this requires most of all moral character and, as far as I can see, has been entirely neglected. Godfrey is a thief—excessive and troublesome—I think professional—Whipple an abusive, weak man of no staunchness or principle. I have treated these men with extreme kindness and with results which show me that I must adopt other measures. I can see ahead of me nothing but dissension and trouble from their presence aboard."

In a later note, Kane writes: "The above I had intended to tear out . . . [but] subsequent matters in connection with John and Godfrey made me fill up and retain the page." In the second, slightly less accusatory rendition, Kane writes that in small crews aboard ship, one man generally leads the rest, "and in our case most unfortunately, for he [John Blake] is turbulent, insubordinate, and powerful, both a good sailor and a smart one, but I fear of a depraved and dangerous character." He describes him as "an inconsiderate drunkard" and notes that three times he had been "injudiciously pardoned for violent behaviour while under the influence of stolen liquors."

Kane recounts the facts in greater detail: "This morning he broke out into a regular burst of mutinous expressions, refusing to obey Mr. Brooks, abusing the condition of things and putting himself completely beyond control. I gave him, very foolishly, a hearing and then after explaining to him the cause of my anxiety to preserve the dogs said that I would nevertheless shoot them for the sake of preserving quiet and content with the crew. Whereupon he broke out into swearing that he would kill the dog himself— a threat made in the presence of the crew and accompanied with abuse of Mr. Grinnell and a complete contempt for order or authority."

Knowing that Blake carried influence, Kane called all hands on deck. He told them that the success of the expedition depended upon their good conduct, and added that their hard labor would be rewarded. But he also "told them of my intention to place in solitary confinement anyone guilty of mutinous expressions or willful disrespect of orders, and that such a scene as we had undergone today would cause me to send the offender to the American consul at Copenhagen if we reached a Greenland port. I then placed John, tied hand and foot, in solitary confinement to see only Mr. Brooks and myself, and his imprisonment to be dependent upon circumstances. The dog I shot."

A few days later, on February 2, Kane wrote and crossed out: "John's confinement has had an excellent effect upon the rest of the crew. The work goes on if anything better than with an additional hand."

o   o   o

When the time came to rework his unpublished journals into *Arctic Explorations,* Kane would spare readers the harsher details of disease symptoms and downplay the tensions that arose among the men. Early in February, for example, he notes that "bleeding piles are general," while one man suffers from a bleeding urethra and another from very painful bleeding lungs. "This last is Mr. Goodfellow," he writes, before reflecting on the young man's growing isolation: "To me his whole conduct has been an incomprehensible enigma. He has one by one by sharp speeches and unsympathizing ways so lost the good will of the officers and men that he is almost without associates. My efforts to bring about a better state of things were met with absolute insult. . . . The memory of Tom [Kane's brother] has made me kind to this poor boy—as kind as he (Tom) would have me be or he (Goodfellow) let me be.

"I have after going through a whole round of conciliatory and coercive expedients made him a gentleman passenger—exempt from all work and all regulations he goes to sleep when, how, and where he pleases, rises late and drinks the same. Scribbles over my papers or drops my books into his wash basin without let or hindrance. He will not let me be his friend for he addresses me a full sheet of foolscap divided into three lawyer-like heads proving that I not being doctor but commander had no right to such a privilege. But he permits me by stealth to make him as comfortable as I can, and at this moment he is the occupant of my state room while I am swinging in a temporary cot."

From such reflections as these, Kane would sometimes move in his journal into deeper, more personal reminiscences. The extant record, expunged of references to Maggie Fox, retains allusions to home and family, and especially to his brothers Tom and the late Willie. After visiting a large ravine at the eastern curve of Rensselaer Bay, Kane describes swirling, limestone protuberances spiraling upward like certain depictions of the Tower of Babel: "One of these abuts against the glories of the sunshine blazing like a yellow topaz. Long before the departure of the day I had watched this rock forming into deeper shadows, and when the winter darkness blotted him out, had caught him in our brightest moonlight rising above the ash-colored snows. I named it Little Willie's Monument. Thinking—as often as I dare allow myself—of this gallant boy-gentleman brother—the idea comes to me with a sort of satisfaction that he lies as much beneath this great Arctic hill as under that planted by Tom's tear watered Cypresses. Not to me is this dear boy's grave the granite or gravel or iron door of any city necropolis. All that I love, and all that I would remember is as much a part of the crust of our planet here as at Laurel Hill [the Philadelphia cemetery where Willie lies]."

This illustration, Life in the Brig, *puts a brave face on an increasingly difficult situation. It depicts a later moment in the expedition, when the men had donned fur clothing, and shows (left to right) Bonsall, Brooks, Kane, Hayes, and Morton.*

o   o   o

Finally, in mid-February, the midday sun began "silvering the ice between headlands of the bay." On the twenty-first, Kane donned sealskin pants, dogskin cap, reindeer jumper, and walrus boots. And when, after a long, solitary walk and a tough climb, he managed to see the sun from a projecting crag, "it was like bathing in perfumed water." As daylight returned, and he could again trace the outline of the shore, Kane saw that overflowing tides and freezing had transformed the ice belt into a bristling wall more than twenty feet high. Still, unlike the rough hummocks and tables littering the pack ice, it promised a secure and level sledge road north.

The death of the dogs, the obstacles of ice, and the fierce cold had forced Kane to revise his plan. Without the dogs for a longer run, he needed to cache provisions far beyond those already deposited near Humboldt Glacier.

He proposed to establish a final depot on the far shore of Kane Basin, on what is now Ellesmere Island. That land, never yet trodden by Western man, lay sixty miles from the nearest point on the Greenland coast. The captain would send a depot party northwest on a journey of seventy-five miles. This would mean leaving the ice belt and slogging through hummocks and drifting snow against icy winds. But to ensure success, it had to be done.

Kane began preparations in February, ordering the building of new sledges and a portable boat. By mid-March, with the sun rising over the horizon and the two main hunters, Hendrik and Petersen, producing rabbits and foxes, the health of the men had improved. On March 18, Kane tested the largest sledge with a small boat strapped atop the supplies. Eight men could scarcely budge this load, and he reduced it by removing the boat and one quarter of the food.

Later, Petersen would claim that he had warned Kane that March was too early to dispatch an expedition. Subsequent commentators would repeat this criticism, blaming Kane for the hardships that ensued—just as other armchair critics would fault Shackleton for leaving the relative comfort of his so-called Ocean Camp, a move that would increase the privations and miseries of his men.

But at that time, and in that place, no visitor could predict the weather. Two years before, in 1852, Kane's explorer friends William Kennedy and Joseph-René Bellot had begun a stupendous Arctic sledging journey on February 28, and ended up traveling for three months and covering more than 1,100 miles. And many subsequent explorers would set out still earlier and in far worse conditions. In 1906, for example, Robert Peary would depart in mid-February from much farther north; and two years after that, Frederick Cook would start for the Pole on February 19, at the first sighting of the sun. Generally, the Inuit would begin going on seal-hunting expeditions around that time, because the snow would finally be thick enough to muffle the sounds of their footsteps on the ice.

So, on March 19, an early but not unreasonable date, with the temperature standing at 49 degrees below zero but trending warmer, Kane dispatched an eight-man depot party northward. To lead this party he chose Henry Brooks, "a picture of faithful bulldog serenity [who] growls like a bear but eats his run of potatoes and does his work well," and who by now had recovered from the worst symptoms of scurvy.

In his journal, Kane wrote that the party "went with the usual three cheers and a special three for myself. These men can make a devil of a clamour." And, alluding to a marriage that took place just before he sailed, he noted that his brother "Tom's wedding cake—in the same box whereon was written for the first time Mrs. T.L. Kane—was totally demolished. The two last bottles of Mr. Grinnell's port were drank and the party laboured on like a parcel of overladen Esquimaux dogs, eight abreast."

Although, before leaving, the men had offloaded 200 pounds of pemmican, they still had trouble dragging the heavy sledge, partly because the extreme cold prevented the ice from melting beneath the narrow runners. From the brig, Kane watched through his telescope. Concerned to see them struggling, he readied a team of dogs and followed their trail. "By 8 p.m. they were camped only five miles from the ship. Here I visited them. Left them no new orders for the morning, but listened quietly to Petersen's assurances that the cold and cold only retarded his Greenland sledge, that no sledge of any other construction could have been moved through −40 snow. After joining in his regrets and laughing at Ohlsen's long baby face I came back, leaving them under their buffalos."

Back on the brig, Kane showed the grit and resourcefulness that made him a leader. Dismissing Petersen's arguments, he roused all hands and put them to work readying a different sledge—the *Faith,* designed by the British Admiralty and featuring broad runners. The men scraped and polished, fitted the sledge with track ropes, and made a snug canvas cover. At 1 a.m., having reloaded the previously discarded pemmican, Kane and four men set out, hauling the sledge into the lingering twilight.

At the camp, without waking their sleeping comrades, the new arrivals quietly transferred the cargo from the first sledge to the second. They picked up the drag ropes to test the result, and Kane said, "Now, boys, when Mr. Brooks gives his third snore, off with you." The *Faith* slipped easily over the ice. Kane and his men waited until the usual hour. Then, before heading back to the brig, they wakened the sleepers with three cheers. Next day, from the crow's nest, a lookout spotted the depot party a dozen miles away, moving easily. The temperature had risen to a moderate 22 degrees below zero, and Kane had every reason to anticipate a successful mission.

22

HEROES IN DELIRIUM

In *Arctic Explorations,* Elisha Kent Kane is unintentionally vague about one of the most crucial dates of his expedition. As a result, some biographers have got it wrong. According to his unpublished logbook, it was late on the night of Friday, March 31, 1854, that Kane, while sewing sealskin moccasins for his anticipated trek north, was startled by the sound of footsteps overhead. Footsteps on deck? Impossible. Only twelve days had elapsed since the depot party had set out to journey seventy-five miles. Surely the chosen eight could not have returned so soon? But as Kane rose to his feet, he later wrote, "Mr. Sonntag staggered in like an intoxicated man. His face wore a strangely wild and haggard expression—and was so bloated as to be hardly recognizable. Immediately after came Ohlsen and Petersen. Three more exhausted men I have seldom seen."

The three men, their faces swollen, collapsed onto the rough benches, so wasted they could scarcely speak. The other men, they said, were disabled. They were freezing to death in a little tent. Where, where? The new arrivals couldn't say. Kane and his awakening men removed the boots and furs of the three and gave them water to drink. Then, with difficulty, they elicited a fearful tale.

Having left the *Advance* under clear skies, the eight men had not traveled far before a blizzard drove them to take shelter behind a large iceberg. They waited out the storm, then resumed dragging their heavily laden sledge through and around hummocks, some of which stood fifteen feet high. Drifting snow forced them to circle back again and again, so they averaged only three or four miles a day. Finally, they abandoned the boat they were dragging, and also some of the pemmican, and slogged on through a thick fog as temperatures again plunged to 40 degrees below zero. Then had come another blizzard, this one so fierce that for two days they could do nothing but huddle in tents.

Ten days out, having traveled less than forty miles, the men realized they would never reach the western shore of the basin. Reluctantly, Henry Brooks ordered a return to the brig. The men began slogging south over rough ice and through deep drifts, and pitched their tent at 8:30 p.m. Exhausted, shivering, utterly wasted, some of the men crawled into their sleeping bags without brushing the snow from their clothes, and without removing so much as their boots.

That night, the temperature plummeted to −57 degrees Fahrenheit. In the morning, four men awoke to find their toes so badly frostbitten they couldn't stand up. The entire party faced death by freezing. The four men who could still walk volunteered to fetch help by trekking the thirty miles back to the brig. Brooks ordered "Irish Tom," the cabin boy, to remain as caregiver, and bid the other three men godspeed. At 10:20 a.m., the three left the tent. They walked and stumbled nonstop through blowing snow, without food or water, for more than twelve hours, and tumbled into the *Advance* just before midnight. "They had evidently travelled a great distance, for they were sinking with fatigue and hunger, and could hardly be rallied enough to tell us the direction in which they had come."

Recognizing the urgency of the situation, Kane acted swiftly. Three of his men were too ill with scurvy to move, and the expedition doctor, Isaac Hayes, would have to remain with them. Kane would lead most of the other men into the night. The temperature had fallen to 46 degrees below zero, and the recent arrivals doubted that a party burdened with supplies could cover the distance, thirty or maybe forty miles, in a single march. Kane resolved to travel as lightly as possible, and to carry no extra clothing, but only a small tent, a package of pemmican, and a cooking pot.

In his journal, he wrote: "To find a little gray canvas tent within a circuit of 240 miles, choked with icebergs and netted with hummock ridges, was not an easy undertaking anywhere, but when I thought of the positive necessity of making this discovery within thirty-six hours without a halt to melt water or a chance to sleep—for our one practicable sledge had been sent with the absent men—I confess that my judgment refused to second my intentions. It only appeared to me as a forced march without resources into a wilderness teaming with Death—to resist that death until the powers failed—or else finding the needle in the haystack.

"Ohlsen and Petersen, our most enduring men, had been unencumbered by sledge or baggage. They had walked as men impelled by desperation— a probable distance of 40 miles—without a drop of water or a moment's halt. I saw their condition. Both were utterly knocked up and one delirious. What chances had we—steering wildly into this frozen labyrinth— dogged by a sledge with time equally pressing—to say the very least it was an appalling prospect."

Of the three returnees, two could no longer stand and had been reduced to incoherence. Only Ohlsen continued to talk sense. Exhausted, utterly spent, he nevertheless volunteered to point the way. Clearly, he would have to be carried. Kane cushioned a small sledge with buffalo robes and strapped Ohlsen onto it, covering him with furs. At two o'clock in the morning, the rescue party plunged into the Arctic night, bent on finding a small gray tent in the frigid waste.

Kane hoped that Ohlsen, "our essential trust and hope for guidance," would point the way by recalling certain icebergs frozen into the pack. The invalid did manage to remain awake past a striking ice tower that the men called the "pinnacly berg," but then, having gone fifty hours without rest, he lost consciousness. Hours later, Ohlsen awoke disoriented. Kane

Hauling loaded sledges across the ice was always a challenge, as can be seen in Crossing the Ice Belt at Coffee Gorge. *In blizzard conditions, or in temperatures of 50 degrees below zero, this activity could be life-threatening.*

would describe him as showing "unequivocal signs of mental disturbance." Certainly, he could deduce nothing from the icebergs, "which in form and colouring endlessly repeated themselves and the uniformity of the vast area of snow utterly forbid the hope of local landmarks." The men kept slogging, following an obvious route along a stretch of colossal icebergs, guided by their foremost tracker, Hans Hendrik. Late in the afternoon, Hendrik lost the trail. Having arrived at a long, level floe, Kane ordered the men to pitch the tent, eat some pemmican, and fan out in search of footprints.

Ohlsen could stand upright, but he raved incoherently. With the temperature dropping to 50 below zero, two of the would-be rescuers, men who had withstood the severest marches, suffered trembling fits and shortness of breath, and Kane himself collapsed twice into the drifting snow. At 7 p.m., seventeen hours after leaving the brig, Hendrik discovered a faint sledge track and a few footprints. After another four hours of floundering along after the sharp-eyed Inuk, the rescuers halted and rubbed their eyes in astonishment: not twenty yards away, an American flag hung from a pole in the stillness, and below it a Masonic banner—clearly the one acquired in St. John's.

Near those two flags, half-buried in snow, the men discerned a small white tent. What waited inside? As Kane described the scene later, none of the first arrivals made a move to find out. Instead, they stood waiting "in silent file on each side" until their leader came up. Kane would write: "With more kindness and delicacy of feeling than is often supposed to belong to sailors, but which is almost characteristic, they intimated their wish that I should go in alone."

Kane kneeled, pulled back the tent flap, and crawled into the darkness. To his joy, he precipitated a rapturous outburst. All five trekkers had survived, the youngest still caring for the other four. "My weakness and my gratitude together almost overcame me," Kane wrote in *Arctic Explorations*. "They had expected me; they were sure I would come."

∘   ∘   ∘

To this point, four eyewitness accounts of varying length—one each by Kane, William Godfrey, Hans Hendrik, and Thomas Hickey—coincide, with one significant difference. According to Godfrey, Ohlsen had suffered so badly from frostbite that Kane amputated all ten of his toes before he left the brig. This assertion is ludicrous. Hendrik would write, for example, that after the return of Petersen and Ohlsen, "we then directly started, taking with us the carpenter, although he had just arrived and was perfectly exhausted. When we had eaten, he lay down upon the sledge, and we started dragging him." No mention of any amputations.

Indeed, Godfrey's account is corroborated by nobody, not even the intensely critical Petersen, and it is repudiated by subsequent events in which Ohlsen played an active role. On close inspection, it stands revealed as one of several fictions that Godfrey created to malign Kane, for he writes: "Who without a shudder could think of permitting a man, whose toes had been amputated on the preceding evening, to walk twenty miles on the ice. The experiment appeared to be both cruel and dangerous."

How could he justify such an egregious falsehood? Let us return to the arrival at the silent tent. In Kane's version, the rescuers waited for him to arrive and enter. Yet Godfrey writes that he reached the site first. He waited for nobody, but immediately pulled back the flap: "Four bodies, apparently lifeless, each one enclosed in a sleeping-bag, were lying close together in the little enclosure." For a moment, he hesitated to examine the bodies, afraid that his worst fears would be realized. He heard no sound—not even a suppressed groan, and no spasmodic breathing. He knelt down beside one of the bodies, which proved to be that of Brooks, and discovered, "with feelings of inexpressible joy," that the first officer still lived: "He fixed his eyes on me and gave me a faint smile of recognition. I sprung to the door of the tent and shouted to my companions, who were still at some distance, in order to relieve them as soon as possible from their painful suspense and to encourage them to hasten onward. I then examined the other three bodies, and found that the vital spark still lingered in them all."

Godfrey writes not a word about Hickey. But the cabin boy, who published his brief memoir after reading the others, supports the version of his "beloved commander"—and almost in the same words—while insisting upon a larger preliminary role for himself. Of the four dying men with whom he had been left at the tent, he writes: "Their cries and moans were heart-rending. My own hands were frozen in taking off their boots, and rubbing them into life." Hickey explains that he deliberately placed the American and Masonic flags as markers, and frequently stepped outside the tent to look for rescuers.

Late on the third day, he writes, "I saw dark spots at a distance moving upon the snow. As they drew nearer, I became certain that they were our deliverers, and, then, firing a gun to guide them to us, I began to prepare coffee and other refreshments to offer to them." The exhausted captain arrived, supported by Morton and Hendrik. "At the desire of the party," Hickey writes, "he entered the tent alone, where he was received with a shout of joy by the poor frozen men. They told him that they had expected him, and that they knew he would come to their relief."

Hickey's loyal testimony notwithstanding, this is the one instance in which, initially, Godfrey's narrative rings truer than Kane's. The captain's version, with its insistence on the unexpected sensitivity of his comrades, seems too perfect to be credible. And one can't help thinking that this harmless exaggeration, which made everyone involved look better than they were, would have helped Godfrey rationalize his shameless lying. If Elisha Kane could indulge himself in a literary fib, why not William Godfrey?

But now comes the clincher. In his hitherto-unseen journal, writing three days after the events, and without any thought he might be challenged, Kane told the story simply: "It is very pleasant to find oneself loved and trusted by one's command, and on that occasion where suffering with its inevitable selfishness breaks down authority and reduces us to a sort of level, the little and unexpected attentions of my comrades always touch me. No man would enter the sick tent before me. Decorously and with the nice tact of sailors, they stood in silent file on either side of the tent curtain and intimated their wish that I should go in alone. As I crawled in and entering into the darkness I heard the great burst of welcome gladness which came from the four poor fellows stretched upon their backs. And then—for the first time—the cheer outside. I felt like breaking into a crying fit."

o   o   o

Whatever the sequence of events, by the time they reached the tent, Kane and the other rescuers had been marching for twenty-one hours. They had eaten nothing but handfuls of pemmican. They needed rest. But the tent could hold eight men at most, and fourteen had now gathered. Kane ordered that each man be allowed to sleep in the tent for two hours, while the others walked around flapping their arms, or else huddled on the ice in buffalo bags. In his journal, he wrote: "Knowing that if our men were to be saved it must be by one forced continuous journey, we selected barely food enough for 50 hours" and buried everything else in the snow. "Few escaped frost bitten fingers," he wrote, and then added more details that he later elided: "The sick we saved by thrusting the fingers in the mouth. Imagine me sucking at two such tits! Our best resource for each other was placing the hand between the scrotum and the thigh, an office which we performed upon each other."

When morning came, Kane bundled blankets around the four invalids and lashed them onto the *Faith*. He added the tent and the remaining food but, lacking space, had to leave behind even the guns. After a short but affecting prayer, with the temperature dipping to 56 degrees below zero, the men started for the brig, dragging a sledge Kane described as "top heavy with its load of maimed men."

The first six hours went well. Kane observed that Ohlsen, "restored by hope, walked steadily at the leading belt of the sledge-lines." Clearly, this man had not endured any recent amputation. But now, nine hours from the tent the rescuers had abandoned during their outward trek, Kane saw the men showing "an alarming failure of energies." Bonsall and Morton, "two of our stoutest men, came to me, begging permission to sleep: they were not cold; the wind did not enter them now; a little sleep was all they wanted." In *Arctic Explorations,* Kane continued: "Presently Hans was found nearly stiff under a drift; and Thomas, bolt upright, had his eyes closed, and could hardly articulate. At last, John Blake threw himself on the snow, and refused to rise. They did not complain of feeling cold; but it was in vain that I wrestled, boxed, ran, argued, jeered, or reprimanded: an immediate halt could not be avoided."

This is a gentler rendition than appears in the unpublished journal, in which Kane writes: "My great hope was that we might reach the halfway halt of yesterday, where we had left our small sledge and tent, for Ohlsen now like a gallant fellow walked steadfastly at his post, taking the leading rue-raddy [shoulder-belted tow rope] of the sledge and never leaving it. But this hope was rendered null by the recreant dastardly unmanliness of one man—beast rather—John Blake, alias William Huzza [also Hussey], a man who had been engaged in the murderous revolt of the packet ship . . . and had under a false name smuggled himself into the expedition. This man always a burden to me by his wickedness was valuable for his strength and I thought fidelity. He was as attached to me as a man of his sort could be and

I hoped this would keep him to his post. He forsook his line and after all my persuasion refused to assist. I could not shoot him as under other circumstances I should have done. So I simply persisted. He continued thus a drag to our little party but still by compulsion an occasional assistance. Finally he flung himself on the snow and refused to proceed."

Kane ordered a four-hour halt. The freezing men pitched a tent, installed the invalids, and crowded as many more inside as they could. That still left two or three outside at all times. Kane declared his intention to push on to the abandoned tent, and the rugged Godfrey agreed to go with him. The two covered the nine miles in four hours—hours that Kane would later remember "as among the most wretched I have ever gone through." He writes: "We were neither of us in our right senses, and retained a very confused recollection of what preceded our arrival at the tent. We both of us, however, remember a bear, who walked leisurely before us and tore up as he went a jumper that Mr. McGary had improvidently thrown off the day before." Kane added that Godfrey saw from a distance that the bear had carried on ahead and begun ransacking the tent, and "probably our approach saved the contents."

After righting the tent with some difficulty, the two men crawled into their sleeping bags and slept for three hours. On waking, Kane found that his long beard had frozen into a solid mass of ice with his sleeping bag, and Godfrey had to cut him out with his jackknife. Before the others arrived, the two melted snow for water and cooked soup.

But here again, Godfrey tells a different story. Writing when Kane could no longer respond, he insists that only the captain became delirious, while he himself retained possession of reason and judgment. He claims that the bear "was a creation of the Doctor's fancy," that Kane mumbled incoherently throughout the trek, and that he had to help him along. As one of the strongest men on the expedition, Godfrey probably did assist Kane. But the ex-boatman would prove a chronic liar. And, with his ghostwriter, he drew on the hoary parable about the Christian sinner who marvels to discover, while looking back at his own footprints in the sand, that Jesus walked with him every step of the way. The sinner wonders about one curiosity: every so often, he discerns only a single set of footprints. Had he traveled alone during those stretches? Jesus tells him no: "During those stretches, my son, I carried you on my back."

In Godfrey's appropriation, Elisha Kane faints several times during this trek, at which points "I carried him on my shoulder." He writes that later, some of his comrades "were much puzzled by the occasional appearance of only one man's tracks in the snow." They wondered if the two men had been amusing themselves by walking single file. "Our people stated that they sometimes found but one pair of tracks for two or three miles together; and this account surprised me, for I really was not aware that I had carried the Doctor so far 'at a stretch.'"

The fabricating is palpable, the source evident. At this juncture, Kane had written generously of Godfrey, suggesting that "the memory of this day's work may atone for many faults of a later time." But the ex-boatman would have none of it: "Had the doctor's extreme modesty allowed him to place a proper estimate on the value of his own life, he might have thought perhaps that the assistance I then rendered him deserved a more handsome acknowledgement."

o　　o　　o

The final leg of the return trek proved excruciating. The previous night, the overcrowded tent had warmed sufficiently to melt frozen toes and feet. Schubert and Baker, in particular, had suffered agonies. Now, some of the men could not refrain from eating snow. Their mouths swelled, and they became unable to talk. According to Thomas Hickey, the men rested frequently, and "we would have been content to lay down and die, had not Dr. Kane urged and cheered us on. He watched us while sleeping, and woke us at intervals, so that we should not sleep the sleep of death."

Kane writes of the party moving on like men in a dream, while Godfrey insists that "the shrieks and groans of our sick people, who endured the most excruciating torments, harassed our minds and distressed us infinitely more than our own toils and corporeal sufferings." He describes periods of group hysteria, when the whole company, himself included, became frantic: "They laughed immoderately, gibbered, uttered the most frightful imprecations, mimicked the screams and groans of the invalids, howled like wild beasts and, in short, exhibited a scene of insane fury which I have never seen equaled in any lunatic asylum."

Periodically, the hubbub would cease, and raving maniacs would become sullen, moping idiots, or else weep and blubber like children. Then, suddenly, the sailors would begin howling again. Kane had written of allowing the men a tablespoon of brandy, and Godfrey, who stole liquor and got drunk at every opportunity, would write that "although this stimulus was used very cautiously, I believe it did much more harm than good; and I attribute to this very cause a good deal of the frenzy which prevailed among our party."

Despite agonies and outbursts, the men made a beeline for the brig. During the last few miles, according to Hickey, they "crawled along like animated stones." The men reached the *Advance* early in the afternoon, although "how we got on board none of us could ever tell." Isaac Hayes, not long out of medical school, was shocked by the ghastly appearance of the arriving men, several of whom failed to recognize him. The rescuers had been outside for seventy-two hours in temperatures as low as 56 degrees below zero. They had traveled eighty miles, most of that dragging a heavy sledge. Later, Hayes would conclude, "This relief expedition was the heroic performance of the cruise."

The men collapsed into their bunks, babbling and raving in delirium. For two days, the brig was like a madhouse. Many seemed to think they were still out on the ice, freezing to death, calling for help or exhorting others to carry on. When finally they surfaced, they often remembered nothing of the past couple of days. Christian Ohlsen, who had been exposed to the cold for something like a hundred hours and had traveled 120 miles, remained mostly unconscious for two and a half days. He would wake, ask for food, eat voraciously, and then fall back asleep and resume raving.

Kane, too, suffered—though he believed himself perfectly sound, as he could recall "the muttering delirium of my comrades when we got back into the cabin of our brig." Still, at one point he ordered Hayes to "call all hands to lay aft and take two reefs in the stovepipe."

Oddly enough, the semi-invalid Kane, one of the last to collapse, was one of the first to recover. When he awoke into sanity, he discerned that, as a result of frostbite, Brooks and Wilson would each lose three toes. And he realized that with two other men—Pierre Schubert, the high-spirited cook from Delmonico's, and Jefferson Baker, a country-boy admirer with whom, as a youth, he had hunted near Lapidea—he would have to amputate feet above the ankle. Having endured these operations, both men would die—Baker of tetanus on April 8, and Schubert a few weeks later of a bacterial infection, "after resisting with iron strength the effects of present exposure and a previously broken constitution."

Kane would be lying delirious when the cook passed away. On coming to, he would write, "Poor Schubert is gone." He could hardly believe that "our gallant, merry-hearted companion" had departed: "It is sad, in this dreary little homestead of ours, to miss his contented face and the joyous troll of his ballads." Schubert loved the music of French songwriter Pierre-Jean de Beranger (1780–1857), known for his clever, convivial, and populist tunes. Later, describing how the men carried his body in a decent pine coffin to its final resting place, the cosmopolitan Kane would write: "He was a gallant man, a universal favorite on board, always singing some Beranger ballad or other, and so elastic in his merriment that even in his last sickness he cheered all that were about him."

With Baker, whom he had known since boyhood, Kane would be awakened by a sound from the man's throat—"one of those the most frightful and ominous that ever startle a physician's ear." Lockjaw had seized his boyhood friend. In *Arctic Explorations,* Kane writes: "His symptoms marched rapidly to their result: he died on the 8th of April." In his unpublished journal, he is far more graphic: "Baker died this morning at twenty-five minutes past four. His sufferings were fearful. The jaw had not relaxed for six hours before his last paroxysm. The utter hopelessness of his case added to his agony. He asked of me the specific question, 'Can I live?' And got from me the specific answer 'You cannot.' His mind was clear up to the last and in the short intervals of speech he alluded to his spasms and nightmares—'living deaths.' His just mumblings which assumed articulation after or even during one of these fits were 'wake me, shake, squeeze burn me I'm dead. Can't move, wake me, wake me,' and thus we went on, he sleeping his frightful nightmares and me according him. Spasm after spasm, agony upon agony, until, at last, shaking and squeezing in answer to the now no longer understood voice we ceased to waken—and he went on in sleep."

Kane would remember Baker as "a man of kind heart and true principles." He would write of spending two happy seasons at a little cottage adjacent to the Baker family farm: "He thought it a privilege to join this expedition, as in those green summer days when I had allowed him to take a gun with me on some shooting-party." Having placed the young man in his coffin, Kane and his crew formed a heavy-hearted procession, "bore him over the broken ice and up the steep side of the ice-foot to Butler Island." They placed the corpse upon two pedestals that normally supported instruments. Kane read the service for the burial of the dead, sprinkled snow over the body in place of dust, and led the men in reciting the Lord's Prayer. The sailors piled stones over the rough tomb, iced up the wall, "and left him in his narrow house."

23

Two Discoveries

The North Pole is defined as a geographical point at the top of the world. In theory, because every location on earth lies south of that point, travelers can approach via an infinite number of routes. In reality, explorers both early and late have found one path far more practical than any other, and have used it far more often. That path is the so-called "American route to the Pole," which runs north through Smith Sound into Kane Basin, and then through the Kennedy Channel. In late April 1854, when Elisha Kent Kane resumed his explorations, that channel remained undiscovered.

Kane knew only that he had yet to investigate and chart the extensive basin in which the *Advance* lay trapped. On what he projected as the "crowning expedition of the campaign," he proposed to travel north along the Greenland coast. He would retrieve the cache left the previous October, then travel westward along the face of the great glacier he had sighted, seeking "round the farthest circle of ice for an outlet to the mysterious channels beyond." While still hoping to find traces of the Franklin expedition, Kane focused increasingly on geographical issues—specifically, on seeking the

Open Polar Sea. A gap in the distant mountains to the west suggested an indentation in the coast—possibly a channel that eventually wended north.

During the winter, as a result of frostbite, several men had had toes amputated. Scurvy had taken down other crew members, rendering them too sick to travel. Also, more than fifty dogs had died of a miserable, scurvy-like illness. Seven remained alive—just enough to haul a single sledge. Kane himself felt weak from scurvy. Yet he proposed to lead a two-pronged expedition.

First, he would send McGary north with five men hauling a sledge. Despite the fragility of his health, Kane would follow in a light, nine-foot dogsled built by Ohlsen and driven by Godfrey. Both parties would travel light. Besides instruments—sextant, chronometer, and telescope—they would carry only pemmican, bread, tea, a small tent, and their caribou-skin sleeping bags. Their kitchen consisted of a soup kettle for melting snow and making tea.

The sledge-haulers set out on April 25. Placing Ohlsen in charge of the brig and nine men, six of whom were disabled, Kane left the next afternoon. Because of his physical condition, he rode whenever possible, though at times, inevitably, he had to climb out and scramble over hummocks. On the third day out, Kane and Godfrey overtook the trekkers. The two parties then proceeded separately, maintaining a slow but steady pace and joining up at the end of each day's work.

The artist in Kane responded to the majesty of the landscape. He thrilled to the dramatic sandstone cliffs, 1,000-foot-high battlements backed by the steep face of the ice sheet that covers more than 80 percent of Greenland. That sheet, according to twenty-first-century science, comprises 10 percent of all the ice on earth, or 630,000 cubic miles—enough, if melted, to raise global sea levels by twenty-three feet. In 1854, the most startling effects of erosion, according to the keen-eyed Kane, were fantastical columns of free-standing rock created by frost, wind, and water. More than once, he insisted on stopping to sketch these phenomena, warming his hands with his breath. He gazed, enchanted, at a sun-splashed gorge guarded by the "dreamy

semblance of a castle, flanked with triple towers, completely isolated and defined"—the Three Brother Turrets.

And he was even more taken with a slender, solitary column that rose from a 280-foot pedestal, whirling another 480 feet into the air and "as sharply finished as if it had been cast for the Place Vendome" in Paris. Often, during the winter, Kane had entertained the men by declaiming *Ulysses* by Alfred Tennyson: "Death closes all; but something ere the end, / Some work of noble note may yet be done, / Not unbecoming men that strove with gods." Now, he sketched and labeled the whirling column Tennyson's Monument, never imagining that the poet himself would one day hang a colored print based on this sketch in one of his rooms.

One week out from the brig, the men encountered snowdrifts that left them floundering. Most were showing signs of scurvy. Three complained of snow blindness and one felt pains in his chest. On May 3, the trekkers discovered that polar bears had ravaged their first cache of provisions, tossing aside boulders that had tested the strength of three men and smashing open iron caskets of pemmican. The next day, while taking observations, Kane felt a pain in his chest and collapsed onto the ice. On waking, he felt stiff and had trouble walking. And he found that he could scarcely tolerate even the relative warmth of 5 degrees below zero. Having frozen his left foot to the instep, he insisted on going forward. His men strapped him into the sledge and pressed onward.

Now, from a distance of twenty miles, Kane got his first clear view of Humboldt Glacier. He made several sketches but felt that his drawings did not do justice to the natural wonder, "the grandeur of the few bold and simple lines of nature being almost entirely lost." That night, he discovered swelling in his legs. And the following day, he became delirious, drifting in

The artistic Kane responded enthusiastically to the grandeur of the Arctic landscape, and was especially taken with a whirling column of rock that soared to a height of 480 feet. He named it Tennyson's Monument after his favorite poet, whose work he would frequently declaim to the men trapped in the brig.

and out of feverish consciousness. He fainted while moving from the tent to the sledge. Finally, he slipped into a stupor.

His comrades, broken down by scurvy and struggling in the drifting snows, turned around and made for the brig. After a forced march of ten days, they reached it. They delivered the delirious Kane into the care of young Doctor Hayes. He would follow his superior in diagnosing scurvy complicated by typhoid symptoms. But doctors of a later era would ascribe the symptoms to endocarditis and rheumatic fever, exacerbated by fatigue and exposure.

Kane remained in bed for two weeks, and wrote later that he owed his life to the brave men who had brought him back to the brig: Morton, Riley, Hickey, Stephenson, and Hendrik. The whaler McGary had traveled on ahead to alert the brig, and Kane made no mention of Godfrey. Hickey, the cabin boy, would recall that "at the moment when [Kane] needed the kindest attention he was alone, and in the hands of Mr. Godfrey, with whom he had remained behind the sledge party, in order to obtain rest. His complaints of illness to Mr. Godfrey were entertained with bad humor, and nothing was done to relieve him. Godfrey, however, carried him forward [in the dog sledge] to join us, when we immediately made a halt, and began to use all the remedies at hand to restore him."

o   o   o

On May 20, 1854, six days after he reached the brig, Elisha Kent Kane—"propped up by pillows and surrounded by sick messmates"—would resume writing in his journal. He noted "that we have failed again to force the passage to the north." But also he began seriously contemplating Humboldt Glacier. His field notes spoke of the "long ever-shining line of cliff diminished to a well-pointed wedge in the perspective," and of "the face of glistening ice, sweeping in a long curve from the low interior, the facets in front intensely illuminated by the sun."

In retrospect, Kane would add that this cliff "rose in a solid glassy wall three hundred feet above the water-level," and that its curved face ran away sixty miles and "vanished into unknown space at not more than a single day's railroad-travel from the Pole." Kane would go on to describe Humboldt Glacier, which he understood to be an extension of the ice sheet that covered most of Greenland, as a "deep unbroken sea of ice that gathers perennial increase from the watershed of vast snow-covered mountains and all the precipitations of the atmosphere upon its own surface."

Kane believed, wrongly, that the glacier formed a "mighty crystal bridge" connecting Greenland and Ellesmere Island. More crucially, he vividly evoked the enormity of this deep, unbroken sea of ice, fed continually by the watershed of vast snow-covered mountains: "Imagine this, moving onwards like a great glacial river, seeking outlets at every fjord and valley, rolling icy cataracts into the Atlantic and Greenland seas; and, having at last reached the northern limit of the land that has borne it up, pouring out a mighty frozen torrent into unknown Arctic space."

Back home in Philadelphia, Kane had savored analogies likening glaciers to mighty rivers. But when he stood staring across the pack ice at Humboldt Glacier, "I could not comprehend at first this complete substitution of ice for water. It was slowly that the conviction dawned on me, that I was looking upon the counterpart of the great river systems of Arctic Asia and America, [only] converted into ice. . . . Here was a plastic, moving, semi-solid mass, obliterating life, swallowing rocks and islands, and ploughing its way with irresistible march through the crust of an investing sea."

Kane's vision of a vast ocean of ice, and his ability to articulate it, would prove transformative. As science writer Edmund Blair Bolles argues in his book *The Ice Finders,* Kane's discovery of the world's largest glacier was "a finding to match discoveries by other mid-century explorers who reported Mount Everest and Lake Victoria." Bolles shows that Kane's vivid descriptions not only transformed men's understanding of glaciers, but enabled and equipped scientists to conceive of the Ice Age—of a time, lasting thousands of years, when the earth was cold and largely covered in ice.

Before Kane, Bolles writes, people thought of glaciers as tongues of ice characterizing the High Alps. Scientists "did not place glaciers among the greatest, most monstrous, most overwhelming structures on the planet." After Kane, they understood: "Forget about rivers and picture an ocean. The heart of the Ice Age is not the glacier, but the central ice sheet. Ice Age glaciers had been just little bays poking beyond the ice ocean's shoreline."

Bolles gave his book a descriptive subtitle: *How a Poet, a Professor, and a Politician Discovered the Ice Age.* The professor is renowned paleontologist Louis Agassiz; the politician is Scottish geologist Charles Lyell; and the poet is Elisha Kent Kane, who had "chased the Ice Age to its lair." His books and drawings "would transform talk of an ice-shrouded world from an imaginary *maybe* into a palpable *is.*"

Inevitably, an accomplishment of this magnitude would attract critics and counter-claimants. One of the first was Dr. Henry Rink, a Danish official who had spent several years in Greenland, and who eventually translated the memoirs of Hans Hendrik. Rink had never traveled much above Upernavik, yet he challenged Kane's charts and descriptions, while obscuring and distorting the explorer's allusions to Humboldt Glacier as an extension of the Greenland ice sheet. Rink claimed also that he had already published the basic facts about the ice sheet. Shouldn't the recognition be his?

Nobody had shown the least interest in Rink's obscure essay. Yet later scientists, even Charles Lyell, would cite Rink rather than Kane as a source of facts. "In the scientific world," Bolles explains, "Kane had no standing. Writers used his Greenland imagery and cited Rink as their source." The scholar Oscar M. Villarejo probably summed it up best when he observed, in *Dr. Kane's Voyage to the Polar Lands,* that Rink's criticisms simply "cannot be sustained today."

Kane's finding of what he called the "Great Glacier of Humboldt," in which nomenclature he included the Greenland Ice Sheet, has yet to be properly recognized. To declare this a mid-century discovery on the scale of Mount Everest might be going too far. But, given the corollary revelation of the Ice Age and its revolutionary consequences, this much is certain: in Humboldt Glacier, Kane made an extraordinary discovery.

o   o   o

Early in May, after an absence of six months, snowbirds returned to the encircling bay, restoring hope and optimism. The increasing daylight melted the snow from the sides of the *Advance* and freed the rigging of ice. Kane saw these changes as "pledges of renewed life, the olive branch of this dreary waste; we feel the spring in all our pulses." Soon he would be rhapsodizing: men were gleaning fresh water from the rocks, icebergs were running with streamlets, and the base of the ice belt was overflowing with water pools—"Winter is gone!"

Kane sent McGary south to Lifeboat Cove to check on the hidden row-boat, the cache of provisions, and, above all, the state of the ice. Traveling by dogsled along the ice belt, McGary accomplished the 100-mile round trip in four days. He reported the site undisturbed, but observed that the pack ice remained intact thirty miles beyond Littleton Island. To Carl Petersen, the immigrant Greenlander, this boded ill.

Kane remained optimistic. When he thought of Sir John Franklin and wondered whether any of his crew might yet survive, he remained convinced that everything depended on locality. Anticipating the "friendly Arctic" arguments of twentieth-century explorer Vilhjalmur Stefansson, Kane insisted that animals could be successfully hunted within twenty-five miles of just about any point in the far north.

If he had been compelled to address the question of Franklin's survival four months before, while engulfed by darkness and disease, he would have turned toward the black hills and the frozen sea and responded despondently. Even so, he had never accepted the "the complete catastrophe, the destruction of all Franklin's crews." And now, with the return of spring, he pictured the men broken into detachments, "and my mind fixes itself on one little group of some thirty, who have found the spot of some tidal eddy, and under the teachings of an Esquimaux or perhaps one of their own Greenland whalers, have set bravely to work, and trapped the fox, speared the bear, and killed the seal and walrus and whale. I think of them ever with hope. I sicken not to be able to reach them."

As May wore on, bringing with it the anniversary of his departure from New York, Kane felt increasingly driven to find both the lost expedition and the Open Polar Sea. After a year in the Arctic, he had yet to venture beyond Humboldt Glacier, or even to reach the western shore of the basin (Ellesmere Island). At the very least, he needed to determine whether any channel led north or west out of this great bay. With seven dogs remaining, and many of his men still sick, he decided to change his approach: relying on the remaining dogs, he would send out smaller parties.

To lead the first he chose the young doctor, Isaac Hayes. Among those able to travel, only Hayes could use the geodesic instruments to take reliable observations. On May 20, in bright afternoon sunshine, Kane sent Hayes to the northwest with Godfrey, the expedition's best dogsled driver. The two were gone twelve days. When they arrived back at the brig, exhausted, bedraggled, and suffering from snowblindness, they reported considerable success—though initially, only verbally. For six weeks, Hayes could not see well enough to write.

He told Kane that crossing the basin had proven far harder than expected. The pack ice had been broken up by huge icebergs, and deep snow filled the hollows between hummocks. As he later wrote, "One moment we were ascending the slippery, sloping surface of a huge elevated table of ice which had been pressed upward; then we were sliding down another, the sledge on top of the dogs, the dogs tangled in their traces, howling piteously; men, dogs, and sledge in wild confusion, plunging into a snow-drift, or against a cake of ice."

Meanwhile, the sun remained visible twenty-four hours a day, always near the horizon, and successively in the north, east, south, and west. Because of the resulting brightness, Hayes became increasingly snow-blind. Six days out, the journey almost ended disastrously when, surrounded by icy spires and overwhelmed by the loneliness of the landscape, William Godfrey broke down. The man himself would pretend this never happened, and assert that Hayes ended their journey "very much to my regret, as I felt a strong inclination to go further."

But in the second edition of his *Arctic Boat Journey,* Hayes detailed an incident that most commentators have overlooked. After acknowledging that the wilderness of icy hummocks and spires presented "an aspect almost fearful, especially to uninstructed minds, where the power of careful reasoning is wanting," Hayes wrote that his traveling companion, "who had but little education . . . became so impressed with the frightful appearance of our surroundings, and the hopelessness of the undertaking,—so overwhelmingly certain did it appear to him that we were running into the very jaws of death,—that his reason seemed to leave him. . . . 'Turn back, turn back,' was the burden of his song morning, noon, and night, until, tears and entreaties failing him, he fell into a fit of madness, and exclaiming, 'If not with you, then without you,' he tried the rifle as a means to an escape. Fortunately for both of us, a short *rencontre* ended in such a manner as to somewhat restore his senses, and to enable me to proceed the next day with less embarrassment, and ultimately to accomplish my purpose."

The two men reached Ellesmere the following day, just to the south of the indentation about which Kane had wondered—but which proved to be a shallow cove. Hayes traveled north along the coast, passing cliffs that soared 2,000 feet into the air, and planted the Stars and Stripes at a farthest-north latitude of 79 degrees, 45 minutes. With both men and dogs exhausted, and food running short, Hayes then turned and hurried south to survey the coastline as far as Cape Sabine, which had been charted by Inglefield in 1852.

From there, increasingly hungry, Hayes and Godfrey began a desperate dash to the brig. They fed the starving dogs chunks of leather trousers, and threw away sleeping bags and clothing to reduce their load by fifty pounds. The men traveled nearly 400 miles and added 200 miles of coastline to the Arctic charts. Yet they had discovered no outlet from Smith Sound either to the west or the north.

Kane remained convinced that such a channel existed, however, because of the movement of icebergs, the character of the tides, and the thrust of the coastline. And so, yearning to venture forth, but still too weak and sick with scurvy to do so, the explorer decided to send yet another party to the northwest. With only six men well enough to make a hard journey, he projected a two-stage expedition. Five men would haul the large sledge to Humboldt Glacier. The sixth, Hans Hendrik, would remain at the brig to hunt, then follow the others, using a dog team and a light sledge to overtake them. Then, while four men ascended the glacier to survey the ice sheet, Hendrik and William Morton would continue north with the dogs. Kane had taught the trusted Morton to make observations, and had supplied him with sextant, artificial horizon, and pocket chronometer. In his journal, he wrote, "I am intensely anxious that this party should succeed; it is my last throw." The first five men left the brig on June 4, and Hendrik followed five days later.

Only now, as he settled in to await results, did Kane discover the disturbing condition of the ice pack. Still recuperating from scurvy and exhaustion, and intently focused on organizing this final sortie, the captain had spent the past three weeks aboard the brig. His men had assured him that the ice was melting rapidly. But when, immediately after the departure of Hendrik, Kane ventured beyond the usual confines, he discovered those reports to be mistaken. Neither the pack nor the ice belt had melted much. Indeed, he judged their unchanged condition to be "a momentous warning."

With a shock, Kane realized that the summer sunshine might not release the *Advance*. He and his men might be forced to spend a second winter here at Rensselaer Harbor, even though they lacked sufficient coal and fresh provisions. Kane sent Ohlsen and Hayes south to check for open water, and found no comfort in their report: even now, the pack ice extended beyond Littleton Island.

On the evening of June 27, after an absence of over three weeks, four men stumbled back to the brig. The leader, McGary, could hardly see as a result of snow blindness. He would be slow to recover. But, having taken observations and verified the charting of the coastline, he also had a story to tell. During their outward journey, the men had encountered heavy, drifting snow. They hunted with success and kept slogging.

One night, while the five men slept in their tent, McGary awoke to a scratching sound. Realizing that a polar bear had begun poking around, he cried out and woke the other men. The trekkers had left their guns on a sledge outside the tent. They lit matches and waved newspaper torches to scare the bear away, but the massive creature, ignoring their antics, sat down at the entrance to the tent and began devouring a seal they had shot the previous day.

Young Tom Hickey, the cabin boy, cut a hole in the rear of the tent and crawled through it. The youth grabbed a boat hook and, while making a dash for the rifles, as Kane wrote later, "made it the instrument of a right valorous attack." Hickey struck the bear on the nose, grabbed a rifle, and sprang back into the tent. The bear came after him, but the steady Amos Bonsall shot it dead. After this, travelers obeyed Kane's standing order to keep at least one firearm in the tent.

After twelve days of steady hauling, the men had reached the main face of Humboldt Glacier—and again found evidence of what a polar bear could do. One or more of the creatures had ransacked their ultimate cache of supplies, tossing aside boulders and dashing even iron-bound caskets to pieces. They had made a frolic of it, ripping old canvas to shreds, rolling bread barrels off the ice foot to explode them, and tying lengths of India rubber into "unimaginable hard knots." Apparently, they had amused themselves by sliding down a forty-five-degree slope on their haunches—a performance, Kane wrote, "in which I afterward caught them myself."

The men tried to scale the face of Humboldt Glacier. But, with nothing but foot clamps and crude apparatus, they made little progress. Kane was glad they had abandoned the attempt and started back to the brig. The return of the four left two men still out. McGary reported that, roughly as planned, Hendrik had overtaken the trekkers on June 16. After resting for a day, he and Morton left the others to travel north beyond the main face of Humboldt Glacier.

Now, as the almost constant sunlight of early July turned stretches of the ice belt to slush, Kane worried that dogsled travel would become impossible. But on the evening of July 10, while out walking with Bonsall, he heard the telltale sounds of braying dogs. With a thrill of joy, he watched two men come into view, stumbling along beside a sled and a team of limping dogs.

o   o   o

Safely installed aboard the *Advance,* William Morton recounted the most astonishing adventure yet. Having pushed on beyond Humboldt Glacier, traveling on the pack ice, Morton and Hendrik had threaded their way through a maze of icebergs, moving "like a blind man in the streets of a strange city." From atop one of the bergs, while getting his bearings, Morton could see the great white plain of Humboldt Glacier extending far into the interior.

A few miles farther north, the men encountered yet another glacier face fronting on the bay, this one filled with stones, earth, and large rocks. Here the chasms between icebergs gaped four feet wide, with water at the bottom. The two men chopped large chunks of ice from the nearby hummocks. They made bridges by rolling these into the holes and filling the cracks, then coaxed the dogs across. Moving west, they emerged from the berg field onto better ice.

On June 21, in misty weather, the men rounded a point of land. When the fog lifted fleetingly, they realized they stood in the middle of a channel. The ice became so thin that the dogs began to tremble. They lay down and, shaking violently, refused to proceed. Hendrik coaxed them toward thicker ice along the shore, encouraging them to crawl along on their bellies. During this adventure, through the fog, the men had glimpsed open water, and suddenly they saw it clearly: open water two miles up the channel. Hendrik could hardly believe it. And except for the great number of birds, mostly eider ducks and dovekies, that also appeared, Morton too would have had to rub his eyes.

Slogging along the ice foot in the sunny calm, the men realized they were traveling north along one side of a horseshoe with open water in its center. They saw still more eider ducks and, covering the rocks, flocks of sea swallows. On reaching an eight-foot wall of land ice, they turned the sledge into a ladder. With Morton pulling from above and Hendrik pushing from below, they managed to haul the dogs over the top.

To test the depth of the remarkably clear water, Morton heaved a head-sized stone off the ice foot and counted twenty-eight seconds before it reached bottom. The water temperature stood at 36 degrees Fahrenheit. As the two men proceeded north toward a prominent cape, the sturdy ice foot became a narrow ledge hugging the cliffs. It shrank to three feet, then gave way to mashed ice. The current ran fast toward the north, driving chunks of ice along as fast as a man could walk.

For three-quarters of a mile, the men struggled forward across mashed ice. Rounding the cape, which Kane would name Andrew Jackson, they looked north and saw nothing but open water. In the far distance, the coastline to the west seemed to meet the eastern shore on which they stood. The men followed the shoreline around a shallow bay, crossed a stretch of glassy ice, and came upon still more birds, among them ducks and brent geese, ivory gulls, mollemokes, and flocks of screeching terns.

Back at the *Advance,* Kane would name this waterway the Kennedy Channel, honoring his staunch supporter John Pendleton Kennedy. Quoting Morton, he wrote that the channel could easily accommodate any frigate: "The little brig, or 'a fleet of her like' could have beat easily to the northward." But now a wind began to blow from that direction, and a rolling fog reduced visibility. Morton estimated that the two men had traveled forty miles up the channel, which was thirty-five miles across. The eider proved so numerous that when Hendrik fired into a flock, he killed two birds with a single shot.

On June 23, the men left the sledge to proceed on foot, carrying instruments, eight pounds of pemmican, and two pounds of bread. They chanced upon two polar bears, mother and cub, and with the help of the dogs managed to kill them. Hendrik stayed behind to skin the creatures while

Morton pushed on alone, determined to reach one more point of land—Cape Constitution, as Kane would call it.

The ice foot grew narrower until, about a mile from cape, it ended altogether. Here, driven by a crosswind, waves broke directly against the cliffs, which soared 2,000 feet into the air. Morton yearned to round this cape so that he could see farther north. Starting from a height of 180 feet, he managed to climb another 300, but then he could climb no farther. He fastened two flags—the American flag belonging to Henry Grinnell, which had sailed to the Antarctic with the Wilkes expedition; and the Masonic emblem from St. John's, Newfoundland—to his walking-stick and jammed it into the rocks.

According to his instruments, Morton had reached 81 degrees, 22 minutes north—the second most northerly position yet attained by Western man. Subsequent geographers would grant this claim while judging his position as closer to 80 degrees, 30 minutes. Edward Parry, working from the Russian side of the Pole in 1827, had reached 82 degrees, 45 minutes on a sledge journey from the island of Spitsbergen. Yet, according to L.H. Neatby, Morton's achievement was of greater significance, "for the American was following the proper route—the best, if not the only way, to the Pole before the airplane made land bases of lesser importance in the logistics of Polar travel."

For an hour and a half, while Hendrik waited—according to his own account—some distance below and behind, William Morton sat perched on a cliff face within 600 miles of the Pole. Except for a range of mountains in the far northwest, which looked like "a succession of sugar loaves and stacked cannon-balls declining slowly in the perspective," he could see nothing but shining water.

o   o   o

Back at the *Advance,* Elisha Kane addressed the obvious question: Had William Morton reached the southernmost edge of the Open Polar Sea? In a letter to his brother Thomas, Kane would write, "The great North Sea,

This illustration, The Open Water from Cape Jefferson, *is meant to suggest that Henry Morton discovered the Open Polar Sea. Certainly Kane believed this, though in fact Morton had gazed out over the Kennedy Channel, which would soon become known as "the American route to the Pole."*

the Polynia, has been reached, and had not the dogs died and so deprived us of boats, we would have gone . . . to God knows where." On a map he included with his official report to the American navy, he placed the words "Open Sea" beyond the northern exit of the Kennedy Channel.

In his published book, Kane expressed himself more circumspectly. He wrote that whether the water "exists simply as a feature of the immediate region, or as part of a great and unexplored area connecting with the Polar basin . . . may be questions for men skilled in scientific deductions. Mine has been the humble duty of recording what we saw. Coming as it did, a mysterious fluidity in the midst of vast plains of solid ice, it was well calculated to arouse emotions of the highest order; and I do not believe there was a man among us who did not long for the means of embarking upon its bright and lonely waters."

The explorer noted that previous such discoveries, although "chronicled with perfect integrity," had sometimes proven illusory. And he understood that his own finding, "though on a larger scale, may one day pass within the same category." Sure enough, subsequent explorations would determine that the open water Morton sighted was not the edge of a Polar Sea, but simply part of the Kennedy Channel, a waterway more open in some years than others.

Still, that channel constituted a second major discovery. For explorers of the late nineteenth and early twentieth centuries, Kane had found virtually the only feasible way to reach the North Pole. Those who followed the route through Smith Sound, Kane Basin and the Kennedy Channel included Isaac Hayes in 1860 and 1869, Charles Francis Hall in 1871, George Nares in 1875, and Adolphus Greely in 1881. In 1908, when Robert E. Peary launched his final attempt to reach the Pole, he too followed the route that Kane discovered. Even today, an overwhelming majority of those who attempt the Pole without flying travel through the Kennedy Channel, acutely aware that they follow "the American route to the North Pole."

24

THE DEFECTION

On July 4, 1854, to celebrate American Independence Day, Elisha Kent Kane decorated the *Advance* with flags and distributed spirits among the men, trying to disguise his growing concern. Last year, the brig had reached this position on August 28, as new ice was forming. Now, less than two months from that date, twenty-five miles of pack ice lay between the vessel and open water. If the ice continued to melt at the current rate, Rensselaer Harbor would not open up until the last day of August, and the ship would need at least another few days to work free.

Already, the men were tired, sick, and hungry. They had exhausted most of the fuel needed for cooking, the lamp oil required for light, and the fresh provisions that defended them against scurvy. Kane worked hard to hide his disquiet. But he feared that "there never was, and I trust never will be, a party worse armed for the encounter of a second Arctic winter."

On July 7, in rough notes for a letter to his brother Tom—an emotional missive that he would never finish—Kane wrote despairingly of the death of the dogs and his two men, and of the widespread breakdowns, amputations, and sufferings from scurvy. The expedition had charted more than 600 miles of coastline, but: "Never dear brother can poor Elish go through all this again—Fresh trials are ahead, for the ice is unbroken around me—and I am well aged and worn."

The next morning, his optimism returning, Kane went with Hendrik and the dogs to the study the edge of the pack ice. During the past two months, open water had approached only four miles nearer the brig. As he looked out, Kane glimpsed the truth: the *Advance* would not be released that summer. Nor could he hope, this late in the season, with so many men sick and suffering from toe amputations, to escape with the whole party to Upernavik. As he wrote that night, "It would be absurd to try escaping in open boats with this ice between us and the water." Besides, how could he desert the *Advance* while he still had a chance of saving her? He needed no list of pros and cons: "My mind is made up; I will not do it."

But nor would he abandon hope of improving conditions aboard the brig. And so he conceived a desperate plan to seek assistance from a squadron of five British ships. These had sailed under Sir Edward Belcher in 1852, intending to establish a base 600 miles away, at Beechey Island in Lancaster Sound. Now, in July 1854, although Kane could not know it, Belcher was on the verge of abandoning four of those vessels to the Arctic ice.

Kane shared his plan with a few of his officers, who welcomed it. To Henry Goodfellow, who would one day be cited for "brave and meritorious service" at the Battle of Gettysburg, the captain consigned his papers and documents for safekeeping. Goodfellow wrote later that at this time, he still remained optimistic that the *Advance* would be released, although "the practiced eye of Dr. Kane had seen that such hopes were delusive." Carl Petersen, the malcontent Greenlander, would insist that he knew Kane would never reach Beechey Island, but made no effort to dissuade him: "I let him depart without expressing my opinion on this subject, and the more so, because he did not at all consult me about it."

Among the officers, only Sonntag could have navigated well enough to reach Beechey Island, and he was down with scurvy. Kane himself would lead this risky sortie. To accompany him, he chose the expert boatman McGary, and Morton, Riley, Hickey, and Hendrik. Kane placed Brooks in command of the brig and, on July 14, left hauling a sledge that carried the *Forlorn Hope*. Ohlsen had improved this flat-bottomed boat—twenty-three feet long, six and a half wide, two and a half deep—by adding a false keel. Even so, as Kane wrote, "she was a mere cockle shell."

After three days of slogging, the men reached open water. They began sailing south. McGary had rigged the little boat with a mainsail, a foresail, and a jib—or, as Kane put it, "what any but a new London whaler would call an inordinate spread of canvas." The craft lacked a rudder; McGary used an old-fashioned steering oar.

At Lifeboat Cove near Littleton Island, Kane rejoiced to find the cache of equipment and provisions untouched. He spotted a great number of ducks, and tracked their flight to a rugged little ledge so thick with wild fowl that a man could not walk without stepping on a nest. The men killed a couple of hundred birds for food. A rocky island crowded with gulls proved especially productive, and Kane named it Hans Island after Hendrik, his best hunter.

Three days out, having entered the open seaway of Baffin Bay, the men encountered a storm so fierce that Kane could compare it only to the hurricanes he had experienced in the Gulf of Mexico. McGary, the only expert steersman, stayed at the oar for twenty-two hours straight. A broken oar or accidental twitch, Kane wrote, would have been fatal, "and none of us could pretend to take his place." The whaler managed to keep the craft from foundering, and when the storm abated, the men found themselves battling loose pack ice.

Hauling, rowing, and occasionally sailing through an open lead, the men proceeded south along the Greenland coast. The battered boat began to leak, but Kane kept one man bailing continuously, and so managed to pass Hakluyt Island. Two weeks out, a second major storm brought a wet and sleepless night. The next day, in the sunshine, the boat entered an alley of pounded ice masses and got "nipped," lifted high up into the air by the pressure of giant ice floes, only to be lowered again after twenty minutes.

On July 31, ten miles from Cape Parry, the men hit a wall of pack ice that prevented further progress. They dragged the boat onto the shelf. Then, with McGary, Kane walked four miles west and climbed an iceberg frozen into the pack. From a height of 120 feet, looking south and west through his spyglass, Kane could see for thirty miles. And in that great vista, all he could see was ice—"a motionless, unbroken, and impenetrable sea." The open North Water through which Inglefield had passed two years before, and where he himself had enjoyed clear sailing last year, lay covered by a thick, unbroken sheet of pack ice. Beechey Island lay far beyond reach.

o   o   o

On August 7, Kane and his party arrived back at the *Advance*. Having fed for three weeks on auks, eider ducks, and scurvy grass, they found themselves healthier than those who had remained on board. "We were fat and strong," Kane wrote. Despite what he had seen, "our thoughts reverted to the feeble chances of our liberation." Certainly, those who had stayed behind remained optimistic. Goodfellow later reported that, while Kane had been absent, "poor Brooks made more confident promises than ever that he intended to go to church in New York that Sunday eight weeks, and Mr. Wilson would lay out his plan for a long rest in the country which was to make him all right again." Now, on the slight chance that some miracle might arise from the expected gales of late August and September, Kane got the brig afloat by sawing through ice, exploding powder canisters, and warping closer to Butler Island.

With four men, he then made another southward dash to study the edge of the pack ice, only to find conditions worsening. Stupendous icebergs had swept into the vicinity and now, freezing into new positions, extended seaward in reefs or chains. The pack ice rose nine feet above the water line, implying a frozen tabular thickness of sixty-three feet: "The prospect was really desolation itself."

In his journal, Kane revealed both despair and a paternalistic sense of responsibility. "Bad! Bad! I must look another winter in the face . . . It is *terrible*—yes, that is the word—to look forward to another year of disease and darkness to be met without fresh food and without fuel. I should meet it with a more tempered sadness if I had no comrades to think for and protect." In *Arctic Explorations,* he omitted the lines that followed, in which hubris colors his concern for his companions, who are, "alas, how dependent upon my brains with their frail perishable housing. Oh body! body! Damned trammeling housing investiture of blood and bones!"

In response to the fuel shortage, Kane cut the allowance of wood for cooking to six pounds per meal. This allotment of wood, one-third of a pound per man, would boil enough water that, daily, each individual could have one cut of pork (the only meat that remained), one bowl of soup, and two cups of coffee. Around this time, Kane changed the breakfast prayer. He stopped saying, "Lord, accept our gratitude and bless our undertaking"; instead, he prayed, "Accept our gratitude and restore us to our homes." According to Hayes, this raised the men's spirits.

Also in mid-August, thinking of the Franklin expedition, Kane decided to store records on Observatory Island. Recalling how sorrowful he had felt on Beechey Island, while standing at the graves of the three dead sailors—mainly because no sign pointed toward the direction taken by the living—Kane chose a conspicuous spot on a cliff and painted in large letters "ADVANCE, a.d. 1853–1854." Here he built a cairn, a pyramid of heavy stones, beneath which he placed the coffins of his two dead comrades.

Nearby, in a rocky niche, he sealed a document that named everyone aboard and summarized the expedition to date, noting that the men had traveled 2,000 miles either on foot or driving dogs. He wrote of Humboldt Glacier and of charting the large bay (now Kane Basin) in which they sat, and highlighted the discovery of the Kennedy Channel, free of ice: "This channel trended nearly due north, and expanded into an apparently open sea, which abounded with birds and bears and marine life."

By now, everybody understood that the future looked grim—though, as Goodfellow wrote, "the thought of a second winter was intolerable to the minds of many of the ship's company." On August 21, the faithful William Morton told the captain that some of the men, and even some officers, were talking of asking his permission to leave with a boat in a bid to escape to

This rough sketch, The Graves by Moonlight, *shows where Kane buried two dead comrades. Aware of the failure of Sir John Franklin to leave any record on Beechey Island, Kane also deposited a sealed document summarizing his expedition to date.*

Upernavik. As an experienced student of the ice, Kane felt certain that such a scheme could only fail. But Carl Petersen, the immigrant Greenlander, thought otherwise. And he had encouraged dreams of escaping south. As Kane wrote later, "They even thought that the safety of all would be promoted by a withdrawal from the brig."

Kane had considered the idea of detaching a party. But the deeper he thought, the more convinced he became that it would be neither right nor practical. For himself, he wrote on August 21, the decision was easy. As captain, he had "a simple duty of honor to remain by the brig." He could not think of leaving until he had seen the effects of autumn gales and tides, and after that it would certainly be too late to escape. Not only that, but as Goodfellow later wrote, Kane faced another absolute obstacle: "Mr. Brooks was still a great invalid—the wound resulting from amputation of his toes was unhealed, and his whole system was prostrate from the effects of his long confinement. Dr. Kane foresaw in the health of Mr. Wilson, too, as well as in that of others, symptoms of disease soon to be developed."

Considering his other companions, however, Kane felt "by no means sure that I ought to hold them bound by my conclusions. Have I the *moral right?*" This was not an official naval expedition. And "among the whalers, when a ship is hopelessly beset, the master's authority gives way, and the crew take counsel for themselves whether to go or stay by her. . . . if the restlessness of suffering make some of [the men] anxious to brave the chances, they may certainly plead that a second winter in the ice was no part of the cruise they bargained for."

Kane's sense of morality contrasts starkly with that demonstrated the previous year—although the American didn't know it—by British naval captain Robert McClure. In spring, with his ship *Investigator* trapped in Arctic ice far to the west and his crew beginning to die of scurvy, McClure conceived a sinister plan to rid himself of his thirty sickest men. Claiming it was the only way to save their lives, he proposed to send them south and east in two sledge parties. They would depart, pathetically weak and radically undersupplied, on a journey to certain death.

With the remaining men, the healthiest, McClure would try to free the *Investigator* as summer came on. If he failed, he would organize an escape attempt. In April 1853, mere days before he acted on this plan, a searcher from the *Resolute,* sailing with Belcher's squadron, chanced upon the trapped *Investigator.* The ensuing rescue precluded other action.

Now, besides considering moral questions, Kane analyzed the psychology of the situation. Desperately short of provisions, he and his crew comprised "a set of scurvy-riddled, broken-down men." His only hope of restoring the health needed to escape next spring "must be a wholesome elastic tone of feeling among the men: a reluctant, brooding, disheartened spirit would sweep our decks like a pestilence." As a medical man and an officer, Kane feared he would "be wearing away the hearts and energies, if not the lives of all, by forcing those who were reluctant to remain."

Kane agonized. Nobody had caused a disturbance or even called a meeting. Yet some of the men had expressed a desire to leave. With several of the party too sick to move, the captain viewed the men's idea of departing as "a gross violation of their agreement and a violation of everything gallant and honourable. Very good! But have I the moral right to detain them?"

o   o   o

Six decades later, at the earth's other pole, Ernest Shackleton would face a similar challenge. His ship's carpenter, frustrated that he had not been allowed to salvage building wood from the *Endurance,* would argue that his duty to obey orders had ended when the crew abandoned ship. Shackleton would respond by reading aloud the ship's articles, announcing that the men would be paid until the day they reached safety, and declaring flatly that they were bound by his orders until that time.

Shackleton would act on the authority of the Royal Navy. The American enjoyed no such official sanction. Kane was an Arctic pioneer forging his own way forward, not a naval captain who could point to a list of regulations. And so he faced a dilemma: "Had I the right to make any judgment binding upon [those who would depart] in a case of life and death? Was I to arrogate to my own opinion such infallibility as to make it control that of others?" More practically, he wondered: "Can I look forward to the horrible contingencies of the coming long winter and see myself and the faithful surrounded by men—my equals as such—whose inclinations I had forced and whose sufferings were upon my own head?"

On August 22, without declaring himself, Kane ventured south by dog-sled yet once more—and again found the ice impervious: "There is no possibility of our release, unless by some extreme intervention of incoming tides." Now he talked with McGary, who confirmed that whaling captains, faced with this situation, would allow the men to make their own choices and put boats at their disposal. Kane decided to follow this precedent. He would call the men together, share his opinions, and allow some to depart if they chose, "telling them freely why I am opposed to the step, what are its dangers, and finally insisting upon a signed paper from such as leave, placing my position in its proper light." The captain spoke also with Goodfellow, who described Kane as saying he would not compel the men to remain, because that would induce "a spirit of bitter discontent or smothered mutiny on board. We have enough to encounter as it is."

At noon on August 24, Kane called all hands into the cabin. He and four other men—Petersen, Hayes, Godfrey, and Goodfellow—would leave written accounts of what ensued. These differ subtly, not dramatically. Kane spelled out the considerations governing his decision to remain with the *Advance* through the winter, including ice conditions and lateness of season. He argued that an escape to open water could not succeed, and that any such effort would be hazardous. He alluded to the men's duties to the expedition and to their ailing comrades, who were unable to leave, and advised them strongly to abandon this undertaking. In his journal, he wrote: "I desired them to understand distinctly that although they carried with them my kindest wishes and anxieties—the step had not my approbation—here I alluded to the sick and disabled—and simply stated that from what I could hear of their intentions the party left on board would be few in number and far from vigorous in health." Goodfellow later added that Kane said the men could leave if they chose, but the public might regard their departure "as a desertion of the flag of their country."

He would allow them twenty-four hours to consider their options. Then, if some still wished to leave, he would allow them to do so. He would require them to elect a commander, renounce any claims upon the expedition, and sign a paper absolving him of responsibility. He would also provide boats, stores, and equipment.

William Godfrey would describe this exhortation as a formal speech announcing "that such of the men as wished to leave the brig for the purpose of traveling homeward had full permission to do so." Godfrey wrote that he "perceived that the apprehended scarcity of provisions led to this generous offer," and as he had never experienced comfort nor kindness aboard the *Advance,* he became "one of the first to embrace this opportunity to depart." Yet, just a couple of months before, when Godfrey had refused a duty, complaining that he was unwell, Kane had written in his journal: "Although I am convinced that this man is malingering, I cannot force him to a step which, desirable as it may be to me, might injure him against his reported wishes. I never send a man upon a journey unless by his full consent." He had added: "This William is a bad, non-reliable man. . . . He and John have done more to disturb the efficiency and comfort of the crew than scurvy, darkness, and cold combined."

Now, as the men talked among themselves, Petersen emerged as a leading proponent of defection. He reminded his shipmates that the previous August he had urged Kane to retreat south before wintering. And he believed that, even at this late date, an escape attempt could succeed. Christian Ohlsen, the only other Dane on the ship, remained noncommittal. But the articulate Hayes sided with Petersen, and suggested that dividing the ship's company would probably increase everybody's chances of survival—it would be "for the public good."

Hayes later explained that making a September boat journey to Upernavik had always been regarded as an alternative to spending a second winter in the ice. Kane had concluded, during his failed expedition to Beechey Island, that the pack ice he had seen in the North Water doomed any such endeavor. Petersen, who had not seen this barrier, but had lived many years in Greenland, argued that this ice was accidental, an anomaly, and would probably disappear in two weeks. Telling himself that Upernavik was hardly farther than Beechey, and that help for the *Advance* could be found there, Hayes "adopted entirely Mr. Petersen's conclusion."

On August 25, Kane again called the men together. Now he would call the roll. Those who wished to leave the brig would say yes; those who chose to remain, no. As he went around the circle, Kane kept his emotions to himself. Of the seventeen men on the brig, eleven voted to go—an overwhelming majority. The ex-whaler McGary postponed his decision. Of the five men who elected to stay with Kane—Brooks, Goodfellow, Hendrik, Morton, and Hickey—only the last two were fit for active duty. And Kane would write: "Hans is not firm in his decision. I fear that he has been talked over."

Shocked and mortified, and trying not to show it, Kane withdrew to write in his journal. He had anticipated the defections of Petersen, Godfrey, and Blake, and believed that one or two others might join them. But eleven men of seventeen! And four of those, officers! The votes of Hayes, Wilson,

Sonntag, and Bonsall shook him to his foundations. In his journal, he absolved Hayes, accepting the argument that those who departed would need medical care. The conduct of August Sonntag, the German astronomer, he regarded as "the most difficult to palliate. He was on confidential relations with his commander, occupied a position of consideration and utility, and up to the moment of reading the roll, was regarded by me as a faithful and honorable gentleman. His conduct has been such as to prohibit between us any future associations of respect." Amos Bonsall he pitied, because his family belonged to Philadelphia society. Kane took him aside, pointed out "the grave error of his course," and warned that he would lose respect and standing at home: "He heard me with tears but adhered to his selfish intentions."

That Kane had been badly shaken emerges in his response to Wilson, who approached him saying that he had changed his mind. He had been thinking about his friend Brooks, who still could not walk properly as a result of amputations, and how Kane had plunged out into the Arctic night to rescue them. He wished to remain with the brig. Kane told him he would have to get permission from the other deserters, which he duly did: "This man has gentlemanly instincts and has been reared a gentleman, but is very weak. I comforted the poor fellow as well as I could." James McGary, having originally reserved his decision, also decided to stay.

Kane now realized that the defectors were in disarray. He mentioned this to Ohlsen, and then, at the carpenter's request, called the defectors together and told them again to choose a leader. They elected Ohlsen himself. Even now, Kane considered Ohlsen the most useful man among them, but also "the instigator of the whole concern, scheming and non-reliable but efficient." In fact, the record suggests that the prime mover was Carl Petersen, who was slightly older than Kane. Like Ohlsen, Petersen came from Denmark, spoke Danish, and could not be swayed by calls to American patriotism— and these circumstances had enabled him to win over the skilled carpenter.

On the evening of August 26, Kane presented a statement to be signed by all the defectors except Petersen, who had never officially joined the crew. In it, according to his journal, he declared: "I wish it to be distinctly understood that I have no responsibility for or connection with your attempt—up to the moment of your departure you will continue under my command and every aid that our stores can afford will be given. Without reserve. But from the moment of your leaving the brig you will be under your own control and your connection with the Expedition will be regarded as closed."

This formulation, which did not anticipate any possible return, would later give rise to misunderstanding. The defector Hayes judged that the statement exempting the commander from responsibility "very properly required as a condition of his consent that we should formally detach our-selves from the brig's company and effect a separate organization under officers elected by ourselves." But Ohlsen, realizing suddenly how posterity would judge his action, now "showed his ambiguous character." According to Kane, Ohlsen "argued, urged, entreated, almost threatened—behaved like a madman." He declined either to remain or to sign the statement, "although he was taking away my carpenter and most necessary man." By now, Kane had regained his usual poise. He told Ohlsen that, "signature or no signature, I now withdrew my permission. He must remain by the brig. With this, I dismissed him." The shaken Ohlsen returned to the defectors.

August Sonntag, explaining that he might sail from Greenland directly to his family in Europe, requested his back pay. Kane not only paid him a cash advance ($100, worth roughly $2,400 today) but, having decided to behave in exemplary fashion, gave him a letter of recommendation. He gave another to Hayes, and for the party as a whole, he wrote a safe conduct to any American consul they might encounter.

Kane provided the defectors with two boats: the *Forlorn Hope,* which Goodfellow would later describe as "decidedly the best of our boats," and the metal lifeboat hidden near Littleton Island. He provided two sledges to haul their goods to open water, arms and ammunition, a compass, a sex-tant, a chronometer, and a spyglass. He allowed the party a fair share of the food, mainly bread, beans, salt pork, dried apples, and coffee—as much, Goodfellow wrote, "as they wished to carry." And he and three other men even donated clothing—the shirts off their backs.

As preparations neared completion, Ohlsen approached Kane. He offered to sign the original statement if he were given permission to depart. The captain responded that he had missed his opportunity: if Ohlsen tried to leave now, Kane would consider him a deserter. Weeping, Ohlsen decided to remain—which left the defectors without their chosen leader.

Hurriedly, they held a second vote. This time, they chose Petersen. Later, omitting to mention the first election, Hayes would write: "We had no hesitation in the choice of leader; for, beside Mr. Petersen, there was no one in the company who had sufficient acquaintance with the region . . . to guide us toward Upernavik." The mutinous Petersen would complain that Kane had contrived to keep Ohlsen, Wilson, and Hendrik on board "partly by persuasion and not without some menace, as it seems to me."

In his published memoir, Hendrik would write: "In autumn, when the new ice was forming, some of our party set out for Upernavik in a boat. Naparsisortak [Petersen] joined them. I should have liked to do the same, but our Commander forbade me, saying they would be frozen up, and be unable to reach Upernavik." Clearly, Hendrik felt torn between Kane and Petersen. With the latter, he could converse in his own language. Also, from first meeting, in Upernavik, Petersen had always treated him well. Yet Hendrik had also hunted often with Kane, and appreciated both his compassion and medical skills. On one occasion, after Hendrik had nearly cut off his own thumb, he returned to the brig with another of the men: "Our commander, who had observed that I did not drive the sledge, came towards us, and when, soon after, we had come on board, he said that he would cure me fairly, and added that if I obeyed him the wound would soon be healed. He began curing me by cutting away part of the inner flesh. To be sure it ached dreadfully when he took out the bad flesh, but it was soon healed."

Hendrik remained with the captain. On August 28, departure day, seven more men did the same: Brooks, McGary, Wilson, Goodfellow, Morton, Ohlsen, and Hickey. A ninth man, Riley, would join this contingent within days, after nearly drowning in a sledging accident. But now Kane assembled all hands in the cabin and produced two bottles of champagne. Using their broken-handled teacups, the men toasted each other's health. The captain ordered the American flag to be run up the mast. Then the nine defectors climbed over the side and moved off, according to Kane, "with the elastic step of men confident in their purpose."

That night in his journal, the commander paraphrased the British poet Charles Lamb: "They are gone, all gone, the old familiar faces." But he proved unable to sustain this elegiac tone. "These men cannot feel as I do. The consciousness of deserting their posts—with or without such a consent as they carry with them—would hang over me like a nightmare. Their commander and the brig are the expedition, and as long as these hang together, every true man should remain. When, in my judgment, the time comes for leaving, my subordinates can leave in safety and honor."

Bonsall, Hayes, and Sonntag, he wrote, had never shown "the associative gallantry and right-mindedness" of McGary, Brooks, and Goodfellow. As for Petersen, Kane wrote that he "was always a cold-blooded sneak, and Ohlsen double-faced and fawning and insecure." Among the crew, Morton and the Irish cabin boy Hickey stood out "as natural gentlemen" when compared with those officers who had deserted their posts.

Kane insisted that he felt sad and anxious but also relieved: he had been disencumbered "of condemned material, worthy heretofore but rotten now." He washed his hands of the defectors as both a man and a Christian: "They have left the expedition and God's blessings go with them, for they carry not the respect of good men." He would omit these judgments from his published book. And Hayes would recall Kane's exemplary dignity, observing that "when the ship's company decided that the chances of safety were enhanced by a separation . . . he proceeded at once hastily to carry out their decision and give them every facility."

The break did not happen as abruptly as expected. The big sled proved so heavy that the defectors could drag it only a few miles each day. For a week, they returned nightly to sleep on the brig. When they came no longer, Kane sent Hendrik to retrieve the big sledge. Petersen kept the hunter with him until Kane sent two men to demand the return of both Hendrik and the sledge under threat of force. The defectors were reduced to loading and unloading the small sledge. But then Kane received news of difficulties that moved him to sympathy. He sent Riley back with the big sledge, ordering him to return with it after the party reached open water.

The return of Riley with the sled on September 5 marked the end of communications. Kane could not help remarking that the defectors had sent no thanks, no goodbyes, no words of any sort: "From my very heart, I can say a blessing go with them. Neither their ingratitude nor their selfishness, shown in clear repulsiveness only after their departure, can make me feel unkindly to these men."

Late that same night, in addition to whatever he wrote to Maggie Fox, Kane poured out darker feelings in a rough letter to his brother John: "I cannot but feel that some of them will return, broken down and suffering, to seek a refuge on board. They shall find it, to the halving of our last chip— but—but—but—if I ever live to get home—home! And should meet Dr. Hayes or Mr. Bonsall or Master Sonntag, let them look out for their skins. If I don't live to thrash them, which I'll try very hard to do, (to live, I mean), why then, dear brother John, seek a solitary orchard and maul them for me. Don't honour them with a bullet or let the mauling be solitary—save to the principals, it would hurt your character to be [seen] wrestling with such low-minded sneaks."

That the fiercely proud Elisha Kent Kane could be reduced to this maudlin outpouring, even in a late-night scrawl, shows how deeply he felt the defection. Betrayed by several officers, mortified by the disrespect of his crew, Kane looked ahead to months of cold and scurvy and darkness. Never had he felt so low.

25

THE ARISTOCRAT GOES NATIVE

To survive in the north without the technologies of the mid-to-late twentieth century, explorers had to apprentice themselves to the Native peoples. The wisest of the new arrivals understood that the Cree, the Dene, and the Inuit, stereotyped by Europeans and Americans as "ignorant savages," had lived for generations in these challenging environs. A humble willingness to learn, combined with an ability to transcend cultural preconceptions, had characterized the eighteenth-century Englishman Samuel Hearne, the first explorer to visit the northern coast of North America. Those same traits distinguished Orkneyman John Rae, who would use knowledge he gleaned from the Cree and the Inuit to solve the riddle of the Northwest Passage. And they differentiated the American Elisha Kent Kane, who had the wisdom, sensitivity, and tact to establish an alliance with the Inuit of northern Greenland—a relationship that would save his own life and the lives of most of his men, and also create a paradigm, a never-to-be-forgotten template, that would benefit every explorer who followed him in the ensuing race to reach the North Pole.

Kane had met some local Inuit early in April, while still recovering from the effects of the rescue mission. He was sitting one morning by the bunk of the dying Jefferson Baker when a sailor burst into the cabin to tell him that people ashore were hailing the brig. Kane had seen signs of hunters in the area, but they were years old. And when he emerged onto the deck, he felt astonished, as he wrote later, to see figures "on all sides of the rocky harbor, dotting the snow-shores and emerging from the bleakness of the cliffs, wild and uncouth, but evidently human beings." They had climbed onto the highest fragments of land ice to stand waving and calling out "singly and conspicuously, like the figures in a tableau of the opera."

In his journal, he wrote: "During this [bedside] scene so full to us of sadness, a strange episode broke in upon our imprisoned ship. In the midst of death came the most unlooked for irruption of life—Esquimaux. Entering from all sides of our rocky harbour—dotting the snow shores and emerging from the blackness of the cliffs came these children of ice. 'Ka—Kaa—Ka—Ka' came breaking from our solitude and almost before I could walk forth twenty paces from the brig, eight fur-clad savages were dangling in ecstasy around the new existence which I represented, and fifty wolfish dogs were baying their satisfaction at their journey's end."

An Inuit hunting party had chanced upon the *Advance*. They wore furs and carried no weapons but knives and spears or lances. Hans Hendrik was out hunting, so Kane roused Carl Petersen from his bunk to serve as interpreter, and the two men hurried out onto the ice, showing their empty hands. The Inuit leader stepped forward. Powerfully built, six inches taller than Kane, with a swarthy complexion and piercing black eyes, he identified himself as Metek.

Kane invited this man aboard, making clear that the others should wait. Metek followed fearlessly and, once aboard, explained that he and his companions came from Etah, a settlement located on the Greenland coast seventy miles south of the brig, not far from Littleton Island, and probably the northernmost permanent habitation in the world. Satisfied with this initial meeting, and aware of the value of having allies in this difficult environment, Kane said the other hunters could come aboard. The men came boisterously, leaving their sledges and planting their lances to secure fifty-six dogs within 200 feet of the brig.

The hunters carried knives in their boots. They wore hooded, fox-fur jumpers, white bearskin breeches, and fur boots, with the feet ending in claws. Only two of them, visitors from Cape York, had ever seen a white man or a beard, and most found both wildly amusing. They also judged the beards worth tugging. The sailors found the visitors rude, unruly, and difficult to restrain or corral. Incessantly in motion, they raced around, opening doors and poking into corners and dark passages, touching and handling and trying to filch anything that caught their fancy. To keep them out of the forecastle, where Baker lay dying, Kane had to employ a "gentle laying-on of hands."

In the midst of this, Hendrik returned from hunting. As he drew near the brig, he wrote later, he noticed a crowd, and saw two "northern natives" come running. One asked, "Are you a native?" He replied, "Yes, I am a native." They then asked whether he had killed any hares. Yes, three. What weapon he had used? He showed the man his musket, and "he did not comprehend, but examined it, how it was."

Hendrik found he could communicate readily with the northerners, though he noticed some language differences. "When first I saw these people, whom I knew nothing about," he would write, "and nobody had examined, I feared they might be murderers, as they lived apart from any Kavdlunak [Christian Greenlanders]; but, on the contrary, they were harmless men."

On board the brig, the shouldering, the pushing and shoving, remained good-humored. The guests roamed the vessel, carried provisions back and forth to the sledges, and stole what they could until late afternoon when, "like tired children, they threw themselves down to sleep." To make them comfortable, Kane ordered the stove lit, and the visitors marveled at the strangeness of the coal. Recognizing immediately that this mysterious fuel might be used to cook as well as heat, they borrowed an iron pot, melted ice for water, and boiled walrus meat, although generally they preferred to eat this raw—a seemingly barbarous practice that, as Kane would eventually realize, protected them against scurvy.

The visitors slept through the night in a seated posture, some of them snoring loudly, and all of them waking sporadically to eat. At some point during their visit, Kane sketched the Inuit sledges, with their runners made of narwhal tusks, as well as their rough bone lances and wooden knives, which were tipped with metal acquired from the Cape York Eskimos who traded with whalers.

In the morning, the hunters proved anxious to leave. Kane asked if they had traveled farther north. According to Petersen, they said yes, and that they had entered a sound that led to more open water. Kane sought "to make them understand what a powerful Prospero they had had for a host," and how generous he could be. He bought walrus meat and four dogs, paying generously with needles, beads, and valuable metal barrel staves. The Inuit "pledged themselves emphatically to return in a few days with more meat, and to allow me to use their dogs and sledges for my excursions to the north." After the visitors left, cracking their whips and driving across the ice to the southwest, the captain discovered they had stolen an axe, a saw, and several knives.

The following day, five hunters arrived on foot—two older men, one middle-aged man, and two gawky boys. Kane welcomed them hospitably. But he also discovered, through stealthy reconnoitering, that they had hidden dogs and a train of sledges beyond a line of hummocks, clearly with questionable intent. Some explorers would have reacted angrily. But Kane felt that he "could not afford to break with the rogues." As enemies, they would make hunting and sledge travel dangerous. Also, they represented the Americans' best chance of acquiring a steady supply of fresh meat. He treated the five hunters with kindness and gave them presents, but also he warned that none of them would again be brought aboard unless they returned the previously stolen goods.

The five went off, protesting their innocence. Yet McGary "caught the incorrigible scamps stealing a coal-barrel as they passed Butler Island, and

Elisha Kane realized that the Inuit of northern Greenland had developed survival skills that he and his men lacked. Soon after meeting the locals, he forged an alliance with them that involved combining forces to go on walrus hunts.

expedited their journey homeward by firing among them a charge of small shot." Even so, one of the party—old Shang-hu, who later became a staunch friend—got hold of Kane's India-rubber boat and hacked it to pieces for the sake of its sturdy wood frame.

A few days after this, "an agile, elfin youth drove up to our floe in an open day." This sprightly young man, Myouk, denied any knowledge of stolen goods or a damaged rubber boat, but Kane ordered him confined to the hold. The disconsolate youth refused to eat, and cried a while, but then he began to sing. When Hendrik arrived from hunting, Kane ordered him to question the young man about who had destroyed the boat. Myouk insisted that he did not know. "The Master said he would shoot him if he did not confess," Hendrik wrote later. "On hearing this I took fright. At once pitying him, and afraid to look at him, I uttered: 'He says he will shoot you if you do not tell.' He replied, 'I have not done it, I don't know it.'"

Late into the night, the young man sang, cried, and talked to himself. In the morning, when Kane appeared, he found that Myouk had escaped with his sledge and his dogs. Hendrik would write: "In the beginning of the night I heard a noise. I went out and saw him running off speedily. I wonder how he managed to get out, the hatch-way being very high." Obviously, Hendrik had freed the youth. Kane made a display of reprimanding the men on watch, but admitted in his journal to feeling relieved that Myouk was gone.

Through the bright Arctic summer, the Americans received no more visitors, except during Kane's failed attempt to reach Beechey Island, when those men left behind enjoyed considerable communication with the Inuit. Then, a couple of weeks after the defectors abandoned the brig, three visitors arrived from Etah: young Myouk and two women. With half his boats and sledges gone—*and* more than half his able-bodied men—this "coincidence" showed Kane that he was under surveillance.

Hoping to re-establish friendly relations, the captain treated the three visitors hospitably. He fed them salt pork and let them sleep in the hold. In the morning, he discovered that—though they had been under guard—the three had made off with his best dog, some cooking utensils, and two buffalo robes. Kane now perceived that the Inuit lived under "some law of general appropriation" according to which clever pilferage warranted not punishment but praise. Still, he felt his generosity had been abused. Even though he had too few men to guard the brig effectively, he armed two of his best walkers with muskets and sent them to overtake the thieves. Thirty or thirty-five miles south of the *Advance,* in a hut at Anoatok, or "the wind-loved spot," Morton and Riley discovered the three miscreants. They had taken cooking utensils and several small items the Americans had not yet missed, and the women were wearing fur jackets, or *kapetahs,* they had already cut and sewn from the stolen buffalo robes. One of them was the wife of Metek, the head man of Etah.

Morton arrested the two women and sent the young man off to inform Metek. Then, making the women carry their stolen goods, as well as a supply of walrus beef, he marched them back to the brig—no small hike. For five days, the women sighed, sang, and wept, and ate voraciously. At last Metek arrived at the brig. He brought Ootuniah, another senior figure, and a sledge piled with stolen goods, including knives, tin cups, and sundry "borrowed" items. Though the Americans had failed to impress Metek with their "fire-death ordnance," they *had* astonished him by overtaking the three culprits within ten hours of their crime and marching them smartly back to the brig: "Such a sixty miles achievement as this," Kane wrote, "they thoroughly understood."

Now began a negotiation that culminated in a solemn treaty. The Inuit promised to steal no more. They would bring fresh meat to the brig. They would sell or lend their dogs, and show Kane's men where to find game. In return, the white men would release the three prisoners and pledge themselves never to harm the people of Etah. Instead, they would use their guns to shoot game on joint hunting expeditions. They would welcome The People aboard ship and, in exchange for walrus and seal meat, trade needles, thread, knives, and other goods. Both sides pledged brotherhood and friendship forever. When the Inuit left for home, Morton and Hendrik followed as ambassadors. They witnessed the ratification of the alliance by a full assembly of the few dozen inhabitants of Etah. As a token, they brought a massive walrus flipper—forty pounds of meat—back to the brig.

o   o   o

This friendship treaty with the people of Etah, although never formalized in writing, would govern future relations between the parties and would never be broken. The sailors and the Inuit would visit back and forth, and sometimes hunt together. One day toward the end of September, for example, Kane, Morton, and Hendrik set out to hunt walrus with three of their "wild allies." For the captain, this was the sixth such outing, so he knew every rock, chasm, and watercourse in the area. After a successful hunt, and making for home, he judged the sledge to be overloaded. But he could not persuade his Inuit companions to jettison part of the load. As a result, although the dogs worked hard, the hunters failed to reach Force Bay in time for a daylight crossing.

To follow the shoreline would have made the journey far longer, and with darkness coming on and snow drifting before a heavy wind, the men trusted the tracks of previous journeys and set out across the ice. At around ten, having lost sight of the land and with no guide to fix the points of the compass, they veered out toward the floating ice of mid-bay. But now the dogs, sensing unsafe ice, began to show alarm—and Kane knew "nothing more subduing to a man than the warnings of unseen peril conveyed by the instinctive fears of the lower animals."

A couple of weeks before, while out chasing seals with Hendrik, Kane had witnessed similar warning signs when the sledge dogs scampered onto a belt of thin ice. On that occasion, unable to stop or turn around, the hunters had raced for a stable floe. Fifty paces out, a sledge runner slipped through the ice. The lead dog, Toodlamik, followed, as did the whole left side of the sledge. Leaning forward to cut Toodla free, Kane slipped and slid into the freezing cold water.

Despite floundering beside the sinking sledge, Kane managed to free the struggling dog. He then discovered that the half-submerged sledge would not support his weight, but crashed through more ice when he climbed onto it. He tried to haul himself onto the ice at edge of the circle, but it kept giving way. Hendrik, meanwhile, having reached solid ice, tried to pull the dogs out while "praying incoherently in English and Esquimaux" and crying out "God!" at every fresh crushing-in of the ice.

Human beings do not last long in icy-cold water, and Kane was nearly exhausted when the remaining dogs, still tied to the sledge and struggling furiously, jammed one of the runners into the edge of the ice. Feeling that this was his last chance, Kane threw himself onto his back, placed the nape of his neck against the rim of the ice, and swung one foot onto the sledge. Bracing himself against the sledge, he slowly edged his head and shoulders onto the ice. With one final push he moved far enough onto the solid floe that Hendrik could haul him to safety before rubbing him down "with frightful zeal."

To avoid frostbite, and quite possibly death, the two men left the sledge, kayak, tent, guns, and snowshoes to be cut out of the ice later, and set out, with the dogs running freely, on a twelve-mile dash to the brig. Once aboard, with the fire lit and a bird cooked up into a meal, Kane felt so cozy and warm that he almost forgot the disaster.

But now, as he marched across thin ice in the gathering darkness and blowing snow with yet another team of terrified dogs, Kane recalled that baptismal experience only too vividly. Unable to camp in the gale, the party had to keep moving. Suddenly, Kane heard the lapping of waves. He scarcely had time to cry "Turn the dogs" before a cloud of frost wafted over the hunters, briefly increasing visibility, and revealed a lead of open water a quarter mile ahead.

The ice was breaking up before the storm. The men could feel the floes undulating beneath their feet. Having at last got his bearings, Kane led the way south toward Godsend Island, where the floes were heaviest and least likely to give way. With the others, he raced between lines of hummocks, stumbling over crags and sinking into puddles of water. It was too dark to see the island, though Kane could discern a lofty cape breaking the line of the horizon.

With the gale turning into an ice storm, the men approached the shore. They all knew that, under ideal conditions, moving from the floe onto land ice meant crossing over a dangerous tangle of irregular, half-floating masses. Now, in the wind and the dark, these chunks of ice surged and rubbed against each other. Kane persuaded Ootuniah, the eldest of the Inuit, to lash a tent pole across his shoulders for safety. Then, after fastening a line around his own waist and handing the end to this man, Kane set out across the surging barricade, feeling his way onto tables of ice in what was now pitch darkness.

Eventually, with those in the rear driving the dogs before them, the party clambered onto the ice foot. To their astonishment, and with shouts of joy, they discovered they had landed not on Godsend Island but on the coast of Greenland—and not 400 yards from Anoatok, "the wind-loved spot," site of an old stone shelter. Less than an hour later, safely inside with their lamps burning, the men set about preparing a walrus-steak stew. Having traveled forty-eight miles while battling rough ice for the past twenty hours, the hunters feasted, chanted, and sang. Kane and his men had shown no sign of weakness, and had at times even carried two of the Inuit along. Now, when they produced technological wonders—a canvas tent and buffalo bags for sleeping, as well as a copper lamp, a soup pot, and an India-rubber floor cloth—they "profoundly impressed" their fellow travelers.

The Inuit chanted and sang their traditional song, "Amna Ayah," improvising a refrain that eulogized Kane as captain, captain, great captain: "Nalegak! Nalegak! Nalegak-soak!" From now on, among the Inuit, he would be called Nalegak-soak. "They nicknamed and adopted all of us," Kane wrote later, "as members of their fraternity, with grave and abundant form; reminding me through all their mummery, solemn and ludicrous at once, of the analogous ceremonies of our North American Indians."

As the Inuit sang his praises, Kane drifted off. He slept for eleven hours.

○   ○   ○

Over the next few days, while sheltering from the storm and participating for the first time in the domestic life of the Inuit, Kane filled pages of his notebook with sketches and descriptions. He drew a sealskin cup, a snow melter, and a stand made of walrus bones. He described the hut at "the wind-loved spot"—a shelter that would later prove crucially important to the survival of the expedition—as a "single rude elliptical apartment, built not unskillfully of stone, the outside lined with sods." Eight feet long and seven wide, with a tunnel entrance adding another two feet, the hut had a low curved roof made of large, flat, overlapping stones. Inside, a man could hardly sit upright.

And so it began. Over the next few months, Kane would add to these sketches, producing detailed descriptions and drawings of life among the Inuit. One historian, L.H. Neatby, would suggest that these writings "make the most interesting part of his *Arctic Explorations*." Certainly, his depictions of clothes, sledges, weapons, housing, and habits, created what, for most Westerners, would become the conventional image of the Inuit. At the same time, by his conduct, Kane created a cross-cultural friendship that would endure long after his departure. The twentieth-century explorer Jean Malaurie, for example, would hail his "extraordinary agreements" with the Inuit, and write in the 1980s that "the favorable memory that Kane has left among my Eskimo friends is vague, certainly, but tenacious."

In forging this unique relationship with the Inuit, an accomplishment that demanded he move beyond himself, Kane again exemplifies the archetypal hero. That figure, according to Joseph Campbell, having crossed a threshold of personal transformation, enters "a dream landscape" in which he undergoes an initiation. He faces a succession of trials that challenge him to assimilate his own dark side—a shadow-self that, for Elisha Kent Kane, comprised the snobberies and prejudices of aristocratic, mid-century Philadelphia. Having emerged from that tight little world, Kane now proved open and humble enough to learn from hunter-gatherers who had inherited a centuries-old tradition of survival in a harsh environment. "I can hardly say how valuable the advice of our Esquimaux friends has been to us upon our hunts," he would write. "Every movement of ice or wind or season is noted, and they predicted its influence upon the course of the birds of passage with the same sagacity that has taught them the habits of the resident animals."

Kane remarked repeatedly on the observational skills of his allies. He recorded the occasion when Carl Petersen, anxious to get traveling during a hunting sortie, pointed to the horizon and insisted that daylight would soon arrive. An Inuk said no, insisting that when *that* star reached *this* position in the sky, only then would it be time to hitch the dogs to the sledge. To Petersen's amazement, the man proved correct—though Kane was not surprised.

The captain also studied and adapted Inuit technologies. He noticed, for example, that while the iron nails of the expedition sledges snapped like glass in extreme cold, and their wooden frames came apart under stress, the skeleton framework of an Inuit sledge, held together by stretched canvas, proved as flexible as a lady's work basket and weighed only forty pounds. He ordered Ohlsen to emulate that design, substituting wood and iron for bone and ivory, and the carpenter produced a twenty-four-pound sledge that Kane welcomed as "just the article our Etah neighbors would delight in for land portages."

Soon after the defection, Kane wrote in his journal, "I have determined to borrow a lesson from our Esquimaux neighbors, and am turning the brig into an igloo." Having concluded that Inuit housing and diet "were the safest and best to which the necessity of our circumstances invited us," Kane put the remaining men to work prying moss and turf from the rocks and applying this material to the quarterdeck for warmth.

Belowdecks, he created a large room roughly eighteen feet square, with interior walls again of moss and turf. Having analyzed the functional ingenuity of the *tossut,* or narrow entrance tunnel to the conventional igloo, which keeps heat loss to a minimum, Kane asked Ohlsen to create a similar entrance to the cabin from the much colder hold of the vessel.

Since the defection, Ohlsen had spent his off-duty hours lying in his bunk, obviously feeling sorry for himself. Now, Kane gave him a severe tongue-lashing, which cleared the air and ended with the two shaking hands. By constructing an efficient *tossut,* the carpenter again proved his worth—as well as the perspicacity of Kane in keeping him aboard. The winter quarters lacked "the dignity of a year ago," the captain wrote, but he and his men had become warriors under siege, hunkered down in a "casemate" or bunker with all their energies "concentrated against the enemy outside."

Recognizing that Inuit attire suited the climate, Kane took to wearing birdskin socks and fur boots; a foxskin jumper or *kapetah,* which is a loose-fitting shirt with an airtight hood; and bearskin breeches, *nannooke,* though he altered these to shelter those "parts which in the civilized countries are shielded most carefully." Outdoors, he learned to use "a fox's tail held between the teeth to protect the nose in the wind."

Kane also thought it important to impress the Inuit. Because they admired endurance, whenever he traveled with them, he avoided showing fatigue or cold. The ruse worked so well that on one occasion, young Myouk calmly hooked himself to Kane for a tow, even after the captain had walked for thirty miles ahead of the sledge. "The fellow was worth four of me," Kane wrote, "but he let me carry him almost as far as the land ice."

Carl Petersen grumbled that this American expedition was neither as well equipped nor as well manned as the British voyage on which he had sailed, and this was undoubtedly true. But when the disgruntled Greenlander insisted that "Doctor Kane was no Captain Penny," he failed to appreciate what the American accomplished by relating so effectively with the Inuit. The cabin boy, Thomas Hickey, later got it right: "When we lived as Esquimaux, we immediately recovered and enjoyed our usual health."

26

An Ignominious Return

Despite Elisha Kane's adjustments, winter brought increasing hardship. By October 21, sunlight ceased to reach the *Advance* and the temperature fell to −23 degrees Fahrenheit. With fuel in short supply, Kane allowed the stove to go out for four hours each night. Inside the cabin, temperatures hovered around 44 degrees—and held even at that only because of the moss-and-turf insulation. As outside temperatures fell still farther, to 35, 40, and then 45 degrees below zero, the men burned seventy pounds of fuel each day, mostly for cooking, and let the fire go out between meals. Kane had re-established friendly relations with Ohlsen, who identified seven or eight tons of wood that could be taken from the *Advance* without rendering the craft unfit to sail. This included bulwarks and outer decking, the bulkheads belowdecks, some lockers, and shelving. To warm the cabin without expending fuel, Kane set Ohlsen and Petersen to tinkering with the stovepipes, and managed to raise the indoor temperature to 55 degrees—vastly more comfortable, though still well below the 68 or 70 degrees favored by most Westerners.

Meanwhile, in response to colder temperatures, mammals hibernated and birds flew south, making hunting more difficult. Having almost exhausted the fresh meat, Kane sent Morton and Hendrik to seek help from their allies. In mid-October, the Inuit had withdrawn to their main settlement at Etah, seventy or eighty miles south of the brig. The men returned with 270 pounds of walrus meat and a couple of foxes, but they understood that this supply, along with what remained of two polar bears, would have to suffice until the return of daylight allowed them to rejoin the Natives in their hunts.

In combating the food shortage, Kane ventured where few of his men cared to follow. During his first Arctic voyage, with De Haven, Kane had ignored well-known warnings and managed to make bear liver a dietary staple. Now, when he again tried this delicacy—not once, but three times—he suffered nausea, vertigo, and diarrhea, and so abandoned the experiment.

"Another article of diet," he wrote, "less inviting at first, but which I found more innocuous, was the rat." Since the great fumigation of the previous autumn, the surviving rats had multiplied dramatically. These repulsive creatures enjoyed the run of the brig: they turned up in storage lockers, cushions, bedding, boots, and mittens, and frequently snarled an impudent resistance. They gnawed and destroyed even items for which they had no use, such as clothing, shoes, and specimens of natural history. In his journal, Kane wrote, "If I was asked what, after darkness and cold and scurvy, are the three besetting curses of our arctic sojourn, I should say, RATS, RATS, RATS."

Before winter ended, Kane would avenge himself by decimating the rat population for his private table. In this, he enjoyed the assistance of Hans Hendrik, who would while away the lonely hours of the watch by shooting these "small deer" with his bow and arrow. Yet neither Hendrik nor anyone else would join the captain in savoring the resulting "fresh-meat soup, which contributed no doubt to my comparative immunity from scurvy." The men rejected the rats even though, by mid-November, Kane had reluctantly reduced the daily food allowance to six pounds of flour, six ounces of dried apples or peaches, three pints of molasses, five pints of rice, and one ounce of butter.

Every man on board suffered from bleeding gums, swollen ankles, and aching joints—all symptoms of scurvy. Morton's case was especially worri-

Polar bears proved formidable adversaries. During the second winter, Kane joined native Greenlanders in more than one polar-bear hunt. He also tried eating bear livers, but abandoned the experiment after repeatedly falling sick.

some, and Kane wrote: "I cannot afford to lose him. He is not only one of my most intelligent men, but he is daring, cool, and everyway trustworthy. His tendon Achilles has been completely perforated, and the surface of the heel-bone exposed. An operation in cold, darkness, and privation would probably bring on lock-jaw." Brooks, having endured an amputation, had developed scurvy in his stump. Also, he was one of four men, including Kane, suffering from painfully contracted tendons.

Added to this general misery was an enveloping claustrophobia. Ten men lived in an apartment measuring at best eighteen by twenty feet, with a ceiling that reached a maximum height of six feet, four inches but included several beams that made constant ducking a necessity. To enter this fetid palace, which had been stripped to the beams for firewood, men groped their way through a dark tunnel three feet high and two and a half feet broad.

The captain understood the importance of remaining cheerful, and he strove to maintain the men's spirits. Even so, the cold, dark, hunger, sickness, rats, and confinement took a heavy toll. James McGary, overcome by homesickness, spent a whole day pacing the deck and refusing to eat. Kane confined his low moments to his journals. What he wrote to Maggie has been lost. But on one occasion, while imagining his mother weeping on her wet pillow, he evoked each of his siblings in turn: "Oh Tom, Pat, John, Bess, oh if I could see you all for but five minutes."

o   o   o

This dark mood broke on December 7, when from on deck a cry went up: "Eskimos coming!" Elisha Kane, who had just taken an extra night watch, hurried on deck and watched as five sledges approached, each of them hauled by six dogs. The drivers proved to be mostly strangers, obviously Inuit from a settlement more distant than Etah, but they brought Amos Bonsall and Carl Petersen. "In this way they came back," Hans Hendrik would write, "the natives carrying them to the ship by sledge. They looked very emaciated and were dreadfully voracious, but the Master bade them not to eat too greedily, fearing it might be hurtful."

As soon as they could, the two returnees reported that, 350 miles south, the other six defectors were huddling in a hut, sick and hungry and almost out of food. These two had come seeking help. Elisha Kane went to work. By the next morning he had assembled 350 pounds of emergency supplies: 100 pounds of salt pork, plus significant quantities of meat biscuit, bread dust, and tea. The newly arrived Inuit knew nothing of any friendship treaty, and he felt uneasy about relying on them to transport the goods to the six desperate men. But of the two returnees, Bonsall could hardly stand upright, and Petersen, "never too reliable in an emergency, was for postponing the time of setting out" until he recovered. Besides himself, only Hendrik and McGary remained fit for travel—and they could not withdraw without jeopardizing the other men.

The captain decided to rely on the solemn promises of the strangers, but his misgivings would prove well founded. He kept one man aboard as an informal hostage, but that individual slipped away. And instead of returning to the faraway hut, the visitors absconded with the emergency rations. Kane discovered this four days later, on December 12, when at three o'clock

238

in the morning, with the temperature standing at 50 degrees below zero, Inuit friends from Etah and Netlik, the next settlement south, arrived with the other six defectors.

Roused from his bunk, Kane was on deck when Isaac Hayes stumbled up the gangway and offered a few prepared words: "We have come here, destitute and exhausted, to claim your hospitality; we know that we have no rights to your indulgence, but we feel that with you, we will find a welcome and a home." Kane hailed the whole party aboard: "Poor fellows, I could only grasp their hands and give them a brother's welcome."

Covered with frost and snow and nearly collapsing with hunger, the newcomers relished the "scanty luxuries" Kane produced—the coffee, meat-biscuit soup, molasses, wheat bread, and even the salt pork avoided by those who, having remained aboard, were suffering from scurvy. Kane used caution in bringing the men below, as the relative warmth of the cabin might have proved torturous after their long exposure. On their final dash to the brig, from a bay near Etah, they had traveled seventy miles through rugged hummocks in temperatures far below zero. All six of the men were ill, and Hayes was suffering from a badly frostbitten foot. Kane abandoned his own berth to the young doctor, and later had to amputate three of his toes.

During the next few days, the defectors shared their story. After reaching open water on September 5, Petersen had climbed an icy outcrop to 300 feet above sea level. To the south, an open channel four miles wide extended along the coast as far as the eye could see. Surely this proved that he had been right? At water's edge, the men loaded the whaleboat, the same *Forlorn Hope* Kane had used in trying to reach Beechey Island. They carried a barrel and a half of pork, fifty pounds of boiled beans, five barrels of bread, fifty pounds of coffee, and five pounds of tea. For fuel, they had a keg of lard or slush and a coil of rope-yarn. Their luxuries included a twenty-pound bag of flour, a two-gallon keg of molasses, a case of Borden's meat biscuit, half a dozen bottles of lime juice, and two bottles of vinegar. These articles would last four to five weeks. After that, they would rely on their guns—and those, too, went into the boat. Each man brought a change of clothing. And Kane had supplied a sextant, a spyglass, a chronometer, a boat-compass barometer, a shotgun, and some necessary ammunition.

The boat was so heavily laden that, when the eight men pushed off, water came within four inches of the gunwales. The defectors sailed south along the coast. Soon enough, at Lifeboat Cove, they retrieved the emergency provisions Kane had hidden there thirteen months before. In addition to the lifeboat, oars, and sail, they acquired two barrels of bread, one each of pork and beef, thirty pounds of rice, the same amount of sugar, and a few cooking utensils.

But now a gale forced them to land on Littleton Island and to huddle in a tent for four days. When the storm abated, they again sailed south. Still hugging the coast, they rounded Cape Parry. On September 18, they reached Netlik, a settlement of twenty-five Inuit, some of whom they had met previously. These people provided fresh water and walrus meat, and the defectors resumed traveling. But one week later, 350 miles south of the brig, the sailors found their way blocked by pack ice. Petersen, it now appeared, had been wrong, and Kane right: the ice had not dissipated. The North Water lay blocked and impassible.

Unable to proceed, the men built a stone hut in the Inuit style, covering boards and sails with lichen and rock moss. In this drafty hovel, which they called Wanderers' Home, they proposed to spend the endless winter. In the spring, they would resume their journey. But as the dark season came on, despite hunting every day, they found almost no game. Soon, they were running so low on fuel that Hayes began burning his medical texts. Hunters from Netlik came upon the encampment. They carried seal and walrus meat, and offered to trade. Kane had supplied a few beads, needles, and other trifles, but the defectors quickly exhausted these.

On October 30, the sun disappeared for the winter. In the twilight that now represented daylight, Petersen and Godfrey walked to Netlik, sixty miles away. But they brought back only a bit of dried meat. And by early November, the defectors, starving and cold, were discussing their alternatives: they could try to shelter in the hut until spring; they could journey to

Netlik and pass the winter with the "Esquimaux"; or they could retreat to the brig. This last, Godfrey declared, was "less acceptable to me than either of the others." He preferred living on husks or moss "to going back with contrition and making a pitiful appeal to benevolence."

Meanwhile, without Kane's guiding hand, relations with the Inuit deteriorated. The head man, Kalutunah, remained friendly. But others, visiting from farther away, grew surly and hostile. They talked of allowing the white men to starve to death, and perhaps of hurrying that process, with a view to inheriting their possessions. The most threatening of this contingent, a large, muscular man called Sip-su, wore on his face "a fierce expression," according to Hayes, "foreign to the countenances of his companions. While they always appeared to be in a good humor, ever laughing and gay, he was seldom seen even to smile." Sip-su boasted that he had killed two men of his own tribe. As unsuccessful hunters, he explained, they had become a burden to his people. He ambushed them among the hummocks and harpooned them to death.

Petersen sought to trade for dogs and a sledge, and offered to pay well. But he lacked Kane's negotiating skills, and Sip-su turned to Kalutunah: "Don't you think we can get his things in a cheaper way?" Hayes would remember all this in his *Arctic Boat Journey,* and Sonntag, Petersen, and Godfrey would corroborate. An Inuit named Tatterat visited the hut while moving his family north. He warned that other families were evacuating the area, as the unusual severity of the season would make living south of Netlik extremely dangerous. He had not seen such a winter in years. Hayes speculated that "had the season remained open two weeks longer, we should, in all probability, have reached Upernavik." This, of course, was precisely what Kane had sought to communicate: that the season was unusually harsh.

Perilously short of food, and with one man, Stephenson, so sick he could not walk, the defectors debated retreating to the brig. By November 23, even Petersen accepted "that we could not spend the winter in this place." It was impossible to avoid famine without the help of the Inuit, or at least the use of their dogs and sledges, and these they refused to lend. Late in November, the defectors set out on foot to reach the brig, hauling Stephenson on a sledge. They traveled twelve miles before, while floundering in drifting snow, they realized they would never make it and turned around and struggled back to the hut.

The following day, leaving six men at the shelter and hauling only a meager supply of blubber and coffee, Petersen and Bonsall left for the brig to seek help. Six defectors remained at the hut—cold, starving, and increasingly desperate. When three hunters arrived from Netlik with two teams of dogs, the sailors talked of using their guns to steal one of them. Hayes proposed an ingenious alternative. From his medical supplies, he slipped a vial of laudanum. He stirred this into a pot of stewed meat, which he then fed to the unsuspecting visitors. The opium tincture did its work. While the hunters slept, the sailors escaped by dogsled.

They drove off the second team of dogs, but these returned to the hut. The Inuit, awakening to their situation, used these animals to overtake the escapees. Hayes brandished his rifle, however, and they chose to treat the whole affair as an excellent joke. Everybody proceeded to Netlik, where the sailors were well received. Various Inuit transported them to Etah, and from there to the *Advance*. Their numbers grew as they neared the vessel, doubtless anticipating some reward, until six drivers reached the brig with forty-two dogs. "Whatever their motive," Kane would write, "their conduct to our poor friends was full of humanity."

Realizing that any history of the expedition would have to treat the defection, Kane set aside and carefully preserved those parts of his journal that treated the withdrawal and the return; in the event of his death, he instructed Cornelius Grinnell to place them in the hands of Judge Kane. Now, the day after the return, the Inuit complained to Kane that the defectors had stolen articles from them—a serious offence under the treaty. The captain summoned all concerned to a stern and cheerless trial on deck. With Petersen as translator, he took both sides through a series of questions. In the end, Kane judged "that an appeal to kind feeling" might have sufficed to achieve the desired end. "I therefore, to the immense satisfaction of our stranger guests, assured them of my approval, and pulled their hair all round."

Kane brought the visitors "into the oriental recess of our dormitory" for the first time. "There, seated on a red blanket, with four pork-fat lamps throwing an illumination over old worsted damask curtains, hunting knives, rifles, beer barrels, galley stove and chronometers, I dealt out to each man five needles, a file and a stick of wood." To two of the leaders, Kalutunah and Shang-hu, Kane also gave knives and other gifts. He returned the fur clothes, boots, and sledges the defectors had taken, explaining that his men did not steal, but had only borrowed these to save their lives. Finally, he spread out his sole remaining buffalo hide near the stove, built a roaring fire, and treated the visitors to as hearty a supper as he could provide.

After the Inuit left, Kane learned that several knives and forks had gone missing. But this, shaking his head and sighing, he decided to overlook. He had reaffirmed the treaty and restored a cross-cultural alliance—and as he wisely surmised, that would be what mattered most in the days to come.

27

A Polar Nightmare

Ascientist studying the effects of extreme stress could hardly do better than to confine nineteen men in a cabin and subject them to intense cold and never-ending darkness while attacking them with scurvy and starvation. Elisha Kane had learned enough from the Inuit that by December, when the defectors resurfaced, he had transformed the brig into a quasi-igloo. Still, the return of the eight rendered this small, moss-lined cabin almost uninhabitable—and certainly, as Kane wrote, "too crowded to be wholesome."

The congestion also proved dangerous. The men had been reduced to burning pork fat for both cooking and lighting, and Kane wrote of "writing by the miserable flicker of my pork fat lamp." The cabin grew intolerably smoky. The captain moved the lamps into a separate cupboard and ordered a constant watch. But once, when someone deserted his post, the cooking room caught fire. Soon, the entire bulkhead was blazing, as well as the brig's dry timbers and walls. As one of the first to arrive on the scene, Kane grabbed the piled furs of the defectors and tried to smother the flames. He then pushed through a burning sailcloth bulkhead to tear down a sheet of canvas that hung behind the men's loaded muskets. Others began passing buckets of water and splashing them onto the fire. In the smoke, Kane fell and almost lost consciousness. He managed to stumble out on deck minus his beard and eyebrows, and with burns on his forehead and palms.

The crew spent half an hour putting out the fire. The smoke forced them all outside, and the transition, Kane wrote, "from the fiery Shadrachian furnace-temperature . . . to forty-six below zero was intolerably trying. Every man suffered, and few escaped without frostbitten fingers." Had the brig been destroyed and left the expedition without shelter, food, or clothing in temperatures almost 80 degrees below the freezing point, not a man would have survived.

Hans Hendrik offered a corollary version in his memoir. He wrote that some of the men "tried to cook meat in the native fashion, imitating the native lamps in their room in the ship. During this time I happened to go outside, and observed that our ship was taking fire. I shouted at once to those inside: 'Our ship is on fire!' They then hurried out, and, drawing salt water from a hole, succeeded in quenching the flames. Our Master gave me many thanks for my quickness."

Now, with Hayes flat on his back, having lost three toes, Kane served as sole doctor for eighteen men, many of whom were sick. This taxed his mood, his patience, and his temper. In his journal, after the arrival of Petersen and Bonsall, Kane poured out his scorn, writing that it made his blood boil to think that the defectors had "set up their puerile opinions against my own drearily earned judgment of the Arctic ice. Petersen, the Dane, weaned away from his usual caution by recollection of his home and family, never thought that the navigation of this great ice sea involved principles and observations very different from the fisherman's pilotage of his little Upernavik home. Sonntag, a child and an abstractionist, never dreamed that meridian transits and lunars would not teach him to steer a bird line in a raging pack; and here is the result—they send to me imploring succour and claiming my aid and direction as their only hope."

Having received the defectors aboard, Kane did not immediately forgive and forget. He reserved regular duties for those who had remained with him, and compelled the others to eat at a separate mess. This reflected the general feeling, as Sonntag would reveal: before returning to the brig, the defectors "resolved, on board, to form a separate society independent of the command of Dr. Kane, and to demand of him only that hospitality which is granted to a crew having suffered shipwreck on the sea."

Two of the defectors, Godfrey and Blake, had alienated even the other six, and ate by themselves. These two, hired from the New York docks at the last moment, had presented problems throughout the voyage. Before allowing the defectors to leave, Kane had elicited a promise that Godfrey and Blake would not be permitted to retrieve the cache near Littleton Island, because it included a quantity of whisky. Despite this pledge, Petersen had allowed the two tough seamen to retrieve the cache. As Kane had anticipated, they not only plundered it and gorged on the food, but got drunk and became bullying and abusive. In other circumstances, Goodfellow wrote later, their thieving might have constituted petty larceny; in these, it should be considered "robbery or even piracy."

Even before reaching open water, Godfrey had caused trouble. While the other men worked, Petersen saw him "moping on the rocks, and gave him 'peremptorily the option to go back to the ship at once or to go to work.'" He chose the latter. Later, at the hut, Blake argued with Bonsall over the serving of coffee and withdrew from the others in a surly, threatening mood. In his book, Godfrey would insist that to join this Arctic expedition he had quit a job that paid three times as much. He had acted out of youthful audacity, patriotic enthusiasm, and an unconquerable love of adventure.

In his unpublished journal, Kane would offer a different perspective: "William Godfrey is a professional thief who smuggled himself into the Expedition by bribing Mr. Grinnell's wharf protégé, the old shopkeeper in the frame house. He has twice threatened me and once attempted my life on the boat going south [while trying to reach Beechey Island]. I have criminal charges against him." As for John Blake, he "is a spotted man; entered the brig by proxy, being concerned in the murder and mutiny on board the ———. He is a truculent, bold, and able fellow."

One week after the defectors returned, an officer reported that Blake and Godfrey had been insubordinate. He had given them a direct order, and they had flatly refused it. What to do? Six decades later, while dealing with men far less rebellious, Ernest Shackleton would resort to force. Some of his crew, having neglected to bring their hats and gloves into a tent, used this omission as an excuse to refuse to work. Shackleton would write, "Only by rather drastic methods were they induced to turn to." One of his officers would add that they were driven to work "none too gently," while another observed that they "were dragged from their bags and set to work."

In the Arctic, to maintain discipline, Kane had taken to administering punishments himself, believing this less humiliating than using one of his officers. "I therefore always took up the offender alone face to face in the darkness," he wrote, "and after a few words seized him and inflicted as much injury as I was able to. This way of meeting them they understood." Now, as he finished dealing physically with the two husky miscreants, who did not dare to strike him back, Whipple arrived on deck. He fell at the captain's feet, begging mercy: "He got up, after a short cuffing with my mittened hands, and went below thanking me." In his journal, Kane acknowledged that "the above reads repulsively." He explained: "Nothing could palliate such a system [of maintaining discipline] but the gross worthlessness and depravity of the subjects—the thief and the mutineer." The exception was Whipple, "a poor weak unfortunate going to be again a useful man, but completely under the influence of John."

o   o   o

On Christmas Day, 1854, Kane insisted that all the men, including Blake and Godfrey, sit down together for dinner. He opened the last bottle of champagne, toasted absent friends, and pledged that the men would spend next Christmas at home. In the dark, smoky cabin, while eating pork and beans, the stranded sailors pretended they were feasting on turkey, roast beef, onions, potatoes, cucumbers, watermelons, and, as Kane put it, "god knows what other cravings of the scurvy-sickened palate." Later, in a quiet moment, he thought so yearningly of Philadelphia that he had a vision of his family sitting round a Christmas table: "I saw my home. How I saw it no journal shall ever recall."

This curious remark makes no sense unless one knows of Kane's secret relationship with Maggie Fox. It becomes meaningful only if the explorer vividly imagined Maggie as part of the Kane family, sitting down to Christmas dinner with him, his parents, and his siblings. That was almost certainly how he saw it, though he dared not put that on paper.

Kane took grim satisfaction in the irony that, where last winter he had been the weakest of the party, this year he remained one of the strongest. Even so, he couldn't help noticing that the general debilitation spared no one: "I don't know what is the matter with me. I can no longer give by the pen an impression of the immediate foreground . . . [I am] so hardworked and care [laden] that I cease to be impressed by the present in thinking of the future. Those little everyday touches which make the sketch pass by me. The same to a lesser degree pervades our company. Ohlsen has lost his memory. 'Can't keep his tools.' Petersen can't catch the words of our Smith Sound dialect. Wilson, Brooks, and Morton complain of enfeebled eyesight and a scant vocabulary."

In these effects, the captain perceived symptoms of scurvy. And so, having learned to combat the disease with fresh meat, he resolved to go to Etah to trade for food. "Our journeys have taught us the wisdom of the Esquimaux appetite," he wrote, "and there are few among us who do not relish a slice of raw blubber or a chunk of frozen walrus-beef."

On December 30, 1854, together with Petersen and eight dogs, Kane set out on the eighty- or ninety-mile journey. The dogs, suffering from an inadequate diet, began breaking down after a few miles, showing "that accursed tetanoid spasm." Petersen wanted to turn back, but Kane insisted on pushing on to the empty hut at Anoatok. With the outdoor temperature falling to 44 degrees below zero, the men spent a long, cold night during which, using the lamp, they managed to raise the indoor temperature to 30 below.

The next morning, the broken-down dogs could not get the sledge through the hummocks and, with a gale coming, the men retreated to the *Advance*.

Early in the New Year, as a result of lethargy, Kane wrote little. But he kept taking observations, and on January 9 the temperature sank to –69.3 degrees Fahrenheit—the lowest yet recorded at Rensselaer Harbor. With the cabin temperature averaging 8 degrees above zero, Kane and his men burned pork grease for light and warmth, though this filled the cabin with smoke and blackened their beds and bedding, as well as their faces. Still, these lamps provided an astonishing amount of heat: one four-wicked lamp could melt enough ice to produce six gallons of water in twelve hours.

Elisha Kane was also taken with the elegance of Inuit sledge travel, which he judged superior to the cumbersome British style: "Give me an eight-pound reindeer fur bag to sleep in, an Esquimaux lamp with a lump of moss, a sheet-iron snow-melter or copper soup-pot, with a tin cylinder to slip over it and defend it from the wind, a good *pièce de résistance* of raw walrus-beef; and I want nothing more for a long journey, if the thermometer will keep itself as high as minus 30. Give me a bear-skin bag and coffee to boot; and with the clothes on my back I am ready for minus 60."

Ready he needed to be, because in mid-January he knew something had to change: "We require meat, and cannot get along without it." With nothing to feed the dogs except the boiled carcasses of their late companions, Kane again set out for Etah to acquire fresh meat. Having judged Petersen "too cautious for the emergency," he left this time with young Hendrik, who is "careful and attached to me, and by temperament daring and adventurous." The men would walk to the hut at Anoatok, so as not to exhaust the dogs. After that, they would drive the animals forward, and camp out where they broke down: "It seems hard to sacrifice the dogs, but the necessity is too palpable and urgent."

The two lead dogs collapsed even before Anoatok, however, with one of them falling into convulsions. In darkness, and with a storm approaching, the two men groped along the ice foot. After fourteen hours of hard, cold work, they reached the dreary shelter. They had scarcely finished cutting blocks of snow to seal the entrance when the blizzard broke. For the next forty-eight hours, the two huddled in the shelter, sleeping, drinking coffee, and sharing "bits out of the raw hind-leg of a fox to give zest to our biscuits spread with frozen tallow."

When the storm abated, the two men drove the dogs several miles south to Hummock Pass, which marked the route to Etah. But the blizzard had deposited so much snow that in trying to get through, they buried both sledge and dogs. As darkness again closed in, they beat their way back to Anoatok. The next morning, Kane decided to try an alternative route along the ice belt. The two men worked nonstop for four hours and accomplished nothing, and young Hendrik, "buoyant as he was, began to cry like a child. Sick, worn out, strength gone, dogs fast and floundering, I am not ashamed to admit that, as I thought of the sick men on board, my own equanimity was also at fault."

In the moonlight, Kane scrambled up a familiar hill, Old Beacon Knob, and looked south. The ridge around Cape Hatherton jutted out of the broken ice, and open water—"that inexplicable North Water"—formed a long, black wedge along the coast. Best of all, Kane saw a trough running south through the hummock ridges. He called Hendrik to climb after him, and they agreed: if not for the fact that the dogs were disabled, they could easily have completed their journey. The two withdrew again to Anoatok, and then to the brig. They arrived without meat, assuaging the men's disappointment with news of the passage through the hummocks: next time, they would certainly reach Etah. Petersen began preparing to make the attempt.

But now another fierce storm confined the men to the *Advance*. The health of the party continued to deteriorate. During the last attempt to reach Etah, a freakish warm wind from the southeast, a kind of Chinook, *foehn,* or Santa Ana, had driven the temperature upward more than 70 degrees, from −44 to +26. The change did not last, but before the temperature plummeted to its usual levels, Kane and Hendrik had both suffered cardiac symptoms.

On the brig, Wilson had endured a bout of spasmodic asthma, and Brooks a renewal of "dyspnoea," or labored breathing.

Now, Hayes remained prostrate with amputated toes, and Sonntag could scarcely hobble. Brooks needed assistance to get up on deck. McGary was off duty, "saturated with articular scurvy." Wilson lay in bed, unable to move because of blotches and nodes in his limbs. Riley was down with stiff legs. Hickey, swollen and blistered, could hardly stand. Ohlsen was on the verge of breaking down as a result of scurvy in his knee. And Goodfellow, suffering from bleeding, scurvied gums, counted himself lucky. "The state of things aboard begin to press on me," Kane wrote. "But by sleeping day hours I manage well. Hans, Ohlsen and myself are the only three sound men of the legitimate ship's company." Not surprisingly, given the circumstances, even Goodfellow disappointed him, as that young man took to ridiculing the less-articulate Brooks with "satirical and goading remarks," which prompted more than one altercation.

Of the eighteen men, only six could hunt, cook, or even nurse. Still, the cautious Petersen delayed his departure for Etah. Finally, on February 3, along with Hendrik and the dogs, he set out. But three days later, at ten o'clock in the evening, the captain heard voices on deck. The Danish Greenlander had broken down, and the Inuk had brought him back. Within a couple of days, Kane would write: "Petersen is well again—a cold. He is an old woman."

Mid-February brought more illness, hunger, and depression. Fortunately, the hunting improved. One of the men, usually Hendrik, shot the occasional fox, rabbit, or ptarmigan, and once a deer. Even so, Kane felt such a need for fresh meat that he allowed Godfrey to try for Etah. But he, too, turned back, complaining of the horrors of solitude in the icy wastes.

About separating the defectors from the faithful, Kane grew less adamant. He allowed Blake to work temporarily as cook, and then let Godfrey do so—"not implying attachment to the roll of the Expedition." Godfrey fainted while on duty, and Kane reported that, with Hendrik and Petersen handling the hunting, "the whole work of the household, cookery included, is done now by self and Bonsall." For three nights, he kept watch from 8 p.m. to 6 a.m., and for five days he never removed his clothes. Everyone but Morton, who was crippled by a frozen heel, showed signs of scurvy.

On February 21, the sun rose above the horizon, although screened by hills. The next day, Hendrik shot a 300-pound deer, and the starving men feasted. The sickest of them, confined to their bunks, yearned to see the sun. Kane believed that such a sight would do them more good than any medicine, and he devised "a clever system of mirrors" for their viewing pleasure. He never yielded to pessimism. Where Petersen, Godfrey, and even Hendrik had declared a journey to Etah impossible, Kane insisted, "I know better." Having himself failed during the long darkness, he believed that, with the light, the journey could be accomplished—"and, if I might venture to leave our sick-bay for a week, I would prove it."

By early March, Kane had developed a detailed escape plan. Around mid-May, when the cold grew less intense, he would lead the men in dragging boats along the ice belt, and then over the pack ice of Smith Sound—a difficult trek of perhaps ninety miles. The men would then climb into boats and sail south, and so complete a journey "of alternating ice and water of more than thirteen hundred miles." At least four of the men would have to be carried—three because of amputations, and one as a result of a frost wound.

To the men, Kane offered an optimistic analysis. The hunting would soon improve, and collectively they would conquer scurvy with fresh meat. Warmer weather would enable them to reach Etah. It would also allow them to clean the cabin, filthy from lampblack, and to dry and air their fetid sleeping gear. Also, he exhorted the men to stick together. Only by doing so could they meet the challenges that lay ahead. He had already begun sorting through documents and records, selecting those he must preserve. He had set the men to working on clothing, boots, bedding, and provisions, and kept them busy cutting up and stitching canvas and skins.

In retrospect, Kane would describe his early-March journal as "little else than a chronicle of sufferings." Every one of the men suffered from scurvy, and most could not leave their bunks. Some proved grateful for any kindness, some were querulous, others despondent, and still others "wanted only strength to become mutinous." The stalwart Brooks "burst into tears when he first saw himself in the glass."

When they had exhausted the latest infusion of fresh meat, the invalids again began to sink. Old wounds reopened. Petersen declared himself unfit to work outdoors, leaving Hendrik to hunt alone. Kane battled to keep up the men's spirits: "I cooked for them . . . brewed up flax-seed and limejuice and quinine and willow-stems into an abomination which was dignified as beer, and which some were persuaded for the time to believe such. But it was becoming more and more certain every hour, that unless we could renew our supplies of fresh meat, the days of the party were numbered. I spare myself, as well as the readers of this hastily compiled volume, when I pass summarily over the details of our condition at this time. I look back at it with recollections like those of a nightmare."

On March 6, nearing desperation but refusing to relinquish hope, Kane sent Hendrik, his only effective huntsman, to try again for Etah. The season had changed, the ice track had improved, and the weather, though still intense, was less cold than before. Hendrik left with the two surviving dogs and the lightest sledge. "If Hans brings meat," Kane wrote, "we can make it." But within a couple of days, he felt his own strength waning. Only he and Bonsall were working—nursing the sick, cutting the ice, cooking and serving the Spartan meals. Kane reminded himself that, if Hendrik brought back walrus meat, the sick would rise again. If the young hunter failed, "the thought is horrible." Not a man aboard could hope to linger much more than one month.

Two days later, while writing in his journal and fretting that Hendrik had not yet returned, Kane heard the barking of dogs. Hans had arrived with fresh food, a fellow hunter, and much to relate: "To men in our condition," Kane wrote, "Hans was as a man from the cities." After spending one night at Anoatok, Hendrik had reached Etah late the next day. He was welcomed, but found himself surrounded by "lean figures of misery." The people of Etah, too, had endured famine, and been reduced even to eating their dogs—twenty-six of thirty.

When Hendrik proposed a walrus hunt, his hosts rolled their eyes. They had tried repeatedly to kill walrus. But when the sea is frozen, that crafty creature can only be taken at an ice hole. With a harpoon, this was proving an insurmountable challenge, because even a struck and wounded walrus would usually escape with the weapon. In response, Hendrik showed the people Kane's rifle, and demonstrated what it could do. They responded by digging out a sledge and harnessing the last four dogs. During the ensuing hunt, the men harpooned and shot not only a walrus, which took five musket balls, but also two seals. The Inuit of Etah feasted.

Now, Hendrik had brought back a considerable supply of meat. Kane had told him to engage an assistant if possible, and he had returned with young Myouk. To the fresh meat, the men of the *Advance* did not respond immediately. "The truth is," Kane wrote, "they are fearfully down." But within three or four days, all except Brooks, Wilson, and Riley began shaking off scurvy, and Kane felt a great surge of optimism.

Then he learned that trouble was brewing.

{ 28 }

GODFREY'S TREACHERY

In mid-March, Morton and Stephenson overhead a whispered conversation. Godfrey and Blake were conspiring to desert the brig and their embattled companions. "I have a couple of men on board," Kane wrote, "whose former history I would give something to know,—bad fellows both of them, but daring, energetic, and strong. They gave me trouble before we reached the coast of Greenland; and they keep me constantly on the watch at this moment, for it is evident to me that they have some secret object in view, involving probably a desertion and escape to the Inuit settlements. A life with the Esquimaux would relieve them from much discomfort, and be temptation enough to make them sacrifice their sick comrades.

"They are both feigning sickness this morning; and, from what I have overheard, it is with the view of getting thoroughly rested before a start. Hendrik's departure with the sledge and dogs would give them a fine chance, if they could only waylay him, of securing all our facilities for travel; and I should not be surprised if they tried to compel him to go along with them. They cannot succeed in this except by force. I am acting very guardedly with them. I cannot punish till I have the evidence of an overt act."

On March 20, with Hendrik having left for Etah, Kane sat up all night. At 6:30 a.m., suspiciously early, he saw Godfrey rise. Pretending to sleep, he watched as the man cooked breakfast. "At first he appeared troubled and had several stealthily whispered interviews with John [Blake]; finally, his manner became more easy and he cooked and served our breakfast meals." Convinced now that the two would meet outside, Kane pulled on his furs and, pistol in hand, slipped out through the dark *tossut* and hid near the entrance. After half an hour, Blake came out and, glancing furtively around, climbed the ladder to the deck. Ten minutes later, when Godfrey emerged, booted for travel and clad in buffalo hide, Kane confronted him and ordered him back inside. He sent Morton to fetch Blake and posted Bonsall at the inner end of the tunnel to prevent escape.

The captain told the ship's company what the two scoundrels had been plotting, explaining their plans step by step. Godfrey confessed, and in response Kane "knocked him down and mauled him until he cried for mercy." Under his mitten, Kane carried a piece of lead he had secretly manufactured for this purpose. Then, showing his usual foresight, Kane "read from the Logbook an affidavit signed by two witnesses that [Godfrey] had regularly stolen property from the brig, specifying how, when, and what articles in detail. Finally I told him that a penitentiary hung over him, and that I would give him a chance to escape it by restoring him to duty and give him another trial."

Lacking manpower and space to confine the would-be deserters, the captain accepted their apologies and avowals and released them. Godfrey "accepted my lenity with thankful hypocrisy, went to duty, and in less than an hour," while Kane was out hunting, fled toward the south. The captain feared, plausibly enough, that he would spend one night at Anoatok before proceeding to Etah. There, from the unsuspecting Hendrik, he would try to steal the sledge dogs, rifle, and trading goods, and with them flee to Netlik and beyond.

His success would spell disaster, as Kane's hopes of transporting the sick, and then of escaping in boats to the south, depended upon the dogs. Yet, he

did not have the men to send after Godfrey—"it is the most culpable desertion I ever knew or heard of." Bonsall, Petersen, and Kane were the only
men able to care for the others. In a rare allusion to his cardiac weakness,
he added, "Save for the warnings of a secret trouble, the fox gnawing under
the jacket, I do better than the rest; but I bear my fox."

During the next several days, while hunting and caring for his scurvy-
stricken comrades, Kane worried that Hendrik had not returned. Perhaps
Godfrey had waylaid him and stolen the dogs? "This wretched man has
been the very bane of the cruise," he wrote. "My conscience tells me that
almost any measure against him would be justifiable as a relief to the rest;
but an instinctive aversion to extreme measures binds my hands."

Finally, on April 2, while standing watch, Bonsall spotted a figure skulking around on the ice belt about a mile from the brig. He called to Kane, and
together they walked out to investigate. They found their sledge and dog
team, but the man turned and fled south. Recognizing Godfrey, Kane followed and called out for him to wait. When the captain drew near enough,
Godfrey told him that Hendrik lay sick at Etah, suffering from exposure.
He himself had traveled south beyond Etah to Netlik and Northumberland
Island. He proposed to return there, to spend his life with Kalutunah and
the other Inuit, and "neither persuasion nor force should divert him from
this purpose."

Suspecting this to be a ruse, and that Godfrey had returned to collect
Blake and escape to the south, Kane drew his pistol and forced the deserter
to walk to the gangway. But here Godfrey refused to go farther. Kane could
not hope to subdue the larger man by force, and he could not bring himself to
shoot him. He ordered Bonsall to stand guard and went to fetch ankle irons.
He returned to see Godfrey scampering away over the ice. Bonsall claimed
his musket had misfired. Kane grabbed a different rifle but he, too, failed to
get off a decent shot, and the fugitive disappeared among the hummocks.

This incident, described in *Arctic Explorations,* would spawn controversy
and contention. In the *North British Review,* an English reviewer would
write: "The attempt to take the life of William Godfrey, which no law,

human or divine, can justify, was, fortunately for Dr. Kane, overruled [by Providence]." The reviewer, spotting a chance to show off his knowledge, drew a comparison with an overland expedition led by John Franklin in 1819–22: "When an officer of a former Arctic expedition shot a ferocious Indian of his party, the world viewed it as an act of stern necessity and personal safety, but Godfrey was neither a madman nor an enemy." In fact, if Godfrey had succeeded in making off with Blake, he would have destroyed Kane's best hope of saving the expedition.

But long after Kane could answer him, Godfrey quoted and elaborated on the reviewer's argument. He contended that he had never been restored to the official roll of the expedition, and so could not be considered a defector. While Kane had recorded the incident in his journal immediately after it happened, on April 2, 1855, and recorded Godfrey's declared intention to spend the rest of his life with the Inuit, the deserter would ridicule this notion. Adopting a tone of injured innocence, Godfrey denied that he intended to flee with the sledge and dogs. He claimed he had brought the sledge-load of meat to the brig for the use of his comrades. And here arises a question of credibility. In his book, Godfrey fails to explain what he and Blake had been planning when Kane apprehended them in mid-desertion. He asserts that he felt entitled to come and go as he pleased, but then fails to account for his skulking and sneaking about.

When he flatly contradicts Kane, as he frequently does, his fabrications border on the ludicrous. A single illustration should suffice. Kane, confiding to his journal soon after the above-described incident, writes that Godfrey turned and ran, "and made good his escape before we could lay hold of another weapon." Godfrey, writing years later, insists that he walked away from the brig—and that Kane, "this amiable and saintly naval officer," fired at him from close range and missed. Apparently, he heard the bullet whistle past his head.

"I then bowed to the Doctor," Godfrey writes, "in acknowledgement of his intended kindness, and advised him to go below and compose himself. 'When your nerves are steadier,' said I, 'perhaps you may shoot with more effect.' He stood gazing at me as if astonished at my audacity. I walked a few paces further, and then turned and addressed him again: 'Dr. Kane, as you will not order your men to unload the sledge, I shall have to go back without it. But no matter; I have walked to Etah once, and I can do so again. I shall borrow a sledge there, and return with another load of meat. In the mean time, you can practice with the rifle until I come back and offer you a chance for another shot.' Then, leaving the sledge, with its load, on the ice, I bowed again to the doctor and departed."

Did Kane shoot at Godfrey to kill him? Almost certainly not. He did rightly believe Godfrey to be a mutineer, and he realized that his mutiny threatened the survival of the entire crew. As captain, he had a responsibility to quell that rebellion, and to use force if necessary. He found himself humanly incapable of discharging that duty—he was simply unable to shoot Godfrey in cold blood. And so Kane drove him off. And, in relating the incident later, rather than confess that he had been unable to shoot the mutineer, and so reveal that he fell short of a certain Victorian ideal of manliness, he wrote that he had tried and failed.

The sledge-load of walrus and seal meat proved a godsend. Within days, the scurvy-ridden crew showed signs of improvement, and soon several men were back on their feet. Of Godfrey and the 450 pounds of meat, Kane wrote, "one may forgive the man in consideration of the good which it has done us all." But he also issued a standing order "that desertion, or the attempt to desert, shall be met at once by the sternest penalty." He felt the crew welcomed this as guaranteeing their safety, and believed it encouraged "a strict, staunch fidelity to the expedition."

Meanwhile, he again grew worried about Hendrik. He feared that Godfrey might have fed him some story, conveyed some threat or reproof, and so discouraged him from returning. While far from healthy, Kane felt honor bound to go in search of the young hunter. And on April 10, in the relative warmth of 10 degrees below zero, Kane set out for Etah. Driving five dogs, he left the brig at 10:30 a.m. On the smallest sledge, wonderfully portable at five and a half by two feet, he carried nothing but a bearskin jacket and sack pants for sleeping, and a ball of walrus meat for sustenance. Comparing this with the sledge outfits of the previous year showed, he wrote, that "we are now more than half Esquimaux."

The dogs hauled well, the ice ran away smoothly, and after covering sixty miles in eleven hours, Kane spotted a black speck moving near the Greenland shore. Approaching, he recognized "the methodical, seal-stalking gait" of Hans Hendrik, and soon he was shaking the young man's hand, the two of them talking excitedly. On his sledge, Kane carried Hendrik to Anoatok, and there heard his story.

At Etah, after hunting for several days, the young man had fallen ill. He spent five days suffering severe stomach pains. He had been nursed by the daughter of Shang-hu and, and as Kane put it, "her sympathies and smiles have, I fear, made an impression on his heart which a certain damsel near Upernavik might be sorry to hear of." While Hendrik lay in bed, Godfrey arrived—and urged him to desert the expedition and drive away south. Hendrik refused, and also prevented Godfrey from taking his rifle.

Before falling sick, the hunter had cached some meat at Littleton Island, which he had urged Godfrey to carry back to the *Advance*. This the man had done, although his intentions remained suspect. The fugitive had now retreated to Etah, where he lived among the Inuit. "Strong and healthy as he is," Kane wrote, "our daily work goes on better for his absence, and the ship seems better when purged by his desertion; but the example is disastrous; and, cost what it may, I must have him back."

During their long talk, Hendrik also reported that Kalutunah, the leader of the people of Netlik on Northumberland Island, had managed to save as many as seven dogs. At this news, the irrepressible Kane thought again of making a northward dash to the Kennedy Channel. He had not yet given up hope of seeing for himself the Open Polar Sea. If he could borrow four dogs from Kalutunah, a final sortie suddenly became feasible. Kane also recognized that he must begin preparing to abandon the *Advance,* in the event that she remained trapped in the ice: "I must have an exact discipline, a rigid routine, and a perfectly-thought-out organization."

From Anoatok, Kane sent Hendrik south with the dogs to retrieve more meat from Littleton Island and to negotiate for the use of additional dogs. With most of his men still on their backs, and a month of preliminary work ahead before he could commence transporting boats eighty miles over the ice to open water, Kane walked the thirty miles back to the brig.

Within a few days, Hendrik returned with the dogs, two visitors, and enough rabbit and walrus meat to provide what Kane called "a supper for a king." The hardships of the past few months had made the captain "more charitable than I used to be with our Esquimaux neighbors," and he turned the smoke-dried cabin into a scene of feasting: "The day provides for itself; or, if it does not, we trust in the morrow, and are happy till tomorrow disappoints us."

Kane learned now that the Inuit of Netlik had suffered through a devastating winter. Since the arrival of the *Advance,* five of them had died. During the past winter, they had been forced to kill most of their dogs. "They are dying out," Kane wrote, "not lingeringly like the American tribes, but so rapidly as to be able to mark within a generation their progress towards extinction. Nothing can be more saddening."

Hendrik had brought along Metek, the headman of Etah, and a youth named Paulik. He had been unable to arrange the loan of any dogs. And he reported that Godfrey "was playing the great man at Etah, defying recapture." Kane decided to address this last situation first. He worried that Godfrey might influence his relations with the Inuit, and so resolved to recapture the deserter.

Kane left Paulik on the *Advance* with Hendrik and, on April 10, having hidden a six-shooter in his clothes, set out for Etah with Metek. Approaching the settlement after a cold, hard journey, Kane pulled his hood over his head to disguise himself as Paulik. The people of the village emerged to welcome the returning hunters, William Godfrey among them, waving his arms and shouting *"Tima!"* as loudly as the rest. "An instant later," Kane wrote, "and I was at his ear, with a short phrase of salutation and its appropriate gesture."

According to Kane, Godfrey yielded unconditionally at once. "He could have crushed me, but he was completely tamed and could not even meet my eye. I even went so far as to order him to clean my pistol; he received it trembling, cleaned, loaded, and returned it to me like a humble lackey. This giving my pistol was a piece of acting on my part. I don't think Bill will attempt my life any more."

The rebellious sailor later offered a different scenario. He wrote that Kane arrived "very much fatigued and very cold," and that he helped remove his clothes, chafed his limbs, and put him to bed. When, after sleeping for several hours, Kane awoke, the two men talked. As in the previous example, much of the discussion is transparently fictitious. This much is certain: Kane told Godfrey that he must return to the brig. The sailor may well have argued that his engagement had dissolved, which meant he was no longer subject to naval discipline. And it is possible that, as Godfrey claims, Kane responded: "These are questions for lawyers to decide; but until a legal decision is given, you are bound to obey my orders. And your refusal to come on board is mutiny."

Both men were trying to reach an understanding. As revealed earlier in his narrative, Godfrey was feeling bored and homesick. Lacking books, all he had to do was smoke a pipe he had made out of the marrowbone of a seal. Now, in answer to questioning, he told Kane that he intended to travel to Upernavik with Metek, as the Inuk "was inclined to visit that place and had offered to convey me thither in his dog-sledge." From there, Godfrey would make his way to the United States.

According to Godfrey, Kane responded: "I am now making preparations to return to our own country, and I find that your assistance is indispensable. It will be much better for you to go home with your comrades, and I now ask you, as a *friend,* to accompany me back to the brig." Apparently, Godfrey now answered without hesitation, "Dr. Kane, since you ask me as a friend, I will go with you."

In *Arctic Explorations,* Kane reports no such negotiation. But he did spend one week at Etah, during which time he went hunting with a group that included Godfrey. Kane suggests that he compelled the seaman to return to the brig, and writes that Godfrey, "after walking and running by turns for some eighty miles before the sledge, with a short respite at Anoatok, is now a prisoner on board." This would appear to be an exaggeration. But Kane did compel Godfrey to abandon his mutiny, return to the *Advance,* and resume his duties. And the captain, with his crew intact and summer coming on, turned his attention to escaping the ice.

29

AWAY LIKE STEVEDORES

The people of Etah, among whom Kane lived for a week before he brought Godfrey back to the brig, belonged to four extended families. During the winter, they had retreated into two large huts buried in snow and completely enclosed except for vent holes. His arrival on April 11 sparked cries of welcome: "*Nalegak! Nalegak! Tima!*" The captain followed Metek through a *tossut* that ran an extraordinary thirty paces. On reaching the hut, a vault measuring fifteen feet by six, he discovered that several other guests had preceded him—"six sturdy denizens of the neighboring settlement" who had been caught by a storm while hunting.

The sudden change in temperature, from 40 degrees below zero to 90 degrees above, would alone have proved overwhelming, but Kane also found himself "gasping the ammoniacal steam of some fourteen vigorous, amply fed, unwashed, unclothed fellow lodgers." This amorphous mass of humanity included men, women, and children sleeping "with nothing but their native dirt to cover them, twined and dovetailed together like the worms in a fishing-basket." The exhausted Kane ate some frozen liver-nuts that Godfrey handed him, and then, "bursting into a profuse perspiration, stripped like the rest, threw my well-tired carcass across Mrs. Eider-duck's extremities, put her left-hand baby under my armpit, pillowed my head on Myouk's somewhat warm stomach, and thus, an honored guest and in the place of honor, fell asleep."

During the next several days, while joining in settlement life, Kane also functioned as an ethnologist, and took notes on the habits and customs of the Greenlanders. In *Arctic Explorations,* he would devote more than twenty pages to elaborating on these, touching on everything from eating utensils to mourning rituals, religious beliefs, and the perquisites of the *Nalegak-soak* or head chief, who enjoyed "the questionable privilege of having as many wives as he could support." He noted that, as with some Asiatic and North American Indian tribes, the practice of carrying off a bride by force was "common among the Esquimaux, and reluctantly abandoned" even by those converted to Christianity by Lutheran or Moravian missionaries.

Like eighteenth-century explorer Samuel Hearne, who traveled with a group of Chipewyan Dene, Kane felt drawn to *angekoks,* or prophets, all of whom believed in their own supernatural powers. "I have known several of them personally," he wrote, "after my skill in pow-wow had given me a sort of correlative rank among them, and can speak with confidence on this point. I could not detect them in any resort to jugglery or natural magic. . . . They have, however, like the members of the learned professions every-where, a certain language or jargon of their own, in which they communi-cate with each other." During this week, Kane also drew sketches that later he would develop into etchings for his book. At some point, using musical notation, and as evidenced in the archives at the American Philosophical Society, he went so far as to transcribe "An Eskimo Round" for six voices.

o　　o　　o

Kane was out hunting walrus near Lifeboat Cove, sharing a sledge with young Myouk, when Hendrik arrived carrying a note from Isaac Hayes. On reading that McGary had become seriously ill, Kane cut short his hunt-ing trip and, with Godfrey and a sledge load of meat, hurried back to the *Advance.* Before racing home, Kane sent Hendrik south to Peteravik on

While sheltering among the Inuit in snowhuts or igloos, Elisha Kane sketched his surroundings and also took notes on the habits and customs of the Greenlanders, focusing on everything from eating utensils to religious beliefs.

Northumberland Island, where the people formerly of Netlik had established a new settlement. The Inuit of Etah had no dogs to spare, but he hoped that Kalutunah and his people might have some. He sent along a valuable iron capstan bar as a gift and an inducement to Kalutunah, whom he regarded as the most cultivated of the Inuit he had met.

On April 24, less than a week after Kane got back to the *Advance*, Hendrik arrived with three men, an astonishing sixteen dogs, and three sledges equipped with harpoons, lances, and other equipment. Kalutunah and two of his fellows, Shang-hu and Tatterat, explained that they were engaged in a polar-bear hunt. With McGary recovered and his own preparations for departure going smoothly, Kane recognized their arrival as an opportunity to travel north beyond Humboldt Glacier, and perhaps to see the channel leading to the Open Polar Sea. He fed the visitors and allowed them to sleep, and then asked to join them on their northward sortie. The following morning, together with Hendrik and the three visitors, Kane set off "with a wild yell of dogs and men in chorus."

After a couple of hours, fifteen miles north of the brig, the hunters reached a towering iceberg where last year Kane had broken through onto a smooth plain. Now the outside channel lay thick with squeezed ice that led only to a jumble of hummocks. Still, the Inuit agreed to forge ahead, and by running along beside the sledges, the men reached a more open area. Thirty miles north of the brig, and the same distance east of the Greenland coast, they stopped to rest.

While cutting away meat, Tatterat discovered a tallow ball that some of the crew had hidden in Kane's sledge as a surprise treat—without the captain's knowledge, but clearly intended for his personal use. Soon the whole party, including Kane, sat feasting on this succulent mixture of liver and cooked muscle—everyone but Hendrik. He felt so "indignant at the liberty taken with my provender," Kane wrote, "[that he] refused to share in the work of demolishing it. My ten-pound ball vanished nevertheless in scarcely as many minutes."

After lunch, the men resumed driving north. Near the northern coastline, and about thirty miles from the central peak of the Three Brother Turrets, Kane perceived a band of stratus clouds hanging over the horizon toward the Kennedy Channel—a clear indication that the waterway remained open. But the hunters had been spotting more and more bear tracks. And now, somewhat to Kane's dismay, the dogs surprised a large polar bear devouring a seal. At that instant, he lost of control of the expedition, becoming part of a howling, pell-mell chase—"the dogs, wolves; the drivers, devils."

After a furious run, the dogs brought the polar bear to bay. The men did their work with lance and rifle, then gorged themselves and buried the remains of the huge carcass for later retrieval. They spent a cold night on the open ice, during which Kalutunah, seeing that Kane was shivering, took his *kapetah* from his back and wrapped it around the *kablunah*'s feet—a gesture that the captain "appreciated very sensibly at the time."

Next day, Kane urged his companions to the northwest. They, however, had discovered bear tracks leading east toward the Greenland coast and insisted on making for the Great Glacier of Humboldt. Kane remonstrated, pleaded, and protested, but Kalutunah pointed out that the men needed bear meat for their families: "It was a strong argument," Kane had to admit, "and withal the argument of the strong."

If he could not proceed north, Kane wished to return to the brig, where perhaps, even now, he could negotiate with Metek for the loan of some dogs. But even this was not to be, as the hunters remained intent on finding more bears. When this endeavor brought the captain closer than ever before to Humboldt Glacier, he felt somewhat mollified: "I had not fully realized the spectacle of this stupendous monument of frost. I had seen it for some hours hanging over ice like a white-mist cloud, but now it rose up before me clearly defined and almost precipitous."

Kane debarked and, while the hunters chased polar bears, sat absorbed with the spectacle of an ice wall that rose 300 feet into the air. Intrigued by "the escaladed structure of the Arctic glacier," he worked away at his sketchbook and took notes. Ultimately, he would devote pages of *Arctic Explorations* to analyzing glaciers and icebergs.

After a couple more nights on the ice, during which he got caught up in further bear hunts, Kane persuaded Kalutunah to return to the brig. The hunters spent one night on the *Advance* and then headed for home. Kalutunah left three dogs on loan, one from each team, and promised to solicit additional animals from Metek. Kane felt pleased to have earned the trust of these people, "at first so suspicious and distrustful." Clearly, he had come some distance from the drawing rooms of aristocratic Philadelphia.

Soon after the three hunters left, Hendrik approached Kane "with a long face" and asked permission to travel south to Peteravik. He wished to acquire some walrus hide for boots. He declined the offer of dogs, insisting that the weather was fine and that he could walk the eighty or ninety miles, resting at Etah. The commander consented, but then waited in vain for his return.

For a while, he worried. But then he gleaned that Hendrik had formed an attachment to a young woman named Mersuk, the daughter of Shang-hu. "Hans was a favorite with all," Kane wrote later, "the fair especially, and, as a match, one of the greatest men in the country." He continued to inquire after him, because "independent of everything like duty, I was very fond of him." Yet the rumors proved true. And alluding to the young man's previous attachment, Kane wrote: "Hans the faithful—yet I fear faithless—was last seen upon a native sledge, with a maiden at his side, and professedly bound for a new principality at Uwarrow Suk-suk, high up Murchison's Sound. Alas for Hans, the married man!"

Later, Hans Hendrik would tell a slightly different story. "Eventually, my companions began to think of abandoning their vessel and repairing to Upernavik," he would write. "I did not believe they would be able to reach it." When, while visiting Etah, he fell sick, the local men "behaved so kindly towards me, I began to think of remaining with them." Still, he says that when he went off for the last time, he intended to return. But the men of Etah "began persuading me to remain. My companions would never reach Upernavik, they said, and they would take me along with them when they removed."

In further justification of abandoning his companions, Hendrik writes, "A pity it was that our Master behaved with haughtiness towards our crew." In offering a single, confused example, he is clearly recalling the arguments Petersen had put forward for defection. Hendrik writes that he had cut off the head of a reindeer skin for sledge meat. He approached Petersen, who was out for a walk, and told him, "The Master intends to shoot me for having cut the head from a reindeer-skin. That is the only reason." Petersen told him: "Don't be afraid. He will never shoot you. I am going to say to him: we have another skin." Hendrik waited on the ice, and eventually Petersen returned and said: "There is no reason for you to be afraid, only remain with us. I will be your protector."

From this point on, Hendrik writes, he "thought more and more of leaving them when they started for Upernavik." Still, when Kane let him depart again, "it was my intention to return. But I began to envy the natives with whom I stayed, who supplied themselves with all their wants and lived happily." He insists that he did not began to think of taking a wife until he had lived several winters with the Etah natives: "First, I went a-wooing to a girl of good morals, but I gave her up, as her father said: 'Take my sister.' The latter was a widow and ill-reputed. Afterwards, I got a sweetheart whom I resolved never to part with, but to keep as my wife in the country of the Christians. Since then, she has been baptized and partaken of the Lord's Supper."

Here, again, various versions of a story become hard to reconcile. Possibly, Hendrik was fudging only the timeline: the "girl of good morals" could well be Mersuk, and the father Shang-hu. More likely, "Mersuk" was the woman Meqru, who married Hendrik, and became the mother of his children. This much is certain: Kane never saw his young friend again. And twice more, starting in 1860 and 1870, Hendrik sailed north with American explorers. On both expeditions, he brought Meqru and their children, the fourth of whom would be born at God Harbor in Greenland, nearer the Pole than any other child.

o　　o　　o

By the spring of 1855, the *Advance* could no longer be saved. During the winter, out of necessity, the men had reduced even the beams to fuel. Yet they had preserved enough wood for Christian Ohlsen to construct two sledges seventeen feet, six inches in length. Late in April, Kane set a departure date. Starting on May 17, using the new sledges, the men would haul the two whaleboats south to open water. They would use a smaller sledge, the rebuilt *Faith,* to haul the *Red Eric.*

Meanwhile, Kane himself would ferry provisions and equipment to Anoatok, using that rough shelter as a staging post. For this activity, he hoped to have the help of Hans Hendrik. Either way, four men—Wilson, Goodfellow, Whipple, and Stephenson—could not walk. Kane would transport them by dogsled, first to Anoatok, and then to the edge of the ice pack, eighty miles away. With preparations proceeding well, Kane assembled his officers—"by which I mean the old stock who abided by the brig"—and announced one final attempt to search the west coast for any trace of Franklin. With this last sortie, he hoped also, of course, to explore the Kennedy Channel.

The Inuit leader Metek, less sympathetic than Kalutunah, had brought no dogs. But after detailing the work to be performed in his absence, Kane took those animals he had and, using the lightest sledge, set out across the ice with William Morton, his most trusted lieutenant. Before long, the two encountered rough ice and high hummocks. They beat forward but, after several harsh nights, admitted defeat and turned back. They reached the brig with Morton broken down and Kane exhausted. Lacking time or energy to detail this last sortie in his journal, Kane would later summarize the end result: "The operations of the search were closed."

Focusing exclusively on the projected evacuation, and determined to avoid anything resembling the debacle in which the defection had culminated, Kane organized everything from the cooking apparatus to the arms and ammunition. He put Ohlsen in charge of the boats. Despite the man's unparalleled abilities as a carpenter, however, and the able assistance of McGary and Bonsall, nobody could confidently declare even one of the three vessels seaworthy.

The two whaleboats—twenty feet long, seven wide, three deep—had been battered by exposure to snow and ice. Ohlsen had reinforced the bottoms and fitted them with a neat housing of light canvas and provided each with a mast that could be unshipped and carried with the oars, boathooks, and ice poles. Yet the planking of both remained so dry that it could hardly be made tight by caulking. The third boat, the little *Red Eric,* was small enough to be mounted on the old sledge, the *Faith,* and could eventually be cut up for firewood.

For cooking equipment, Kane had called on Petersen, the best tinker on the expedition. The Greenlander used old stovepipe to create two portable stoves: iron cylinders fourteen inches in diameter and eighteen inches high.

He fitted these with iron saucers in which travelers could create a roaring fire by using melted pork fat for fuel and spun yarn for a wick. As well, Petersen had fashioned an entire dinner service out of meat-biscuit canisters.

Under Kane's direction, various men had pounded ship's bread into a more portable powder using a capstan bar. They melted pork fat and tallow, poured the resulting mixture into bags, and allowed it to freeze. They placed both flour and meat biscuit into double bags to protect against moisture. For additional sustenance, they would rely on their guns. Kane put Bonsall in charge of arms and ammunition, and of distributing powder and shot. And he himself kept the percussion cups.

With the departure date looming, Kane allowed each man twenty-four hours to select and prepare eight pounds of personal effects. During the preceding weeks, some of the scurvy-ridden crew had begun sewing important articles of apparel, only to throw them down "in a sick man's pet." Kane quietly assigned others to finish these items. Each man had woolen underclothes and a complete fur suit in the Inuit style, including *kapetah, nessak,* and *nannooke,* or shirt, hood, and trousers. Each had one pair of canvas boots faced with walrus hide, and another made of carpeting. Each carried extra socks and a rue-raddy—a long canvas strap for hauling, adjusted to the proper length. Kane had also stipulated such personal kit items as Inuit-style goggles to protect against snow blindness; sleeping bags of buffalo fur; eiderdown quilts covered in waterproof canvas; and canvas bags for personal effects, all of them numbered to avoid confusion.

By now, the captain had wrapped the expedition records in waterproof bags. Compelled to abandon his heavy theodolite, Kane boxed and padded the chronometers and wrapped them in sheets. He also packed his extensive natural-history collections, though he would have to abandon these, with deep regret, along the way.

Despite these extensive preparations for departure, some men remained sunk in a skeptical lethargy, and the captain felt displeased "with the moody indifference with which many went about the tasks to which I put them." Some of the men doubted his purpose. They whispered that he intended only to transport the sick to the hunting grounds farther south, retaining the brig as a retreat. A few thought he meant to establish a camp on some promontory, and wait there for rescue by whalers or searchers.

On May 17, as Kane had planned, the men stored the provisions on the sledges, adjusted the whaleboats to their cradles, and began hauling both to the ice belt. Initially, the men showed little spirit or enthusiasm; yet after they had struggled through the first day, their tone improved. Everyone delighted in seeing "our little arks of safety hauled upon the higher plain of the ice foot." There the boats sat trimmed with jaunty little flags Kane had made using an old linen shirt, red strips of paper, and pieces cut from a blue bag. That evening, for supper, he provided a minor feast, and the men turned in feeling good.

Over the next couple of days, though the weather remained superb, the crews hauled the boat-laden sledges only a few miles, and returned each night to sleep on the brig. The captain realized that the men were unaccustomed to hard exercise, and took care not to push them too hard.

On Sunday, May 20, 1855, Kane summoned all hands into the dismantled winter cabin to say a formal goodbye to the brig. The moss walls had been torn down and the wood supports burned. Most of the bedding had been stored on the boats and the galley sat cold and empty. In these bleak surroundings, Kane said a prayer, read a chapter from the Bible, and took down the inspirational portrait of Sir John Franklin. Having removed the picture from its frame, he cased it for protection in an India-rubber scroll. Then he read aloud the officers' reports of their final inspections of the *Advance,* describing its dilapidated condition and explaining the need to abandon ship.

Kane assured the men that they could overcome difficulties by energy and subordination to command, and reminded them that their first duty was to protect the sick and wounded. He had one of the officers draw up a note of engagement, duly signed by all hands: "The undersigned, being convinced of the impossibility of the liberation of the brig, and equally convinced of the impossibility of remaining in the ice a third winter, do fervently concur with the commander in his attempt to reach the South by boats." The men pledged to travel in a spirit of union, harmony, and discipline, and to abide by the expedition and their sick comrades.

To a stanchion near the foot of the gangway, Kane fixed a note justifying the abandonment of the vessel and explaining that "a third winter would force us . . . to resort to Esquimaux habits and give up all hope of remaining by the vessel and her resources. It would therefore in no manner advance the search after Sir John Franklin."

After saying a temporary goodbye to the four invalids who could not walk and would, for a while, remain on the brig, all the other hands went up on deck. Kane hoisted and saluted the American flag, then hauled it down for the last time. The men proceeded down the gangway and, walking around the brig for a last look, proposed to take along the brig's figurehead—"the fair Augusta, the little blue girl with pink cheeks, who had lost her breast by an iceberg and her nose by a nip off Bedevilled Reach." When he hesitated about adding the weight, the men pointed out that Augusta was made of wood, "and if we cannot carry her far we can burn her."

Kane dispensed with further ceremony. He believed that cheers would be a mockery and, lacking alcohol, proposed no final toast. "When all hands were quite ready," he would write, "we scrambled off over the ice together, much like a gang of stevedores going to work over a quayful of broken cargo."

30

THE ICE TAKES A MAN

Determined to maintain discipline, the lack of which had doomed the defection, Elisha Kent Kane established clear lines of control. He gave Henry Brooks command of both whaleboats and specific responsibility for the *Faith,* and he put Isaac Hayes in charge of the *Hope.* To Brooks he assigned James McGary, Christian Ohlsen, Amos Bonsall, Carl Petersen, and Thomas Hickey. With Hayes, he placed William Morton, August Sonntag, George Riley, John Blake, and William Godfrey. These groups would cook and eat separately.

Kane assigned each man a fixed place in the drag lines, and ordered everyone except the whaleboat captains to take a turn at cooking. Hayes would maintain the logbook, and Sonntag would handle observations. On realizing, even before departure, that six worn-down men could not hope to haul the heavily laden sledges, Kane stipulated that the entire party (with, initially, three exceptions) would first haul one sledge and then the other. They would slog three miles to accomplish one, fifteen to advance five.

By May 24, the men had moved both whaleboats to First Ravine, seven miles from the *Advance.* That night, instead of returning, they began a routine of sleeping beside the boats beneath canvas housing. The next day, having patched and caulked the *Red Eric,* Ohlsen, Petersen, and Morton hauled it across the ice and joined the rotation. Temperatures remained below zero, though now the sun scarcely set. To avoid glare, the men slept by day and traveled through the twilight hours.

In the absence of Hendrik, Kane alone began moving the four invalids, one by one, to Anoatok. He had already led several men in refurbishing the rough stone shelter, to which the men had added a door and a stove-pipe. They had cleaned the stone platform, covered it with shavings, and laid down cushions and blankets. They hung tapestries over the walls and inserted a rough pane of glass in the door. If this "gloomy hospital" looked more like a cave than a human habitation, as Kane admitted, yet it sig-naled inclusion, and would prove far less depressing than remaining on the deserted brig.

Ultimately, Kane believed that the refuge hut at Anoatok saved the lives of the invalids. When he began transporting them, three of the men— Goodfellow, Wilson, and Whipple—were suffering so severely from scurvy that they remained flat on their backs. Wilson's stump had yet to heal, and Whipple's tendons were so contracted that he could not extend his legs. Only Stephenson could crawl around to melt snow, warm food, and keep lamps burning. Had Kane tried to move these men forward in tandem with the boat sledges, he probably would have jeopardized their lives.

Using six dogs and a light sledge, Kane also shuttled provisions from the brig to Anoatok, until the total reached 1,500 pounds—as much as the two boats could carry. During the first fortnight after departure, he traveled roughly fifty-seven miles a day. By checking frequently on the invalids, he kept their spirits up. As temperatures rose, the invalids gained strength, and eventually they could crawl out of the shelter, sit in the sun, and breathe fresh air.

One night, Kane was shuttling between stations when the dogs gave out. He slept on the rocks in below-zero temperatures, alone and unprotected. Next morning, when finally he approached the boat haulers, he felt a pang to see how wearily they moved—Brooks with his swollen legs, Hayes stum-

Hauling boats across the ice belt was always dangerous. But when heavy snows and widening chasms forced Kane and his men out among the ever-shifting floes, the journey south became increasingly perilous.

bling along on his stumps, all the men so obviously weakened by scurvy.

Happily, some Inuit friends from Etah, having discovered the evacuation in progress, had begun lending a hand without being asked. Already, an older man, Nessark, had used his dogs to transport supplies, and helped Kane bake bread on the brig. Now, realizing that to keep working, the men needed fresh meat and bread, the captain divided the dogs. He sent William Godfrey south to Etah to trade for walrus meat, while he and Morton returned to the brig, where they lit fires, melted pork, and baked a large batch of bread.

At Anoatok, while returning to the whaleboats in a gale, the two found the lamps out, the shelter dark, and the invalids weak, hungry, and disheartened. They built a fire, dried the bedding, and prepared a porridge of meat biscuit and pea soup, then refastened the door in the frame and crafted some new lamp wicks. They talked and laughed with the invalids into the night, and with the snow blowing hard, kept burning rope and fat in "a regular tea-drinking frolic, till not an icicle or even a frost-mark was to be seen on the roof."

Godfrey arrived with Metek and two sledge loads of meat. Those two now remained at Anoatok to rest, while Kane hurried to the whaleboats carrying bread and meat. Next, with Metek and Morton, Kane revisited the brig to bake more bread. While continuing to bake, he sent Metek to the whaleboats with 150 pounds of bread and a letter directing Brooks to send him back for another load. "It was something like a breach of faith," Kane admitted, "but his services were indispensable, his dogs more so."

With the sun climbing higher each day, temperatures rose and the ice belt softened. On June 5, the sledge carrying the *Hope* crashed through the ice and dragged six men into the water. They managed to crawl onto the ice, but Kane began to worry that he might be cut off from the relief hut at Anoatok. He decided to move the stores forward to two temporary stations—one on a headland, Navialik, opposite Cape Hatherton, the other on the level ice plain near Littleton Island. To the latter he sent Metek with 180 pounds of bread dust, and he himself transported 300 pounds of food to Navialik.

Heavy snow and widening chasms rendered the ice belt almost impassible. Driven out onto the floes, Kane saw with growing concern that the ice had become sodden and stained with water from below. Besides the loads in transit, nearly 900 pounds of provisions remained at Anoatok, and 200 pounds more, including shot and bullet bags, waited to be removed from Cape Hatherton. Kane recalled Robinson Crusoe and his powder, and wondered: "Good God! What will become of us if all this is destroyed?"

He decided to ask the people of Etah to lend him two of their four dogs. He sent word ordering the invalids at Anoatok to be ready for instant removal and pressed on to Etah, arriving near midnight with the sun low in the sky. Despite the temperature, 5 degrees below zero, he found thirty people gathered outside on the bare rocks. Melting snow had reduced their huts to a shambles, so now they camped out, variously socializing, sleeping, cooking auks, or chomping on bird skins. Around old Kresut, the blind patriarch of the settlement, men, women, and children formed a coil "as perplexing to unravel as a skein of eels."

By now, Kane knew these people well. And before he could say a word, Aningnah, an influential woman he had helped with a medical problem, "summarily banished" poor Kresut from the seat of honor to install the exhausted *nalegak*. Having learned not to question the privileges of rank, Kane accepted some auk livers, a *kapetah* coverlet, and a two-year-old child as a pillow, and soon drifted into sleep. In the morning, he left his tired dogs and took the settlement's only team in an unequal exchange. Old Nessark piled Kane's sledge with walrus meat, and two young men came partway to assist him through the broken ice between Littleton Island and the mainland.

Though he did not stay long at Etah, Kent took a morning walk with an insistent youngster to a playground where laughing boys were engaged in sport. "Each of them had a walrus rib for a *golph* or *shinny-stick*, and they were contending to drive a *hurley*, made out of the round knob of a flipper-joint, up a bank of frozen snow." Kane found the sight curious: "Strange that these famine-pinched wanderers of the ice should rejoice in sports and playthings like the children of our own smiling sky, and that parents should fashion for them toy sledges, and harpoons, and nets, miniature emblems of a life of suffering and peril! How strange this joyous merriment under the monitory shadow of these jagged ice-cliffs."

Later, in his book, Kane would describe, admiringly and in detail, how the "rude Esquimaux of these icy solitudes" measure their lives in winters, as the American Indians measure theirs in summers. He would remember familiar faces with melancholy: "It pains me when I think of their approaching destiny,—in the region of night and winter, where the earth yields no fruit and the waters are locked,—without the resorts of skill or even the rude materials of art, and walled in from the world by barriers of ice without an outlet."

Along the way, Kane prepared a census, "exactly confirmed by three separate informants," that identified 140 souls scattered along the 600 miles of coast from the Great River near Cape Melville to the wind-loved hut of Anoatok. Within this narrow range, he wrote, the people exist "in love and community of resources as a single family." They situated their huts one dog-march apart. They named each rock and hill, so even the youngest hunter could go to retrieve a cache of meat deposited anywhere in the region.

But now, Kane had no time to reflect. From Etah, with fresh dogs and a sledge-load of meat, he raced back to the whaleboats, which had arrived within three miles of Anoatok. Warmer weather, improved hunting and diet, and increased exercise had made all the men healthier—but also hungrier. Some food remained on the brig. But, more urgently still, Kane needed to move the portable stores from Anoatok to the stations farther south. So, assigning that task and the requisite dogs to Petersen and Godfrey, he took young Thomas Hickey, who had previously worked as a baker, and walked back to the brig—a trek of sixteen hours. With Hickey, he sacrificed the *Penny Cyclopedia of Useful Knowledge* to the flames, and converted all the remaining flour into bread.

As arranged, Godfrey arrived with the dogs to transport the bread. For a couple of days, a howling gale confined the three men to the brig. But then they made their way south, calling first at Anoatok, where they found the invalids stronger and more cheerful. At the whaleboats, the men were still recovering from the storm. During the past week, each man had consumed three pounds of food a day. They had eaten all their meat and most of their bread. Kane thought fleetingly of reducing rations, but for men working this hard, that remained out of the question. He would return to Etah and seek more food.

During the storm, six Inuit, including three women, had taken refuge at the whaleboats. With them and Petersen, Kane set out for Etah. The party made slow progress, as they were forced to circle around great patches of discolored ice. As the travelers neared Littleton Island, yet another storm broke—one of the fiercest gales Kane had ever experienced. "It had the character and force of a cyclone. The dogs were literally blown from their harness, and it was only by throwing ourselves on our faces that we saved ourselves from being swept away."

A brief lull enabled the travelers to scramble to the cliffs of a tiny island, where they huddled against the rock face in the howling whiteness, unable to see each other or the dogs. The captain realized they must move or die. With Petersen protesting and the ice cracking and breaking, Kane led the way across a windblown channel to the mainland, where a dark rock thirty feet high formed a barricade that created a great drift of snow. The travelers burrowed into this. They dragged the dogs and sledges in behind them, and soon found themselves "so roofed in and quilted round that the storm seemed to rage far outside of us."

Here at "Cape Misery" the group huddled, cramped and seething, and enduring more than one dogfight, until hunger drove them back out into the waning but still powerful storm. Unable to beat south against the gale, the eight retreated with the wind toward the whaleboats, completing the floundering, forty-mile journey in twenty hours.

By the time the storm abated and the sun again stood high in the sky, the food shortage had grown acute. Etah remained the best hope for help, and the exhausted Kane, unable to travel himself, sent the trusted Morton south with two of the Inuit, Marsumah and Nessark. Meanwhile, the sledgers resumed hauling the whaleboats with new urgency. The snowfields were saturated and damp, and large areas around frozen icebergs were dotted with pools. Again a sledge broke through the ice, dragging six men into the water, and only a desperate struggle saved the *Hope* from sinking forever.

Increasingly fearful of getting cut off from Anoatok, Kane sent Nessark with his dogs to bring Goodfellow forward and begin shuttling invalids. The next day, Morton returned from Etah. The settlement had responded to Kane's brotherly appeal, and he brought men, sledges piled with meat and blubber, and every sound dog that remained. Once again, Kane controlled a serviceable dog team: "The comfort and security of such a possession to men in our critical position can hardly be realized," he would write. "It was more than an addition of ten strong men to our party."

With Metek and two dog sledges, Kane set off immediately—first for the *Advance,* to fetch the last bit of burnable pork fat, so necessary to the looming boat journey, and then for Anoatok, to retrieve the sick men. Traveling along beneath the cliffs, he marveled at the dramatic changes in the landscape. The hot sun released rocks that had been frozen into the ice, and they rolled down the debris-strewn slopes "with the din of a battle-field . . . clogging the ice-belt at the foot."

At Anoatok, having retrieved all he could from the *Advance,* and having sent Metek straight back with a full load, Kane took Stephenson onto his heavily loaded sledge, leaving only Wilson and Whipple to be removed. As he drew within a few miles of the whaleboats, Kane began worrying when he came upon a gaping hole in the ice where some accident had obviously occurred. Then he noticed a lone figure reclining against a large chunk of ice near the sledge track. As he drew near, he recognized Christian Ohlsen, white-faced and faint with pain.

Ohlsen told Kane to carry on, and pointed toward the whaleboats, now halted three miles ahead. In a faint voice, he explained that he had injured himself slightly, but had refused to detain the party. He "had a little cramp in the small of the back" but would soon recover. Unable to walk, yet downplaying his injury, the carpenter had insisted that his companions keep dragging the sledges, and promised to catch up. Seeing his condition, and with Stephenson agreeing to wait, Kane took Ohlsen onto his sledge and drove him to the whaleboats. There, muffling him in buffalo robes, he installed Ohlsen in the stern sheets of the *Faith.*

After retrieving Stephenson, Kane learned the full story from others. A couple of hours before he arrived, while the men crossed a tide hole, a sledge runner had broken through the thin ice. The sledge started to slide into the water, bringing the *Hope* down with it. Ohlsen managed to pass a capstan bar under the rear of the sledge and hold its weight while the men struggled to haul it out. He was a strong man, and might well have managed, but his footing gave way beneath him, forcing him, as Kane understood it, "to make a still more desperate effort to extricate himself."

That night, despite constant attention, Ohlsen failed to improve. And during the next couple of days, he grew worse. He refused to eat and complained of pains in his back and a "paralysis of the bladder." On June 12, after weeping for his wife and young child, Christian Ohlsen passed away.

Kane wrote that, from the first, Ohlsen's symptoms bore "a certain obscure but fatal resemblance to our winter's tetanus, which filled us with forebodings." Decades later, drawing on more advanced medical knowledge, Dr. George Corner would suggest that Ohlsen had suffered the collapse of a lumbar vertebra that had been weakened by a loss of calcium due to malnutrition. He surmised that this had led to the crushing of the spinal cord and acute spinal shock—fatal in this instance because Ohlsen, like the other men, had been weakened by extended exposure to cold, harsh conditions.

At the whaleboats, the struggling men could spare no more than two hours to mourn their comrade—"a tried and courageous man," according to Kane, "who met his death in the gallant discharge of duty." The captain ordered the body sewn up in a blanket and carried in procession to the head of a small gorge on Littleton Island. Here, by digging furiously, the men gouged a trench out of the frozen earth. Kane had slipped away and, stealing sheet lead from the short supply necessary to repair the leaky boats, chiseled the carpenter's name and age into a small tablet: Christian Ohlsen, age thirty-six—which he placed on the dead man's chest.

Kane ordered the remains covered with rocks to protect against bears and foxes, and named the nearest landmark "Cape Ohlsen." He had long since got over chagrin at the carpenter's near-defection. He knew that the sensitive, talented Ohlsen had been one of his most capable and valuable hands, and mourned him deeply. If any of the remaining men retained illusions about the stakes involved in this desperate dash for safety, they died with Ohlsen. Nobody could fail to understand that, in this unpredictable barrens, one of the most extreme environments on earth, they were fighting for their lives.

31

An Incredible Journey

On June 16, 1855, four days after the death of Christian Ohlsen, Kane and his men began stowing cargo in their boats at the mouth of the bay near Etah, less than a mile from open water and roughly three miles from Cape Alexander. The men had been steadily hauling for one month, except for a brief spell when, with a breeze blowing from the north, they managed to sail across a stretch of smooth ice, using the long steering oars as booms. Thrilling to this new sensation, the men broke into song: "Storm along, my hearty boys!"

But mostly they had slogged ahead, battling hummocks and snowdrifts with capstan bars and levers, or proceeding carefully over "salt ice marshes" scattered with threatening black pools. Without the help of the Inuit, Kane wrote, the escape might have foundered. The local people supplied the visitors with enormous numbers of small auks, which men and dogs together consumed at a rate of 8,000 a week. Once, when a sledge sank so deeply into the ice that the whaleboat floated loose, five Inuit men and two women worked with the sailors for more than half a day, asking nothing in return. Sip-su and old Nessark used their dogs to visit Anoatok and fetch Wilson and Whipple, the last of the waiting invalids.

Even so, disaster threatened always. One day, Kane heard some of his men hollering for help: the *Red Eric* had slipped beneath the ice. Scrambling toward them, he realized that the tiny craft contained all the expedition documents—logbooks, journals, meteorological records, even collections of natural history. By the time he arrived, Blake was standing knee-deep in icy sludge with a line around his waste, groping for the documents box, and a soaking-wet Bonsall was on his stomach, struggling to lay his hands on provision bags. Because the boat was light, other men were able to hold it steady and finally haul it onto the ice—at which point, spontaneously, they erupted into three cheers.

With all the boats, sledges, and men gathered together, a storm arose. But Kane had already covered the 1,400 pounds of food scattered about on the rocks, to keep it safe and dry. Virtually the whole settlement had come out to say goodbye—at this time, twenty-two men, women, and children. With blowing rain making departure impossible, Kane hiked into Etah to pay his respects to Kresut, the blind elder who had remained behind with two nurses. He listened to the old man's long farewell speech, and inquired one last time about Hans Hendrik. Kresut said the young man had gone traveling with Shang-hu and one of his grown sons, prompting Kane later to declare: "Lover as he was, and *nalegak* by the all-hail hereafter, joy go with him, for he was a right good fellow."

Back at the water's edge, moved by affection and gratitude, Kane distributed gifts among the people—mainly needles, thread, and items of clothing. He gave the greatest treasures, his surgical amputation knives, to Metek and Nessark. The sled dogs he donated to the community as a whole, taking only Toodlamik and Whitey into the boats: "I could not part with them, the leaders of my team." For the other men, the dogs were an insurance policy: "Meat on the hoof," McGary called them, "able to carry their own fat over the floes."

Some of the Inuit wept, and Kane felt his heart go out to them—"so long our neighbors, and of late so staunchly our friends." Without these people, he wrote, "our dreary journey would have been prolonged at least a fortnight, and we are so late even now that hours may measure our lives." Early on, relations had been difficult, and Kane believed that, driven by superstitious fears, some of the locals had considered treachery. "But the day of all this has passed away. When trouble came to us and to them, and we bent ourselves to their habits . . . then we were so blended in our interests as well as modes of life that every trace of enmity wore away."

With Petersen translating, Kane observed to Metek that his people had lately stolen nothing, though much of value had been scattered about on the rocks. The Inuit leader responded: "You have done us good. We are not hungry; we will not steal. You have done us good; we want to help you; we are friends."

As the wind continued to blow, Kane gathered "these desolate and con-fiding people" around him on the ice beach and spoke to them as to brothers and sisters. He told them that other groups of Inuit lived a few hundred miles to the south, where the cold was less intense, the season of daylight longer, and the hunting better. He told them that, if they acted boldly and carefully, in a few seasons of patient march, they could reach that more wel-coming environment. He implored them to make that march.

o   o   o

On the afternoon of June 19, the storm abated. The sea grew quiet and the sky cleared. At four o'clock, Kane and his men readied the boats, lashing the sledges and slinging them outside the gunwales. The three vessels were small and heavily laden. Split with frost, warped by sunshine, and open at the seams, they would need to be caulked repeatedly. In these frail craft, Kane proposed to sail almost 500 miles. With the sea looking smooth as a garden lake, and despite overhanging black nimbus clouds, the captain and his men pushed off from the ice beach. Stars and stripes flying, they were making for home.

Kane embarked in the *Faith* with McGary, Petersen, and Hickey, plus three men still in recovery: Stephenson, Whipple, and Wilson. In the *Hope*, Brooks commanded Hayes, Sonntag, Morton, Goodfellow, and Blake. And three men—Bonsall, Riley, and Godfrey—put to sea in the tiny *Red Eric.* Kane hoped to eat supper on Sutherland Island, just beyond Cape Alexander, but a freshening wind made landing impossible, so the men cooked and ate in the boats, then made for Hakluyt Island.

With the wind picking up, a choppy sea swamped the *Red Eric.* Riley and Godfrey scrambled aboard the *Faith,* and Bonsall joined those in the *Hope.* The men got a towrope onto the water-filled *Red Eric,* but now the *Hope* showed signs of leaking faster than the men could bail. Kane managed to find an inlet that led through the floes to Hakluyt Island, where the sailors raised a tent for the sick, caulked the leaky boats, and shot a few birds.

Back in the water on June 22, the men sailed through a snowstorm to Northumberland Island. Here, myriads of auks greeted them, "and we returned their greeting," Kane wrote, "by the appropriate invitation to our table." During the next couple of days, the three boats reached Cape Parry and then Fitz Clarence Rock, which the irrepressible Kane declared one of the most interesting monuments along this stretch of coast: "It rises from a field of ice like an Egyptian pyramid surmounted by an obelisk."

The next day, the sailors caught a favorable wind. To take full advantage, Kane remained at the steering oar in the *Faith* for sixteen hours straight. Still, the previous delays forced him to cut daily rations to what he then thought the minimum possible. Eating at intervals, each man would consume a broth comprising six ounces of bread dust and a walnut-size lump of tallow. They found their energies waning. After another couple of days, near Wolstenholme Sound, a heavy fog forced the men to take refuge in a crack in the ice along the shore. Here, they struggled so hard to haul the boats out of the water that they searched for some unusual impediment, and realized only when they found none how much hunger had reduced their collective strength.

A gale arose out of the northwest, driving a massive ice sheet toward their precarious resting place. Working furiously, the men hauled the boats higher and climbed into them. But the platform on whose edge they rested, an icy circle hundreds of yards in diameter, began shaking, cracking, and crumbling. Suddenly—and inexplicably, given the tumult—just as they expected to be crushed or flung into the water, the men found themselves floating free. Kane knew only that "in the midst of a clamor utterly inde-scribable, through which the braying of a thousand trumpets could no more have been heard than the voice of a man, we were shaken and raised and whirled and let down again in a swelling waste of broken hummocks, and, as the men grasped their boathooks in the stillness that followed, the boats eddied away in a tumultuous screed of ice and snow and water."

The boats were whirled along, the men powerless and catching the occa-sional glimpse of "the brazen headland that looked down on us through the snowy sky." At last the boats neared the rocky shore, and using their oars and boathooks, the men were able to regain some control. Finding themselves in a narrow channel, they rowed along beside a wall of belt ice, seeking a refuge. The gale rose and the driving ice stove a hole in the bot-tom of the *Hope,* carrying off part of her weather boarding. The men baled desperately, and finally the tide rose high enough that some of them could scramble onto the ice cliff.

Working together, the men pushed and dragged the boats up onto a nar-row shelf, and then into a deep, narrow gorge that opened in the cliffs. They had found a sheltering ice cave—a "crystal retreat." And as they shored up the last of the boats with ice blocks, they heard a sound that brought tears to their eyes: eider ducks whooshing past in such numbers that their breed-ing grounds had to be nearby. During the next three days, while outside the storm raged, the men scouted around from "Weary Man's Rest" and col-lected duck eggs at a rate of 1,200 a day. Never, Kane wrote, could one hope to find "a merrier set of gourmands."

On July 4, after marking American Independence Day by quaffing a "patriotic eggnog," the men resumed their southward voyage. Rowing and sailing in the open lane between the pack and the ice belt, the men made slow progress for a week. Then they reached an impassable wall of ice—the side of a great tongue protruding from a glacial mass. For sixteen hours, they tried to work around or through the berg-strewn ice to seaward.

The men hauled the boats onto a narrow shelf and then into a gorge in the cliffs, a "crystal retreat" Kane dubbed Weary Man's Rest. They stayed three days while a storm raged, collecting ducks eggs at a rate of 1,200 a day.

Finally, they hauled the boats onto the ice and rested. Kane climbed an iceberg to a height of 200 feet. Looking west, he perceived a possible lead. But then, from Brooks and McGary, he learned that the boats—especially the *Hope*—could not proceed without repairs.

The birds and eider ducks so numerous at Weary Man's Rest were nowhere to be found, probably dispersed by the storm. Once again, Kane was forced to put the men on short rations. The lead had disappeared and he decided to remain inshore and battle the barricades of ice in hopes of finding game. The men spent fifty-two hours dragging the boats across the tongue of ice—terrible work that succeeded, according to Kane, only because of "the disciplined endurance of the men."

Once across the ice barrier, the men resumed sailing south. Approaching Cape Dudley Digges, they came upon yet another tongue of ice, this one extending still farther out to sea than the one they had just crossed. Because the men were so weak, Kane resolved to sail around it. He tried forcing the boats into the only available lead, which was filled with icy sludge, and found the craft too frail and weather-beaten to make headway.

Again, Kane climbed the tallest iceberg. Looking south, he could see as far as Cape York, which marked the northern end of Melville Bay. Across hundreds of square miles, Kane could see no open water—nothing but pack ice. Later, he would write: "My eyes never looked on a spectacle more painful."

o   o   o

The advancing summer, Kane fervently hoped, would melt some of that ice. Now he could do nothing but make for the cliffs and seek another refuge. Rowing along beneath the shadowing cliffs, some of which rose to a height of more than 1,100 feet, Kane at last spotted a possible perch for the boats: a fragment of decaying ice belt situated in front of a cavern. As they hauled the boats onto this ice, the men heard a cacophony of cawing and screeching, and realized that the terraces above were alive with nesting seabirds. The captain declared the site a perfect resting place, and named it Providence Halt. Several men grumbled about stopping again so soon, but Kane kept secret what he had seen from the iceberg. To describe that depressing vista would only destroy hope.

With the boats safe, Kane climbed a craggy, north-facing hill and viewed the interior glacier, savoring "a sublime prospect of this great frozen ocean, which seems to form the continental axis of Greenland—a vast undulating plain of purple-tinted ice, studded with islands, and absolutely gemming the horizon with the varied glitter of sun-tipped crystal." With the temperature in the sunshine standing at 90 degrees, torrents of water poured down the front of the glacier. Yet Kane felt more excited by the abundance of food—the lumme and their eggs, and an arctic cress called *cochlearia*.

Kane and his "scurvy-broken, hunger-stricken men" spent a week feasting at Providence Halt. He allowed two of the party to look out on the bleak ice field to the south, but only after he had pledged them to silence. By July 18, however, the bright sun had melted enough of the nearby ice that Kane felt ready to leave. As if to illustrate the hazardous, unpredictable nature of the entire enterprise, the departure proved nearly disastrous. Launching the *Hope* into the water, the men lost control. The ice snapped off part of the rail and bulwark and sent their best shotgun and only teakettle spiraling into the depths. From now on, whether making soup, bread paste, or tea, they would heat water in a tin can.

Continuing south along the Greenland coast, following leads that opened up under the heat of the sun, the men rejoiced at seeing signs of spring. "Our happy oarsmen," Kane wrote later, "after a hard day's work, made easy by the promise ahead, would stretch themselves in the sunshine and dream happily away till called to the morning wash and payers. We enjoyed it the more, for we all of us knew it could not last."

Approaching Cape York, which at best marked the beginning of a rough, three-week voyage, the men encountered more impassable shore ice. Kane took inventory. Before leaving Providence Halt, he had stored 195 birds, each weighing four ounces, and several dozen eggs. Besides this, to feed seventeen men, including himself, he had 112 pounds of pork slush, 348 pounds of bread, fifty pounds of flour, fifty of Indian meal, and eighty of meat biscuit. The total ran to 640 pounds of provisions, or thirty-six pounds per man.

The captain judged the fuel situation equally dire. At Providence Halt, Hickey had discovered a peat-like turf that would serve to boil water. But at a rate of just two boilings per day, even this, together with sledge runners, spare oars, and empty provision bags, would provide fuel for no more than seventeen days. Fortunately, the men still had the *Red Eric*—though they would soon reduce that to firewood.

Kane faced the choice squarely: either they could camp and wait for a lead to open in the shore ice along the coast, or they could turn seaward and try to sail around the ice. With McGary, he studied one well-defined lead wending to seaward—clearly, their best hope. He called his officers together and explained his choice. After burning some planks from the *Red Eric* to brew broth, coffee, and tea, Kane built a cairn on a prominent headland. Here he deposited a written record of his intentions, and marked it, reluctantly, with a red flannel shirt from his pack.

The men beat southwest into the ice fields. Slowly, the ice became more impacted, and Kane had to use all his expertise to determine which leads would prove navigable. Despite frozen icebergs and frequent fogs, the whaleboats made good progress through the narrow, zig-zagging leads. But even a captain must sometimes sleep, and Kane awoke one evening after a nap to discover that the steersman of the leading boat, whom he never named, had gotten confused by an irregular iceberg and veered shoreward instead of seaward. The two whaleboats were locked into a channel not twenty yards wide, and narrowing. With darkness falling, Kane ordered the boats hauled onto the ice.

The next morning, accompanied by McGary, he climbed a 300-foot iceberg, and again saw a view that was "truly fearful"—nothing but stupendous bergs and jumbled floes whichever way he looked. His sturdy second officer shed tears at the prospect. The men had only one option. Heavy with disappointment, they mounted the boats back onto the sledges, attached the drag ropes, and began hauling westward, back the way they had come. After three days of hard labor, exhausted, they reached the irregular iceberg that had caused the confusion. They hauled the boats over its tongue and, on the other side, regained the lead and resumed sailing.

The detour had cost them much. The men had enough fuel to last eight days. Game had grown scarce and, after quietly analyzing the provisions, Kane cut the daily ration to five ounces of bread dust, four ounces of tallow, and three of bird meat. Later, Amos Bonsall would write admiringly that these measures sparked no dissent: "During our passage through the ice in open boats on that perilous journey of more than eighty days, by his judicious management [Kane] not only cheered the dispirited and quieted the querulous and discontented, but he so dispensed the provisions as to give no one the slightest cause for complaint (a most difficult operation, as anyone who has had to do with starving men can testify)."

On their restricted diet, augmented only by tea and the occasional bird, the men felt their strength waning. Kane sought now to reach Cape Shackleton, known to be rich in birds, and steered by compass, sailing south-southwest as best the leads would allow. One afternoon, while hauling the *Hope* over a tongue of ice—formerly a simple task for half a dozen men—the sailors discovered that they needed the entire crew to keep the boat moving.

Now came another near-disaster. While the men worked to move the *Hope,* heaving and sweating in the dazzling sunshine, the ice behind them cracked and the *Faith* drifted rapidly away from her berth. Several of the men responded almost hysterically. Fortunately, the wind brought a cake of ice near the main floe. Kane and McGary leapt onto this, and managed to float across to the drifting boat, the loss of which would have proven fatal.

Having reached partly open waters, Kane sailed south in the great ice drift of Baffin Bay. The boats had taken such a battering that, to keep them afloat, the exhausted men had to bail day and night. They were experiencing shortness of breath, swollen feet, mild fever, and insomnia—all signs of malnutrition. Some of them broached the subject of killing the dogs, but Kane refused to entertain the idea.

Several times during the voyage, someone had spotted a seal or walrus lolling on a floe. But always the creature had slipped away as the sailors approached. One afternoon toward the end of July, while gazing out from the bow of the *Faith,* Kane spotted another seal. Apparently asleep, it lay basking in the sun on a patch of ice—a mammal so large that at first he thought it was a walrus. Having devised a series of signals for just such an eventuality, Kane waved furiously for silence. The men muffled their oars with stockings and approached quietly from 300 yards. Petersen, the party's best shot, moved to the bow of the *Faith* with the large English hunting rifle.

As the starving men drew within range, several of them trembling with anxiety and anticipation, the massive seal raised its head and looked around. The writer in Kane would surface in retrospect: "To this day I can remember the hard, careworn, almost despairing expression of the men's thin faces as they saw him move; their lives depended on his capture." Nobody moved.

Petersen, almost paralyzed, struggled vainly to rest the rifle against the cut-water of the boat.

The seal rose onto its flippers, gazed at the interlopers in alarm, and coiled for a quick plunge. Petersen fired—and the seal "relaxed his long length on the ice." At the brink of the water, his head lolled onto one side. Before Kane could order a second shot, the men yelled and exploded onto the floe, grabbing the seal and hauling it onto safer ice. The captain had not realized how much famine had reduced his party. Crying and laughing, they fell upon the seal brandishing knives, and within five minutes, every man was "sucking his bloody fingers or mouthing long strips of raw blubber."

Within a couple of days, the men would shoot a second seal. From then on, they would acquire sufficient meat. But that first immense seal would prove to be a turning point. Come evening, encamped on the large floe, Kane devoted two planks from the *Red Eric* to build a cooking fire, and with the men partook of "a rare and savage feast." As George Stephenson later recalled, "The charm was broken, and the dogs were safe."

o   o   o

On August 1, Kane spotted the Devil's Thumb of Melville Bay. Approaching the Duck Islands, he decided to end the voyage, probably the most difficult in Arctic history, not with a reckless display of derring-do, but by wending cautiously through the labyrinth of islands along the coast. The men began spending their nights on shore.

One morning, an excited Carl Petersen woke Kane to report that he had just seen an Inuk he recognized, paddling past in his kayak. According to an unpublished boat journal kept by Stephenson, foggy weather had forced the men ashore at three o'clock in the morning. At about nine, with the fog lifting, Petersen ascended a hill "to see if he could recognize the land, when he saw an Esquimaux in the way." Petersen hailed him by name and asked a question. The man replied, "Who are you?"

"Paul Zacharias, don't you know me? I am Carl Petersen!"

The man stared intently at the emaciated, heavily bearded Petersen,

The snowy peak of Sanderson's Hope rises above Upernavik. Here, on August 6, 1855, the men hauled their boats ashore for the last time.

then cried: "No! His wife says he's dead!" He then paddled furiously away, believing he had seen a ghost.

Soon enough, while rowing through the islands, Kane heard someone calling out, "Halloo!" He ordered the men to hold their oars and listen. Finally, Petersen exclaimed in a half-whisper, "Dannemarkers!" The men resumed rowing. They rounded a cape and, scanning the shoreline, spotted a single-masted vessel at anchor in a small bay. Petersen, who had remained quiet and grave, burst into an incoherent babbling: "It's the Upernavik oil boat! The *Fraulein Flaischer!* Carlie Mossyn, the assistant cooper, must be sailing to Kingatok for blubber. The *Mariane* has come, and Carlie Mossyn is on his way to Kingatok!"

Petersen proved correct. The annual supply ship from Denmark had arrived at Upernavik and the assistant cooper was indeed sailing to fetch a store of blubber. From the Greenlanders on the oil boat, Kane and his men received their first news in two years. They learned that two American vessels, a steamer and a barque, had passed this way a fortnight before and proceeded north in search of them. And what of the lost expedition of Sir

John Franklin—any word? Yes: a newspaper had recently arrived from Europe. The sailors could remember few details, but some explorer had retrieved relics far to the southwest. Kane and his men had been searching the wrong area.

Yet even this could not lower their spirits. Late the following day, on August 6, 1855, the men rounded a cape and spotted the snowy peak of Sanderson's Hope, which rises above Upernavik. They heard the barking of the dogs, and then the six-o'clock tolling of the workmen's bells. Could this be a dream? Hugging the shoreline, they rowed past the old brew house, and then, in a crowd of children, hauled their boats ashore for the last time.

o   o   o

Over the next few days, Kane learned that the American searchers who had passed this way included his brother John. He learned, from a German newspaper translated by the local pastor that a thousand miles to the southwest, another explorer—John Rae of the Hudson's Bay Company—had discovered relics from the lost Franklin expedition, and that some of the final survivors had been driven "to the last resource" to remain alive.

Finally, Kane learned that Edward Inglefield had never entered Smith Sound in the *Phoenix*. Instead, with his old friend Joseph-René Bellot aboard, the British navigator had sailed west to Beechey Island. There, while voluntarily delivering dispatches, Bellot slipped off an ice floe and drowned. "His last letter to me," Kane later wrote, "just before I left New York, promised me the hope that we were to meet again in Baffin Bay, and that he would unite himself with our party as a volunteer. The French service never lost a more chivalrous spirit."

The Danes of Upernavik proved more than generous. They fitted up a loft for Kane and his men, and shared their meager stores. The captain of the *Mariane,* who would soon sail for Denmark, offered to transport the Americans to the Shetland Islands, where they could catch a vessel home. Given that the alternative would probably mean remaining in Greenland through another winter, Kane accepted the offer. On September 6, with the

Faith strapped on deck and Toodlamik and Whitey chained to a rail, Kane and his men sailed out of Upernavik.

Five days later, the *Mariane* put in at Godhavn on Disco Island, its last port in Greenland. The Danes delayed their departure in case the American rescue ships returned. On the final night before sailing, a lookout stationed on a hill spotted a steamer on the horizon—and then a smaller vessel with it. Peering through his looking glass, Kane recognized the American flag. Spontaneously, he ordered the *Faith* into the water. Then, accompanied by every vessel in Godhavn, he sailed out to greet his countrymen.

{ III }

Return of the Hero

32

DR. KANE HOME AGAIN!

According to mythology, a returning hero, to complete his adventure, must survive a difficult re-entry into the world he left behind. In *The Hero with a Thousand Faces,* Joseph Campbell presents three scenarios. The returning adventurer can suffer the fate of Rip van Winkle, who, having slipped into his experience unconsciously, returned without any idea of where he had been, and so emerged confused and ridiculous—a figure of fun. The Irish hero Oisin, by comparison, made it back from a transformative adventure in full consciousness, but then lost his balance and hard-earned perspective, and with them all hope of communicating his experience. The successful return, Campbell suggests, is more like that of the Persian prince Kamar-al-Zaman. He arrived home carrying a ring, a talisman of his supernatural experience so convincing that it enabled him "to retain his self-assurance in the face of every sobering disillusionment."

To mid-nineteenth-century America, Elisha Kent Kane returned with what Campbell would call talismanic "runes of wisdom" in the form of his journals and logbooks. Building on these, he would create a two-volume masterpiece detailing his polar visitation. At the same time, true to mythology, he would become thoroughly familiar with "sobering disillusionment."

Initially, as he approached New York City in the *Release* on Thursday, October 11, 1855, the returning explorer foresaw no insurmountable difficulties. Early in the afternoon, while passing just off Sandy Hook, New Jersey, a triumphant Kane sent a note to his friend John P. Kennedy, the former secretary of the navy: "We are back again safe and sound, after an open-air travel by boats and sledges of thirteen hundred miles." As the rescue vessel neared Battery Landing, cheering crowds appeared and cannons roared. In the harbor, while eager well-wishers thronged the docks, reporters came aboard to interview the conquering hero.

Typically, Kane arrived well briefed. His brother Thomas had never ceased to serve as self-appointed publicist and literary agent. Having married the British-born Elizabeth Dennistoun Wood—a remarkable second cousin, more than a decade younger, who would become a medical doctor, father his four children, and help him create a town in western Pennsylvania—an older, wiser Thomas had sent a cautionary letter with the relief expedition, advising the explorer that "fortune has made you the child of *your whole country.*" He recalled that they used to discuss "how much more this place and the North had done for the Franklin search than the rest of the Union. In the search after you, it has not been so." The call for a rescue mission had united politicians from north and south, he explained, and elicited support from groups as diverse as ladies' seminaries and "the ugly gritty of your naval men."

Thomas urged restraint in making geographical claims, and offered unsolicited but acute advice on general conduct: "When a nation makes a pet of a man, all it requires of him is to take his petting gracefully. . . . Your tack will be the official Scientifics—Science with the brevet of sword spunk and gentlemanly savoir faire." He called for "a concise sham modesty of speech in public, and a composed and courteous demeanor universally." What's more, he advised, "remember your newspaper friends. . . . It is they who *made us and not we ourselves.*"

Having survived "first contact," Kane found himself whisked away to Astor House on Broadway, probably the finest hotel in the country, to be

Elisha Kane arrived in New York looking bronzed and fit and wearing what the Times *described as a "heavy black beard." Kane described his own health as "almost absurd: I have grown like a walrus." His father would warn him that much work lay ahead once he got "clear of Arctic ice, beard and breeches."*

swarmed by well-wishers at the Rotunda Bar during an impromptu welcome-home party. With newspaper reporters still in tow, Kane emerged, piled into a carriage, and drove to the elegant home, at 17 Bond Street, of his patron Henry Grinnell. According to the *Herald,* that gentleman "received the Doctor with such a welcome as comes only from the depths of the heart." According to this report, Kane said sadly, "I have no *Advance* with me." And Grinnell responded: "Never mind. You are safe. That is all we care about. Come into the parlor and tell us the whole story."

The following day, October 12, 1855, the *New York Tribune* would report: "Few events within the range of possibility could have produced a livelier feeling of public joy than did the announcement yesterday of the safe return of the gallant Arctic Adventurer, Dr. Kane, and his exploring party." The *New York Daily Times,* not to be outdone, devoted its entire front page to the expedition's return, its headlines trumpeting: "DR. KANE HOME AGAIN! / The *Advance* Left in the Ice / New Lands Found / An Open Sea Found / No Traces of Sir John Franklin / Life in the Frozen Regions / On Sledges for Thirty Days / DR. KANE'S OWN ACCOUNT."

Despite his ordeal, the *Times* reported, "The Doctor has improved in personal appearance in his absence. He brings home a bronzed face, a long and heavy black beard, a shock of hair just whitening a little—a sort of iron grey,—a stouter body and a hand with a hearty grip." In another note to Kennedy, Kane himself would observe, "My health is almost absurd: I have grown like a walrus."

The *Times* recapitulated Kane's expedition as he described it, highlighting his discovery of an Open Polar Sea—for which, as counseled by his younger brother, he properly credited William Morton—and his extraordinary escape. Originally, in his journal, Kane had calculated that while hauling the boats across the ice, frequently doubling back, the men had marched 316 miles; and he himself, traveling by dogsled, had shuttled back and forth over a distance exceeding 1,100 miles. In talking to the press, he reduced these numbers, and estimated that he and his men had traveled about 1,300 miles. He included 240 miles the men trekked while hauling sledges; another 600 that he had covered while ferrying men and supplies; and 500 miles the party had sailed in small boats, tracing the Greenland coast between Cape Alexander and Upernavik.

On October 13, two days after Kane reached New York, newspapers in Boston, Philadelphia, and Washington reprinted stories of his triumphant return. Within the week, virtually every newspaper in the United States had carried at least one article, and news of the heroic expedition began reaching the entire English-speaking world. Almost overnight, these reports turned Elisha Kent Kane into an international celebrity.

o   o   o

Against this sensational public welcome, and almost immediately, the lionized Kane encountered his first re-entry challenge: the opposition of his family to his relationship with Maggie Fox. In battling this familial antagonism, and defending his integrity as an individual, the explorer would expend vast amounts of energy. He would lose the occasional skirmish and embarrass himself, but he would always retake the high ground. This war, only partially visible to the public, would fuel his desire to complete his great book as quickly as possible.

The skirmishing began on his arrival at the home of Henry Grinnell.

*Judge John Kane ruled his
family with an iron fist.*

Caught up in the whirl of arriving family, Kane received word that Maggie
Fox was in New York City. While still based in the hamlet of Crookville,
she had chanced to be visiting the city when the explorer arrived. She was
staying with a friend of the Grinnells, a widow named Ellen Walter, and
sent word of her whereabouts—then waited in a fever of anticipation.

Maggie had endured two grim years in limbo. Accustomed to admiration, attention, and independence, she had endured loneliness and privation,
and had been reduced to pleading for money from Cornelius Grinnell. Early
in 1854, however, Cornelius had exchanged revealing letters with Robert
Patterson Kane, now a twenty-seven-year-old lawyer who worked alongside
the Judge. To Patterson, Cornelius had written of Maggie: "It has occurred
to me whether by withholding funds from her she could not be induced to
return to her parents . . . I am desirous of doing everything in my power to
carry out your brother's wishes, and at the same time to promote his happiness . . . A deep friendship for your brother alone prompts me to make this
suggestion, and I shall be governed . . . by your views in the matter."

Patterson, seven years younger than Elisha, had responded in the same
spirit: "It does strike me that the opportunity of letting the young lady know

your own impression of the position which she bears to the doctor should not be lost. We know her only as a dependent; as one to whom the doctor bears the relation of a kind-hearted friend whose interest in the young lady shows itself by furnishing her with the means of leading an honest life and resisting the temptations which beset a poor girl with a pretty face and already disreputable association. My dear brother resembles our very lovable Don Quixote, but then this resemblance must not be construed into anything affecting his reputation."

Patterson laid out the strategy: "The funds in your hands are exhausted. The trustee reports accordingly. The Doctor is your friend, but—. [Maggie] is not his mistress and holds to him no other relation than that of the recipient of his charity, and to you no other than that of a purely business correspondent. Do you take my drift?

"Burn this," Patterson concluded, "for I am really ashamed of such a scrawl."

Whether the young man felt shame for his handwriting or his machinations, Cornelius preserved the letter. Yet he did catch Patterson's drift, and Maggie struggled along on a miserable stipend. On departure, Elisha Kane had imagined her moving from Mrs. Turner's to some lively boarding school. But his betrothed had been reduced to writing his best friend: "My dear Sir, I am very lonely and should love very much to go and spend a few days with my friend Mrs. Walter. Will you please do me the kindness to write to Mrs. Turner and tell her to let me spend say one week with Mrs. Walter."

By 1855, when the explorer returned from the Arctic, Maggie had suffered so much that, when Kane did not fly to join her the day after he reached New York, she collapsed in nervous desperation, and moved a few blocks across town to stay with her mother and sister, who conducted séances out of a house on Tenth Street.

What happened at the Grinnell mansion, meanwhile, can only be roughly reconstructed from subsequent events. At least one writer suggests that Kane wished to break off his relationship with Maggie, and that his family supported him in this. The biographer George Corner, who expressed particular thanks to the descendants of Robert Patterson Kane, observes that, in his surviving Arctic journals, the explorer made no reference to Maggie. Kane wrote those volumes knowing, of course, that whatever happened, his family would control access—and that his first readers would include his parents and his siblings. The emotionality of his parting from Maggie suggests that Kane kept a separate journal devoted to her—and, in retrospect, that this volume has been destroyed. As indicated earlier, certain of Kane's surviving letters, including several that might have included references to Maggie, no longer exist in their original form, but have been copied in some other hand.

In 1855, Elisha Kane did not arrive in New York completely unprepared. His brother Thomas, the nearest of his siblings in age, temperament, and talent, had hinted that trouble was brewing on the home front. In March 1854, a couple of months after Patterson laid out the family line to Cornelius Grinnell, Tom wrote a letter to Elisha touching on everything except Maggie Fox, observing: "I wish I could feel that my words would not be lost, or exposed to a stranger's view. I have a great deal to say, but what is most upon my mind, my dear friend, I must let remain unsaid." Elisha Kane would have deciphered this allusion as relating to Maggie Fox.

Now, at the Grinnell home in New York, as family members welcomed the explorer, having been alerted to his imminent arrival by telegraph, the name Maggie Fox came up almost immediately. Spiritualism had lately been making headlines in conjunction with free-love societies, and Kane's mother felt heartsick at the idea, repeatedly suggested in the press, that her son had become engaged to a spirit rapper. Jane Leiper Kane was an educated woman, but as a mid-century Philadelphian, she was not a cosmopolitan intellectual like her oldest son. In anyone associated with Spiritualism, she could perceive nothing but godless immorality.

At the Grinnell home, she probably withdrew from the discussion as it grew stormy. Probably, too, judging from what ensued, the supportive Thomas was absent. In March of the previous year, in a long letter to Elisha, he had reported that his wife, now seventeen, "miscarried in July [three months after they wed] . . . no ill effects. If any one has a welcome for you out of our family it is this dear child. She has the notion you were her particular friend before she was married, and I believe she never forgets such things." Thomas, having transgressed a few boundaries of his own, would have stood shoulder to shoulder with the explorer.

Almost certainly, then, three men conducted the emotional ambush: Kane's father, the Judge; his lawyer-brother Patterson; and his friend Cornelius Grinnell. These three contended, judging from subsequently planted newspaper articles, that Kane should break off the relationship with Maggie Fox and present himself as a gentleman-philanthropist who had been seeking to assist a deserving unfortunate.

Still reeling from his public welcome, and with half his mind yet in the Arctic, Kane responded at some point that, even if he wished to break off the relationship, which he did not, Maggie possessed certain letters he had written that gave the lie to any such posturing. We know he revealed this because, on the night of October 12, the night after he reached New York, Cornelius Grinnell visited the home of Mrs. Walter. Finding Maggie absent, he said Kane was suffering from rheumatism, but would call on the young woman within the next few days. Then, announcing that he was acting on behalf of the Kane family, he asked for the letters that Kane had written to Maggie.

Mrs. Walter, shocked, said she did not know where they were. Meanwhile, Maggie had been summoned to Mrs. Walter's home. She arrived too late to see Cornelius, and the widow could not bring herself to communicate what had just transpired. Maggie was still at that house at nine o'clock the following morning when, resplendent in his naval uniform, Elisha Kane came calling. At first, Maggie refused to see him. When she finally came down the stairs, the explorer covered her face in kisses and declared that his feelings remained unchanged.

Soon afterward, however, he informed her gently that their marriage had to be "indefinitely postponed on account of the violent opposition" of his family. For now, they must "be to each other only as brother and sister."

Kane then produced a statement, which he described as necessary to calm his mother, and which he asked Maggie to copy and sign. "Do it for me, Maggie! It is for my mother."

Stunned, the young woman did as her lover asked. She wrote that their relations had always been "merely friendly and fraternal" and that "no matrimonial engagement had subsisted." When she had finished copying, Kane called Mrs. Walter into the room and, to her surprise, asked her to witness the statement. The older woman said, "Maggie, is this true?" And Maggie replied, "No, no. It is not so! Doctor Kane knows it is not."

Turning to him, and alluding to a discussion of wedding plans, she said, "Remember what you said in the carriage!" A testy exchange ensued, with Kane declaring, "You are not the Maggie I took you for." He left with the statement in his pocket. A couple of days later, having collected his thoughts and recovered some personal territory, he brought it back and sheepishly handed it to Maggie, saying, "The wicked shall not inherit the kingdom of heaven."

The young woman tore the letter to shreds on the spot.

33

RUMORS & REBUTTALS

O n October 19, just eight days after the explorer arrived home, the *Troy Daily Whig,* a newspaper in upstate New York, announced that Kane was "soon to be married to Miss Margaretta Fox, the second sister of the 'Fox Girls.'" The Kane family immediately planted a rebuttal in the *Boston Traveller,* and that same denial soon surfaced in Philadelphia's *Daily Pennsylvanian.* The rebuttal denounced the "foolish story of the engagement of Dr. Kane, the Arctic navigator, to one of the spirit-rapping Fox girls." And it sounded the familiar refrain that Kane was one of several "liberal, kind-hearted gentlemen" who had undertaken to educate a remarkably bright, intelligent girl "worthy of better employment than 'spirit rapping.'" With notable shamelessness, this article added that such philanthropic zeal was an honorable peculiarity of the Kane family.

By now, several New York newspapers had picked up the original report of a looming marriage, among them the *Herald* and the *Express.* The *Evening Post* then declared the story to be "without a shadow of foundation." Horace Greeley, the influential editor of the *Tribune,* and a man friendly with both Maggie Fox and the Kane family, complained that newspapers publishing such articles, either pro or con, have "perverted their columns to the

Elizabeth Ellet impressed Kane with her spirit, energy, and eloquence.

gratification of an impertinent curiosity. What right has the public to know anything about an 'engagement' or semi-engagement between these young people?"

Greeley thundered to no avail. The *New York Times* followed the *Post* and denied the truth of the rumored engagement. But then it retracted this denial, which had been precipitated by "some party furious in the Kane interest—who threatened vengeance against the person who had made the assertion, could he learn who it was." The *Times* refused to name its source. But the woman herself, Maggie's friend Elizabeth Ellet, wrote an anonymous letter to Kane declaring that, until she heard a denial from the explorer's own lips, she would not believe it, as she "could not conceive of a gentleman being so cowardly or so wicked as to be influenced by fears of the prejudices of stupid people to repudiate an engagement to a lovely and virtuous girl."

The articulate Ellet, best known as the author of a two-volume work entitled *Women of the American Revolution,* had published several books and also survived a scandalous flirtation with Edgar Allan Poe. Elisha Kane admired the spirit, energy, and eloquence of her communication, and shared his reaction with Maggie and her mother. Contrary to what Ellet and others surmised, however, he feared public opinion mainly insofar as it hurt his beloved mother. Also, he maintained a complex relationship with his father, the Judge. At one point during his first Arctic expedition, alluding to his notes on ice formation and a projected book on glacial geology, he had written, "If only I can only get home again to report to Father and Grinnell the result of all this, my satisfaction and gratitude will surpass my hopes . . . I may advance myself in my father's eyes."

Yet now, having exhausted his financial resources on this latest expedition, he worried that his father might cut off his income—and in this regard he had reason. Judge Kane, who once almost had his son Thomas jailed over the tone of a resignation letter, showed no signs of mellowing. Recently, he had issued a severe judgment against the abolitionist Passmore Williams, condemning him to prison for having freed a group of slaves. In response, the *New York Herald* accused the Judge of self-righteousness, of making "every state a slave state," and subtly contrasted father and son: "Judge Kane is the Columbus of the new world of slave-whips and shackles which he has just annexed, and is entitled to all the rank of a discoverer. His insulting inhuman persistence . . . is the acme of outrage and cruelty."

John Kintzing Kane loved his eldest son dearly. But everyone in the family, and many people outside it, understood that he was not a man who would allow paternal feelings to take priority over his public reputation. By now, the Judge would have warned his son that, if he were to marry Maggie Fox, he would put himself outside the family orbit, and be treated accordingly. Given his precarious financial situation, the explorer feared being disinherited. This same, well-founded concern almost certainly increased his mother's anxiety on his behalf.

But now, as a result of the newspaper articles, Kane's aunt Eliza—wife of his uncle George Leiper—got wind of the controversy. Having helped to find a place for Maggie in Crookville, and gleaned something of the secret circumstances, she wrote her nephew expressing her outrage at the denials. She told him to clear himself of the imputation that he had deceived this young woman, or he would never enter her house again. According to *Love-*

Life, Kane produced this letter and said: "See, Maggie. Here is my favorite aunt turning against me for your sake!"

o   o   o

On November 15, 1855, while visiting New York on business, Kane went to dinner with Henry Grinnell at the prestigious Century Club. During the after-dinner informalities, while the men drank sherry and smoked cigars, someone introduced him to William Makepeace Thackeray. The British novelist, who had become famous with his 1848 work *Vanity Fair,* was touring the United States giving a series of lectures entitled *The Four Georges.* Under prompting, according to a columnist from *Harper's Monthly Magazine,* Elisha Kane began describing his recent expedition. Thackeray and the other guests "listened like schoolboys might listen to Sinbad the Sailor," he wrote. "The tale was marvelous, but the Centurions believed it." One man likened the experience to listening to Marco Polo. When the explorer had finished, Thackeray rose from his chair, approached Kane, and asked Grinnell, "Do you think the Doctor will permit me to stoop down and kiss his boots?"

On the same evening that Kane dazzled Thackeray and the Centurions, the *New York Evening Post* reported that he had signed a contract with a Philadelphia publisher, Childs & Peterson, to write an account of his latest expedition. The book would be illustrated by well-known artist James Hamilton, who had designed the plates for his earlier work. That 522-page opus had appeared while Kane was in the Arctic, and elicited nothing but praise. One American critic spoke for most when he declared *The United States Grinnell Expedition* superior to the celebrated narrative of John Franklin's first journey: "This far exceeds it in clearness and picturesqueness of description and conveys a much more distinct image of the perils and marvels of the Polar ice." In London, the *Athenaeum* opined that the work was "profusely and admirably illustrated, one of the most interesting of the kind that we have seen, and deserves a place by the side of our own most cherished records of Arctic adventure."

Judge Kane had relayed news of laudatory letters "from the best officers of the British Admiralty, altogether flattering, and much is expected from your 'Narrative' of your present cruise. Be prepared therefore for a two years' writing and printing labour when you get clear of Arctic ice, beard and breeches. I am offered a large price for the right of publishing it."

Kane's first book, so critically successful, earned little money. Just before Christmas 1853, when the work was ready to ship, a fire destroyed the first print run of nearly 5,000 copies. The publisher, Harper & Brothers, charged those against the author, and as Judge Kane reported, made the explorer "debtor besides for the cost of all the illustrations save only one half of the wood cuts. The result is that they leave you in debt on an edition of some 9,000 copies in all. It is a rascally account."

In response to this book-trade accounting, and encouraged by his father, Kane switched publishers, contracting his work-in-progress to the aggressive new firm of Childs & Peterson. From the outset, the sales-minded George Childs urged Kane to write not for a specialist audience of geographers and scientists, but for the general public, as he had already shown himself capable of doing. Childs also recognized the importance of timeliness, and urged Kane to deliver as quickly as possible.

Kane was prepared to meet this demand. Throughout the expedition, he had kept detailed journals. Now, using these as a blueprint, and to provide color, authority, and detail, he began working night and day. He scoured his journals and, as authors have done since time immemorial, removed repetitions, banalities, and emotional excesses. Six decades in the future, Ernest Shackleton would do the same, glossing over incidents and omitting entirely the rebellion of his ship's carpenter.

Now, Kane exercised the author's prerogative, eliding and elaborating as necessary, and adding contextual information while shaping the whole into a lively, coherent narrative. He wisely retained much about Esquimaux life, including descriptions of seal-hunting, bear-hunting, and life in the igloo; nor did he minimize the suffering induced by cold, starvation, and scurvy. In this regard, his literary instincts won out over his scientific training—although to Childs he complained: "Most certainly my efforts to make this book readable will destroy its permanency and injure me. It is a sacrifice." Kane worked feverishly enough that, in mid-December 1855, just two months after arriving home, and while insisting that he might yet do further revising, he could deliver 300 pages for typesetting.

o o o

Meanwhile, Kane persisted in his affair with Maggie Fox. At Christmas, he sent both her and her sister Kate boxes of chocolate-covered bonbons. Through January, he visited her frequently in New York, where she was living with her mother and sister on Tenth Street. He took both young women for a sleigh ride along the still-bucolic Bloomingdale Road, now upper Broadway. Kate's recent conquests included Canadian writer Susanna Moodie and her husband, and Kane worried that Maggie might return to spirit rapping. He urged her toward Catholicism, which denounced the practice as anathema, and he took her to vespers at Saint Anne's Roman Catholic Church.

For her part, Mrs. Fox fretted, justifiably, about Maggie's reputation, which might be damaged beyond repair by the continuing attentions of a man unwilling to marry her. Early in December, she had tried to end the relationship. She wrote Kane that a woman friend had begged "with tears in her eyes never to let my daughter see you, or exchange words with you."

Mrs. Fox warned that, if he persevered, she would feel justified in publicizing his deplorable conduct: "I from this moment forbid you ever again entering my house. I forbid my daughter from receiving you." She felt she had "done wrong to have allowed Margaretta to see you." His visits were "injuring her hitherto unblemished name. I am her mother and must protect her and she must obey me. . . . My child is as pure as an angel, and if you are seen coming here the world will censure her."

Kane tried to stop seeing Maggie but could not. He explained to Mrs. Fox that he had spent all his money on his Arctic expedition—and so, for a time, remained financially dependent on his father. He was working on a book, however. Once published, this work would produce sufficient funds that he would be able to "spurn the interference of friends who had already wrought so much mischief."

Around they went. Mrs. Walter and other friends urged Maggie to stop seeing Kane, though any such suggestion induced depression and fits of weeping. At one point, Maggie gave in. She wrote Kane: "I have seen you for the last time. I have been deceived." She must either give him up forever, "or give up those who are very dear to me, and who hold my name and reputation as sacred." Since their romance was over, she added that she would return his love letters. "You can have your letters if you wish them. No one can prevent me from returning them to you. Do as you please; if you want them, send Morton, and every letter shall be returned; but do not call on me again; for it will only give me more pain and trouble."

To this, Kane responded that he was very much distressed: "As to your dear generous offer of returning my letters, I tremble—not at the letters— but at the fear that you have not understood me. I have never distrusted you or even asked for those notes. With or without them, you were always the same to me. . . . I only felt and feared that suspicious, designing friends or enemies might see and abuse these letters." He would not deprive her of them, or give her pain by requesting them: "If of your own free choice you send them to me, I will regard it as the highest proof of trust and love."

Subsequently, he flatly refused to accept them. Like countless lovers before and since, these two could not remain apart, and they resorted to using Kate as an intermediary. In March, Mrs. Fox intercepted a letter that, she wrote Kane, she "deemed it proper to open and read." Clearly, it contained suggestive remarks, for she wrote: "It is best for the happiness and interest of my child that you should discontinue your visits and also leave off writing to her. My motives I hope you will understand, and respect my feelings."

On April 21, Kane sent Maggie an engraved self-portrait. "Although a mere trifle, it may serve as evidence of my high respect for your character, and will, I hope, assure you of my continued and brotherly interest in your welfare." A few days later, Kane turned up unexpectedly and proclaimed his interest to be more than brotherly. Allowed into the house by a maid uncertain of protocol, he surprised Maggie as she arrived home.

According to *The Love-Life of Doctor Kane,* he took her in his arms: "My own Maggie,—you are again mine—the betrothed wife of Dr. Kane." After kissing her head, he removed a ring from his hand, which he said he had found in the Arctic, and placed it on her finger. He also presented her with an engraved locket containing a lock of his late brother Willie's hair. He no longer cared, he said, "for the world's opinions or its sneers. His beloved wife was all in all to him."

Maggie surmised later that, because Kane had come directly from a friend's funeral, he had been moved to reflect on the brevity of life, and so to seize the moment. More probably, the explorer was acting in response to a wonderfully encouraging meeting with his publisher. George Childs, having failed to persuade the U.S. Congress to buy copies of the forthcoming book for schools and colleges, had begun selling excerpts to newspapers— with great success.

Kane had sought and received an advance against royalties of $600. In contemporary terms, this equates roughly to $13,500. Childs would also have revealed to Kane that, based on advance orders, this amount represented a small percentage of what he would receive after the book appeared. Kane responded euphorically to these proofs and promises of looming solvency and escape from paternal decree, and acted on his heart's desire.

His tokens must have persuaded Mrs. Fox, because he again became a regular visitor to her home. During his frequent visits to New York from Philadelphia, he escorted Maggie to dinners, lectures, and theatrical performances. The young woman had taken to calling the Kanes "the Royal Family," and in one note, Kane adopted this usage: "The Royal Family keep me in our quiet city to attend a ball; and on Friday I have to talk science and stupidity to a society of learned philosophers. Pity me, for truly I had rather be with you, resting after my hard work like a boy in his holiday time."

That spring, the three Fox women—mother and two daughters—moved to a larger house on East Twenty-Second Street. Here, Kane would often spend time alone with Maggie in a third-floor parlor. In a letter, he described the room as "a sort of sanctuary: a retreat to which we are driven by mischief-making eyes and tongues. There like wounded deer, we escape from the hunters; and if we, both of us, are conscious of doing no wrong, whose business is it if we seek a shelter?"

34

THE WRITER DELIVERS

esides keeping written records, Kane produced more than 200 sketches while in the Arctic. And while he prepared his narrative, and shuttled between the family home, Fern Rock, and the offices of his publisher on Arch Street in downtown Philadelphia, he also turned his attention to these. During the spring of 1856, at Kane's invitation, artist James Hamilton lived at Fern Rock for a month, during which he turned some of the explorer's drawings into watercolors from which to produce engravings for the book. Hamilton, an Irish immigrant a year older than Kane, had trained with a well-known Philadelphia engraver and had long since emerged, in the words of one critic, as "the ablest marine painter of this period."

In his preface, Kane would write of the illustrations: "Although largely, and in same cases exclusively, indebted for their interest to the artistic skill of Mr. Hamilton, they are, with scarcely an exception, from sketches made on the spot." And Hamilton, widely known as "the American Turner," would elaborate on this in an 1857 note he sent to Kane's first biographer, William Elder. The artist praised Kane's sketches for "the air of simple, earnest truthfulness which pervades them. These qualities, without which the most labored efforts are comparatively worthless, exist to an extent which confers importance on the most insignificant of them."

Of Kane's lead-pencil original of Tennyson's Monument, Hamilton noted that "every fragment is jotted down with a perception and feeling which seize the special character of the minutest particle defined, and yet its minutiae in no way conflicting with the grandeur of the subject." If Kane's pen-and-ink sketches could be placed before the public, Hamilton insisted, "they would add still further, if that were possible, to his reputation as an Arctic explorer." In a postscript, he added: "Another very note-worthy feature of the doctor's sketching was the extreme rapidity with which it was executed. In illustrating his wishes upon any particular subject, I have frequently seen him make slight drawings which required but a very few additional touches to render them complete."

Preparing the book meant reliving the Arctic experience, which took an emotional toll. Early in April, when Childs was still seeking support from Congress, Kane had tried to dissuade him: "It gives me pain to look back upon [the expedition]; one-sixth of our little party perished in the field, and, of those who survive, a majority are mutilated or broken down. I cannot mingle with the associations of this cruise any thing so degrading as that of a pecuniary recompense; and I can only trust that my hard-earned labors will establish their own and best claim to the sympathy and consideration of good men."

Since returning from the Arctic, Kane had maintained a feverish pace. And yet, while writing his book and conducting his tempestuous affair with Maggie Fox, whenever he was away from Philadelphia he found time to write warm, nostalgic letters to one especially close friend and confidante: his mother. In February 1856, having briefly retreated to Massachusetts for the sake of his health, Kane wrote: "I have arrived at Stockbridge, a sweet tranquil place—the more pleasing because there is now that about me which, perhaps for the first time in my life, finds congenial influence in tranquility. Mrs. Watts is like a sister to me and her cottage . . . is open, windowed, open-doored and to me a dear little palace of refinement and comfort—yet there is not a gilt-looking nor a decent piece of furniture in the whole concern . . . As to my health, I did not leave the watering mountains a jot too soon. I don't know what is in store for me but I have *missed my fever for four nights*. A real god's blessing, for I was very weak."

Having attended a concert, he recalls visiting the area as a youth: "Then there were Uncle Patterson and aunt and you and Father all young and happy and gaily dressed—and tramping home to . . . suppers and whiskey punches. We the boys a great crew, brim full of the music, were running along side of you." A few months later, writing from a health spa, he again grows nostalgic, noting that his mother's latest letter "with Father's appendix carried me back to old times. Just such letters have I watched for in far back early days—such as the Latin boarding school or the University of Virginia; just such letters in my first buffetings with the world, China, India and Manila; just such in the middle period—'Africa so gay and Mexico so low'—just such in the . . . wearing voyages of exile—these later Arctic wayfarings which have made or unmade me.

"I cannot realize that you are older. Father's 'God bless you' and your 'ever devoted mother' read as they used to twenty-five years ago. I see no difference in the hands. But then, dear people, I may measure your aging by my own and it needs no looking glass nor stiff muscles to tell me where the years are. This water cure so far has not answered its end but I am determined to try it fairly."

Back in Philadelphia, having addressed—informally—only the American Philosophical Society about this latest expedition, Kane declined repeated requests for public lectures to concentrate on the book. At times he toiled until three-thirty in the morning, retiring only when his vision went blurry. During this period, he also conducted five trips to New York and Washington to consult experts at the U.S. Coast Survey headquarters and the Smithsonian Institution. The predictable results of maintaining this pace emerged in his letters to Childs. On June 7, he wrote: "Authordom has again overdone me. I will have to take a spell soon." A week later, he observed, "My health is nothing extraordinary under this extreme heat; but

I think that I have accumulated enough of nerve-force to carry me through to that ominously pleasant word, 'Finis.'"

By early July, Kane had delivered the complete narrative. On the fourth, he wrote: "With little spirit of congratulation and much weariness, I send you this preface, which completes my task. Drained and unaccountably weary . . . Now that the holy day [of publication] is at hand, I am ungrateful enough to complain that it finds me without capacity to enjoy it." He spent a couple of days on the beach at Long Island with Cornelius Grinnell, but on July 30 he admitted to Childs: "My health goes on as usual. Something is the matter, for I get weaker every day. I tried Long Island bathing with my friend Grinnell, but could not stand it."

Kane was now working on supporting materials. Feeling responsible to his scientific supporters, he insisted on incorporating eighteen appendices that eventually ran to an incredible 168 printed pages. These included not only various individual reports but tables and lists on everything from Arctic plants to magnetic dip, wind velocity, and temperatures, as well as a fold-out chart entitled *Mean Monthly Isothermal Lines of Baffin Bay.*

For the sake of readability, Childs had wisely stipulated that this technical data be confined to the back of the book—though today, any scientist studying global warming in the Arctic might well find it the most valuable part of the book. Aware of such considerations, the disgruntled scientist in Kane would tell Childs, "After the *opus magnum* now in your hands, I hope to publish, either through the Smithsonian or the Government, a work on Ice, for reputation sake."

Meanwhile, the appendices required yet another expenditure of energy. By August 9, Kane would write, "I am now convinced that my enemy is a combination of rheumatism and the Arctic scourge of scurvy." Twelve days later, he wrote, "My motion being impeded by my maladies, I would regard it as a favor if you could come to me for a few minutes." On September 18, he confessed, "I am unable to announce any improvement in my health." And five days after that, he added: "At present I see no possible chance of being able to work in any way; and the unanswered letters which crowd around me might well appall an abler man. . . . The book, poor as it is, has been my coffin."

o   o   o

Late in September 1856, less than a year after Kane arrived back in New York, Childs & Peterson published *Arctic Explorations: The Second Grinnell Expedition in Search of Sir John Franklin, 1853, '54, '55*. This sounds incredibly fast, given that the two volumes together total 931 pages and include more than 200 illustrations. But the publisher had typeset the work as Kane produced it, all the while calling for more.

The ambitious Childs conducted a superb marketing campaign. He provided booksellers with illustrated broadsides and secured endorsements from such influential figures as Alfred Tennyson, Louis Agassiz, William Cullen Bryant, and Washington Irving. He also planted glowing advance articles in newspapers, including a long biographical sketch by Dr. William Elder, who would later produce the first biography of Kane.

None of this would have mattered if Kane had failed to deliver. But in the U.S., soon after the book appeared, the man of letters George William Curtis wrote, "As a personal narrative, it is unquestionably at the head of our Arctic literature, which is a literature by itself—and there is not a boy in the land to whom your name will not be as famous and dear as Robinson Crusoe. So young to be so famous, and to have deserved such fame to its utmost reward—is not that something?"

In the U.K., a discerning review in the *Saturday Review* can be considered representative: "Looked at merely from a literary point of view, the book is a very remarkable one. It consists almost entirely of extracts from a journal kept at the time, connected by narrative matter more or less compressed from it. An attentive reader can trace the feelings and prospects of the little knot of icebound prisoners, and of their gallant leader, with extraordinary clearness, for Dr. Kane is obviously a cultivated man, and by no means unaccustomed to watch the processes of his own mind. The hoping against hope, the determination to look at the bright side of things, and the effort to write himself into a cheerful frame of mind . . . seems to us far better worth having than any amount of artistic composition."

Such was the critical reception. Before *Arctic Explorations* appeared, the publisher had pre-sold 20,000 copies. Within its first year, the two-volume work would sell 65,000 copies, and so earn Kane, under the existing royalty agreement, $65,000. In contemporary terms, this equates to $1.5 million, and denotes a spectacular commercial success. Within three years, *Arctic Explorations* would sell 145,000 copies, generating the equivalent today of $3.4 million. For Elisha Kent Kane, tragically, this rapid success would arrive too late.

35

TWO BECOME ONE

In May 1856, thanks to the enthusiastic sponsorship of Jane Franklin, Elisha Kent Kane received the gold medal of the Royal Geographical Society—the highest honor the society could bestow—"for his distinguished services and important discoveries in the polar regions, while in charge of the expedition fitted out in America to search for Sir John Franklin, and for his valuable memoir and charts."

Lady Franklin anticipated—indeed, her expectation was almost a decree—that Kane would lead yet another "final" search expedition to the west coast of King William Island. That was where, according to convincing evidence provided by explorer John Rae, the Franklin expedition had come to grief. Initially, Kane leapt at the chance to lead that endeavor. Despite ominous symptoms—weight loss, emaciation, physical weakness, lack of energy—the explorer convinced himself that all he needed was rest.

By mid-July, however, he realized that he would not be able to undertake a proposed lecture tour, much less lead an Arctic expedition. Henry Grinnell wrote to Jane Franklin that Kane had visited for an hour: "I never saw him look so bad; he is but a skeleton or the shadow of one; he has worked too hard." Kane dreamed of traveling to France and Switzerland,

and regaining his health among the glaciers before proceeding to England. But Grinnell noted, "He is every day attacked with the remittent fever, better known here as fever and ague."

Jane Franklin was embroiled in a battle over a British ship called the *Resolute*. In 1854, to his everlasting disgrace, Edward Belcher had abandoned that ship and three others in the Arctic ice. The following year, an American whaler, James Buddington, chanced upon the *Resolute,* which was by then floating freely. With a skeleton crew, he sailed it home to the United States. The American navy, urged on by Henry Grinnell, purchased the salvaged vessel, refurbished it, and proposed to return it to Britain as a goodwill gesture.

Meanwhile, Lady Franklin had launched a furious campaign to acquire the *Resolute* for yet another "final" search expedition. Over the years, however, she had made powerful enemies at the Admiralty, and she needed allies. Elisha Kane had established himself as almost without peer, and she clamored for his presence with her usual relentless energy. He was not just the most famous of contemporary explorers, but also the most eloquent and engaging. If he could not lead the expedition, then she hoped he would at least assist her in gaining control of the *Resolute*.

Her niece and confidential secretary, Sophy Cracroft, wrote to Kane: "My aunt sends you 2 letters which we know will have weight with you, and if you can act upon the suggestions they contain, there is no doubt that the Admiralty would at once place the *Resolute* in my aunt's hands for the search. . . . All that is wanted is to have a representation of your wish that the ship should be made over to my aunt signed by a few friends." Soon afterward, she sent another letter: "Sir Roderick Murchison [vice-president of the Royal Geographical Society] is so increasingly convinced of the all importance of such a representation on your part that (without of course presuming to say it will be made) he intends intimating the probability of it to Sir Charles Wood [First Lord of the Admiralty], as an inducement to make him give up the ship to my aunt."

Lady Franklin did not appreciate the seriousness of Kane's condition. And the explorer himself could not accept that rheumatic fever and endocarditis had begun their final assault. With the *Resolute* slated to arrive in England in November, he wrote: "It was my intention to have sought repose and health by a few weeks' sojourn in Switzerland, but I will come to England to confer with you [Jane Franklin], and return for a longer visit after I have attempted to relieve your cares. . . . My book, 900 pages of *ad captandum* sacrifice, has left my hands. . . . I have no fault of health but a complete inability to withstand hot weather and indoor life." That Kane had established a rapport with the widow is evident in his use of the Latin phrase *ad captandum,* which suggests a "meretricious attempt to catch or win popular favor." Of all those to whom he wrote, with perhaps the exception of his father, she was the only one who would appreciate such a phrase.

On August 31, while seeking to regain his health at Brattleboro, a well-known health clinic in Vermont, Kane wrote to his father in support of Lady Franklin's campaign, asking the Judge to use his influence with the U.S. secretary of state. He noted that he himself would decide whether to command the expedition: "Looking ahead and feeling as I now do—*this dream must be over*—my health is gone—on this head I say nothing more. You may imagine all that I feel. But Lady Franklin's means are limited and my intermediation and influence with Admiralty could procure her from the Naval Dock Yards nearly all that she would need; my withdrawal would be on the other hand both a loss and a misfortune." A few days later, he instructed his father: "Make the concluding chapter of my book expressive of sympathy with and hope for Sir John Franklin. My closing words as you see them in the manuscript."

The advance from his publisher made a transatlantic voyage possible. Some observers have suggested that Kane looked forward to being feted in England and to meeting such eminent British figures as poet laureate Alfred Tennyson. That reserved author had, uncharacteristically, sent Kane not one but two effusive letters, writing of *Arctic Explorations:* "I believe I never met with [a book] which gives such vivid pictures of Arctic scenery. Nay, I am quite sure I never did: & indeed I feel that I owe you more thanks for it, & for your warm-hearted inscription, & your memorial of me in the wilderness than I could well enclose in as many words." Tennyson sent a signed copy of "that volume of my poems containing the line which . . . came into your mind when you stood first before the great greenstone monument." Certainly, Kane hoped to meet Tennyson and others—mainly explorers. In the end, however, the decision to go came down to what he told the Judge: "I think that duty requires my presence."

o   o   o

The previous week, Maggie Fox had traveled to Canada West (now Ontario) with her mother to visit her ailing grandfather. As she left, Maggie wrote of leaving Manhattan immediately, "as Mamma's father is not expected to live. It will therefore be impossible for us to meet, until we return [from Canada]." From Philadelphia, Kane responded: "I am very sick, and go this afternoon to Brattleboro, Vermont [site of the "water-cure" sanitorium], to which address send me a letter at once, saying when you will be back. . . . But just to think of it! You will see me again before I cross the water, for I cannot leave until [October] the tenth; and as soon as your letter reaches me, will hasten to New York."

Patients at the unorthodox sanitorium, which combined homeopathy and hydrotherapy, would be wakened at four in the morning, overheated in warm blankets, and then plunged into cold water. After enduring three weeks of this treatment, unhelpful at best, Kane spent a couple of weeks in the Berkshire Hills of Massachusetts, at the home of a friend of Henry Grinnell. His condition failed to improve.

To Maggie, before she left, the jealous lover in Kane had said, "You must remember that you are mine; you must hold yourself sacred, as my wife should be; there must be no flirting; you must receive no attentions from gentlemen." Laughing, Maggie asked, "Should I then disclose our engagement?" To which Kane replied, "Yes—if brought to it."

From Cobourg, Maggie wrote: "Have you visited our home in Twenty-Second Street? I suppose if you have you found it solitary enough. . . . I have often dreamt of you since I left, and have twice dreamt that you were *very* ill, and wakened each time weeping bitterly. But fortunately my dreams always prove false, unless they are of a pleasing character." In another missive, she declared: "Without you all is darkness, and every place seems a grave. You ask if I mix in company. No, no. I join no merry scenes. 'Lish, I have not laughed since we parted. By the time we meet again I fear I shall quite have forgotten how to laugh." She added a teasing note: "You will clothe me in the habiliments of a nun, and send me to a convent to count my rosary," but she closed, "On the wings of angels, I send you ten thousand kisses."

When Maggie wrote of laughter, she conjured Kane's gift for mimicry. He often convulsed her and her family with his imitations, she revealed later, and once persuaded Mrs. Fox to tell a curious visitor that a renowned professor was in the parlor. When the woman entered, he commenced "a discourse on abstruse scientific subjections in the most elaborate style, and in a loud tone of voice, for her edification. In such boyish pastimes he delighted, and his return to them showed a heart once more at ease."

In the third week of September, with Maggie due to arrive home, Kane moved back to New York—officially, into the residence of Henry Grinnell, though in fact he spent more time at East Twenty-Second Street. As a welcome-home gift, he gave Maggie a bound galley of *Arctic Explorations,* far more valuable than a first edition. Also, he bought her a diamond bracelet from Tiffany's, and told her as they went to collect it, "They will all know now, Maggie, that I want it for my betrothed."

One evening, while Kane waited for her in the third-floor parlor, Maggie surprised him by emerging from a closet, wearing an exotic costume and laughing self-consciously. Kane found her enchanting. He declared that she was Eve, that she was woman eternal, or perhaps some nymph out of Greek mythology. He insisted that she have an ambrotype photograph taken in this dress. To the photographer, he specified a "large plate—figure erect—complete profile—eyelids drooping, countenance pensive and looking down." Next morning, when Maggie expressed a fear that perhaps the costume was too revealing, he urged her forward: "Don't be afraid of your neck and shoulders. I want you to look like Circe, for you have already changed me into a wild boar."

Kane booked passage to Liverpool on October 11. The steamship company, the Collins Line, was providing free passage on the *Baltic* for both him and his former steward William Morton, who joined him as a valet. Meanwhile, he took Maggie and her sister Kate to the opera at Niblo's Garden, and brought her with him when he went to say goodbye to several friends and acquaintances, among them General Winfield Scott—as near a public announcement of engagement as, under such hurried circumstances, he could make.

As departure day drew near, and his health showed no sign of improving, Kane had a presentiment that his death might be imminent: "Maggie, what if I should die away from you? Oh, my own Maggie, could I but die in your arms, I would ask no more! I can part from all the rest,—even from my mother—with calmness; it is parting with you, Maggie, that kills me."

If he died, what would happen to Maggie Fox? Kane prepared a new last will and testament, a document witnessed by Henry Grinnell and his wife and daughter. Not realizing, yet, quite how much his new book would earn in royalties, he stipulated that $5,000 be paid out immediately to his brother Robert. This sum, the equivalent today of roughly $115,000, he intended for Maggie. Both Mrs. Fox and the Grinnells understood this, as well as Maggie.

A couple of nights before he sailed, Kane asked, "If I send for you, Maggie, will you come to me?" She answered, "Certainly, I will." Reflecting on how this might be judged, Kane said, "I fear you would hesitate. And yet you are my own! My wife! You remember what I have told you." He paused, according to *Love-Life,* then asked Maggie, "Would you like me to repeat what I have said, formally, in the presence of your mother?"

A declaration of connection in the presence of witnesses, he rightly told her, constituted a legal and binding marriage: "Attend to me, Maggie. Listen: would you be willing *now* to enter into such a bond?"

Maggie said yes. Kane summoned everyone in the house to the third-floor parlor—Kate, Mrs. Fox, a servant, and a young woman visitor. He explained that he wanted them to witness a solemn declaration. Then, putting his left arm around Maggie and taking her hand in his, Kane said: "Maggie is my wife, and I am her husband. Wherever we are, she is mine, and I am hers. Do you understand and consent to this, Maggie?"

The young woman said she did. Kane then explained that he did this to provide against any eventuality. The ceremony, he said, made the two as indissolubly one as if performed in a church. And, thinking ahead to the time by which he would be financially independent, he added that the marriage "shall be made public in May."

To the lovers, only a short while remained. To spend a last night with Maggie, Kane pleaded ill health and declined an invitation to a celebration dinner with the mayor of Philadelphia and two dozen leading citizens. On the morning of Saturday, October 11, 1856, with both of them weeping, Elisha Kent Kane left his wife, Maggie Fox, at the door of her mother's house. He climbed into a carriage and, with her portrait sitting on the seat beside him, and grim foreboding in his heart, set out for the docks to board the *Baltic*.

36

The Land of Fog

After a smooth Atlantic crossing, on October 22, 1856, the *Baltic* steamed into Liverpool. Elisha Kane had spent most of the voyage in his berth, although he did not suffer his usual seasickness. Accompanied by William Morton, he strolled the deck occasionally. An old acquaintance and fellow traveler, Dr. Betton, later reported that "when his strength would permit, he seemed to rise above his maladies and enjoy all around him, contributing his share to the general happiness."

In Liverpool, Kane went to the Adelphi Hotel. Built thirty years before, it still offered the city's finest accommodation. Here he received the mayor, who came to pay his respects. But the soot and coal dust of the industrial city exacerbated Kane's condition, and he developed a miserable cold with a bronchial cough. On arrival, he wrote to his mother: "We reached this foggy smoke palled city at 7 o'clock last night and after a night at a tolerably comfortless inn, I try with rheumatic hand—head is out of the question—to write you my safe arrival. . . . Lady Franklin—dear woman . . . has been actively reading and posting herself about hot baths. What will be the result of her review? I cannot tell. My present idea or rather [Doctor] Betton's idea is the south of France, but every body tells me that December and November are most disagreeable months every where in Europe, and I truly believe it." He closed: "My hand so aches that, paper ending, I end too. Bye bye."

After three nights in Liverpool, Kane left by train for London. Jane Franklin had arranged for him to stay at the home of scientist and explorer Edward Sabine, who had once sailed as an astronomer with Sir John Ross, Kane's "old man" mentor. When she returned to the city, she began visiting Kane every day. Not yet realizing how ill he was, she believed he might recover sufficiently to lead her next expedition. Kane yearned to escape both her expectations and the polluted, coal-dusty city, where people walked the streets holding handkerchiefs to their faces, and just the next year, the stink of the Thames would force parliamentarians to abandon sitting. Kane dreamed of sailing to the more salubrious climes of Algiers, Madeira, or Cuba.

To his father, Kane wrote that the sixty-four-year-old Lady Franklin "offers to go to Madeira with me. She comes here daily and kisses 'my pale. forehead.' Dear Father, the woman would use me, if she could, even now. . . . She wants me to go to Madeira simply because it insures my return to England when she has a scheme for me to urge her case before Prince Albert. She has been skirmishing around this for some time and I shall not be sorry when the proper moment enables me to say, 'As long, Lady Franklin, as I was the recognized leader of your party I would have felt it a duty to apply, etc., but my health having forced me to withdraw, any application on my part as an American would be an impertinence.'"

Kane enjoyed little of the attention that might have been his—the discussion of his charts with geographers, the lectures he would have given to scientific societies. He did receive notification, from Rear Admiral Frederick Beechey, that the Royal Geographical Society had acclaimed a resolution expressing its admiration for his conduct. That society, according to the *Illustrated London News,* passed a motion expressing sincere regret that "this distinguished man should have been prevented by ill health from appearing at the meeting to receive the unanimous and hearty welcome which awaited him." Kane did manage to visit Whitehall, where the Lords of the Admiralty presented him with a silver service comprising coffee pot, tea pot, sugar bowl, and pitcher, along with an inscribed tray thanking him "for his gallant and generous exertions in command of the American Arctic Expedition dispatched to afford assistance to Sir John Franklin and the officers and crews" of the *Erebus* and *Terror*.

But Sir Roderick Murchison would write that, by the time he encountered Kane, "alas! the hand of death was already upon him. . . . I at once saw that his eagle eye beamed forth from a wasted and all but expiring body." He added that, while staying in the city, Kane called once or twice on Lady Franklin, "but the fogs of London, so thick at mid-day that the street-lamps were invisible and flambeaus were carried before the carriages, overcame him: he grew worse rapidly."

From his country estate, Captain Richard Collinson spoke for many when he wrote to Kane: "My dear Sir: I regret to find by a letter from Lady Franklin that the state of your health is such as to demand immediate departure from our island, and that I shall not have an opportunity which I had hoped to do of expressing in person my congratulations on your return from an enterprise which . . . will ever reflect honour upon your home."

Kane's health continued to deteriorate, and after eight days in London his friends took him to a residence outside the city. The eminent physician Henry Holland diagnosed the explorer as suffering from rheumatic swellings of the joints, as well as chills, fever, rapid pulse, and a dry cough. While noting that Kane had lost weight and strength, he detected no heart problems. Dr. William Elder, writing in the 1850s, suggested that "a rheumatic affliction of the heart looks like the better explanation of the anomalous symptoms so often exhibited," and in the 1970s Dr. George Corner would write that Kane's symptoms pointed clearly to "bacterial endocarditis with subacute bronchitis."

All the doctors agreed, Kane himself wrote, that his inability to recover "is explained by my extreme want of power and this wretched land of fogs. They all urge the 'exaltation' of vital function to be expected from a warmer climate." With a view to getting nearer the U.S., Kane decided to go to Cuba. Jane Franklin, realizing finally that Kane was deathly ill, sent for Cornelius Grinnell, who was visiting Paris on business. He hurried to London and booked passage for Kane and Morton on the steamer *Orinoco,* which would sail from Southampton on November 17.

While preparing to sail, Kane gave Jane Franklin a portrait of himself— a work she would frame in gold and crimson velvet and hang in a place of honor. Sophy Cracroft, Lady Franklin's niece and amanuensis, wrote to Henry Grinnell, "I cannot tell you how unhappy and absorbed my aunt has been by Dr. Kane's illness." In another letter to Grinnell, dated November 21, 1856, Cracroft spoke of Lady Franklin's distress over the explorer's ill health, but also deplored "the painful impression created by the disclosures of Dr. Kane's book. Day by day, we have now the task of facing the—to us—terrible result, viz: that its horrors will probably prevent the sending out a vessel to complete the search."

Those opposed to dispatching a naval expedition, Cracroft explained, refused to consider "whether such sufferings have ever been encountered before, in any modern Arctic Expedition, public or private," and whether they were likely to be repeated. "I need not tell you what must be my Aunt's feelings as she slowly but surely receives this dreadful impression, that a result so contrary to Dr. Kane's intuition, and yet I fear, too naturally following from his recital, is impending." Her fears proved well founded: the Admiralty would refuse to finance another search, leaving Lady Franklin to sponsor one more private expedition, that of Leopold McClintock in the *Fox.*

Now, before leaving London, Kane wrote his mother that William Morton, formerly an Arctic companion, now his steward, had returned to the metropolis after visiting his parents in Ireland. "His conduct is most exemplary and I could not do without him. He goes to Southampton in advance to prepare all things for my comfort." Sending along his warm love, he added, "My life has been marked by crises, and I trust that this, like others, will be but to establish better things . . . so avoiding the harsher regions of the Atlantic, I cross the tropic winds and work my way homeward in sunshine."

His closest friends, however, proved less optimistic. After communicating with Lady Franklin and his son Cornelius, Henry Grinnell wrote to Judge Kane: "My heart is bad, bad, bad, so is that of Mrs. G. and all my family. I am preparing my mind for the worst. May God in his infinite mercy avert so great an affliction as depriving us of your noble son." The Judge responded that he remained confident: "I have waited in suspense for weeks, when the army surgeon's letter had assured me that he must die before morning of his wounds in Mexico. I have heard of him prostrate and hopeless with the fever of the African coast, and, before that, with the plague; I have twice bidden him a last goodbye, when he sailed upon his crises for the Arctic; and but little more than a year ago, when he was fairly out of time, I gave him almost up for ten days before he reached New York. And now I cannot realize that so noble a spirit, so well tried in suffering and peril, so full of love and fortitude and daring, is to be the victim of ordinary disease."

o   o   o

On the *Orinoco,* which sailed from Britain to the Caribbean, Kane enjoyed a smooth passage, though he suffered from swelling and pain in the joints. To Maggie Fox, whose daily letters to him had gone astray, Kane had written as he left Liverpool: "I have just time to catch the steamer, dear Tutie, to tell you of my safe arrival, and to beg you to write should you need anything. Pardon the haste of this letter, and believe me always as of old."

At Southampton, according to William Morton, Kane was "in a very bad way. . . . His rheumatism was so bad that he . . . had to be lifted out of his carriage to the train and from it again to the docks. Even to stand upright gave him great pain. It was not only in his feet and legs, however, but shifted about into every portion of his body." During the voyage, Morton added, "His night sweats were tremendous. I had to keep a fire burning every night, and some nights changed his shirts and drawers every half hour."

While sailing on the *Orinoco,* his fingers swollen, Kane managed to write a brief note to Maggie Fox—the last letter he would ever write: "Dear Tutie: I am quite sick and have gone to Havana; only one week from New York.

336

I have received no letters from you; but write at once to E.K. Kane, care of American consul, Havana."

The *Orinoco* reached the Caribbean island of St. Thomas on December 2, 1856. During the next couple of weeks, while awaiting a ship to Havana, Kane became the guest of an American named Robert Swift. He endured fevers and night sweats, yet proved able to walk from bedroom to dining room, a distance of thirty feet. He believed himself to be recovering as a result of the warmer climate. In his journal, Morton noted that Kane's face grew fatter and "lost the weary expression and haggard old look it had in England."

Kane took quinine to ward off the fever. On the afternoon of December 20, despite a strong wind and a heavy, rough sea, Kane felt well enough to sail for Havana. The next morning, complaining of nausea, he took a strong dose of quinine. Morton went up on deck to breathe for a few moments, and had just arrived back when Kane awoke and sat bolt upright. He lay down, but after a couple of minutes, in a thick voice, he called Morton and asked for medicine. The steward told him it was all gone, but soon saw he had misunderstood. Kane "lay on his back and moaned. I asked him what was the matter and he went on regardless of me as if in pain. And I said are you sick, and he said yes, and I said shall I go and seek the ship's doctor, to which he answered yes also."

Morton, who described these events in a detailed journal, summoned the ship's doctor, who gave Kane a pain reliever. After the man left, Morton said, "What is the matter? You scare me, sir." Kane "replied pretty plain, though as if his tongue was swollen: 'You may well be scared, poor fellow. You will not have me to trouble you long.'" The explorer fell silent, Morton wrote, though "he squeezed my hand repeatedly in a manner which I understood to be bidding goodbye."

Later, doctors diagnosed an apoplectic stroke. A fragment of heart-valve tissue, damaged by bacterial infection, had broken off and been carried along by the bloodstream to block an artery leading to the brain. Yet, over the next couple of days, Kane revived somewhat. He sat up without support, and watched keenly as, on December 25, the vessel sailed into Havana.

Here he was met by his brother Thomas, whose own health had been damaged by pulmonary tuberculosis and who had hurried south after learning of the situation. Within four days, Kane was able to move his right leg, though his right arm remained paralyzed. Over the next couple of weeks, while installed at a Mrs. Almy's hotel, Kane slowly regained the use of his right hand, wrist, and forearm. But he continued to slur his words, and clearly he had lost some memory.

As December ended, Thomas Kane sent a letter to the Judge, telling him to open it in privacy. "I give you bad news," he wrote. "Things look better here these three days past; but Elisha has had a paralytic stroke! A week has passed since he had it, which has been on the whole a week of improvement . . . but you must fully resign yourself to regard it as a calamity of the gravest kind."

To his mother, Thomas wrote: "If anything can comfort you in this affliction, it may be in the surpassing love which Elisha has shown himself to bear you. Other thoughts often trouble him, but your name he seems to rest upon invariably with a comfort and support that is unmistakeable. When we meet, I will give you many particulars of this which are too affecting for me to be able at present to dwell upon; but I trust you will still see him at New Orleans where he *may* land within eight days of this date. Mother, you have my word for it, that he not only understood your not coming, as explained in your letter, but approves of it. He would have you meet him at New Orleans, if this be so ordered; but finds a reason to reconcile him to this delay in the hope that you may see him improved in appearance when the time comes. Your interview would have been too trying to both of you had it taken place when he first landed here."

Kane proved unable to sail to New Orleans. But his mother could not stay away. While his father, the Judge, remained at work in his courtroom, Jane Leiper Kane traveled to Havana with Elisha's brother Patterson. The once-brilliant explorer, reduced now to childhood memories, expressed a yearning to return home. His family booked passage on a ship to New York, but awaited favorable weather.

Mrs. Almy's Hotel in Havana: Elisha Kane died here at age thirty-seven.

On February 10, while waiting, Elisha Kane suffered a second stroke, more terrible than the first. He regained partial consciousness, but lay now completely paralyzed. He lingered still, prompting a doctor familiar with his medical history to marvel, "One can hardly conceive how life could have been sustained for so long a period as five days after the last shock." On February 16, 1857, at age thirty-seven, while his mother sat reading at his bedside, Elisha Kent Kane passed forever into the land of fog.

37

THE JUDGMENT OF 1857

The very next day, on February 17, 1857, the *New York Daily Times* printed a front-page headline that shocked and saddened tens of thousands of Americans: "Dr. Elisha Kane Dies in Havana." The short report that followed carried few details. But regular readers of the *Times* would have remembered that, less than two years before, they had thrilled to the saga of Kane's triumphant return from a two-year ordeal in the Arctic.

To read that now he was dead? Impossible!

As news of the explorer's death sank in throughout the land, it inspired an outpouring of grief on a scale unprecedented in America. The mourning began in Havana the day after Kane died, when every American in the city turned out at a public square. The consul read them a letter from the captain-general of Cuba, who offered the state barge to convey the explorer's body to the ship that would carry his remains to the United States.

Three days later, a procession of 800 people followed the casket to a central square, the Plaza de Armas, while two military bands played dirges. Starting from the waterfront, and flying the Stars and Stripes, the barge transported the casket to the packet *Cahawba,* accompanied by a flotilla of boats. During a ceremony aboard the steamer, the governor of Havana spoke of Kane's heroic ideals, and the American consul responded. Three family members—Kane's mother and two brothers—and his faithful steward, Henry Morton, sailed with the casket, and arrived in the United States on February 22.

In New Orleans, the mayor came aboard and offered a military escort. The Continental Guards carried the coffin to City Hall, where Kane's body lay in state until a paddle steamer was ready to carry it north up the Mississippi River. A dozen officers of the army and navy carried the casket to that vessel, accompanied by hundreds of people, among them military men, foreign dignitaries, members of a Masonic lodge, and an imposing British delegation.

The riverboat spent one full week traveling the Mississippi and Ohio rivers, as at every small town, people gathered on the wharves and levees and insisted on paying homage. The explorer's parents and one of his brothers met the riverboat in Paducah, Kentucky, near the confluence of the Ohio and Tennessee rivers. At Louisville, a procession of carriages, horses, and marchers accompanied the casket to a public square, where dignitaries spoke for more than an hour.

The next day, a boat from Cincinnati met the riverboat. It transported the casket to that city, where several mayors and the governor of Ohio were among the hundreds of people who followed two dozen pallbearers from the wharf to the railway station. Here began a train journey that, in the next 150 years, would be matched or superseded only twice: once in 1865, during the public mourning for Abraham Lincoln, and again in 1968, when Americans marked the death of Robert Kennedy.

At every town along the route, church bells tolled and mourners lined the tracks and bowed their heads at the passing of the railway car draped in black. Again and again, people spilled over the tracks and delayed the train. At Columbus, Elisha Kane's body lay in state in the senate chamber while people stood with their heads bowed, attending to eulogy after eulogy. At smaller cities, where the casket remained on the train, mourners congregated at railway stations. Baltimore produced the grandest procession and the biggest crowds yet—including, according to one observer, an unusually large number of ladies, "who numbered thousands in the houses and on the sidewalks." Church bells tolled from eleven in the morning until four in the afternoon, and speakers included some of the most prominent citizens in Maryland.

On March 11, more than three weeks after Kane's death, the funeral train finally reached his native Philadelphia. The waiting throngs included a dozen committees, a cavalry troop, an artillery company, and several hundred police officers. A light rain fell as the hearse moved slowly through the city toward Independence Hall, the casket draped in the flag of the brigantine in which Kane had sailed farther north than any other explorer. Eight of those who had accompanied him now followed his body on foot.

In the Assembly Room at Independence Hall, birthplace of both the Declaration of Independence (1776) and the United States Constitution (1787), the body of Elisha Kent Kane lay in state within a few feet of the Liberty Bell. In being so honored, the explorer followed former president John Quincy Adams (1848) and preceded future president Abraham Lincoln (1865). Now, in 1857, attendants placed a ceremonial sword on the coffin, along with a magnificent wreath bearing the words, "To the Memory of Dr. Kane, from Two Ladies." For three days, people lined up and walked past to pay their respects.

Finally, on March 14, a group of seamen placed the casket on a twelve-foot funeral carriage that was drawn by four black horses and festooned with the national flags of several nations. Leaving Independence Hall, the cortege wound through the streets of Philadelphia. It passed the house on fashionable Walnut Street where Kane had been born, and continued to the Second Presbyterian Church in what one reporter called "a scene of solemn grandeur." After a final service here, where Elisha Kane had been baptized and attended Sunday school, distinguished honorary pallbearers—among them bishops and chief justices and shipping magnates—accompanied the coffin to Laurel Hill Cemetery. Before Kane's remains were interred in the

(Above) A present-day view of Independence Hall in Philadelphia.
In the Assembly Room, depicted in the engraving (below), the body
of Elisha Kent Kane lay in state for three days.

343

Elisha Kane was laid to rest in the family vault at Laurel Hill Cemetery. This vault, the lower of the two depicted in this photo from the 1950s, is now separated from most of the cemetery by an inconvenient fence.

family's hillside vault, which looked out over the Schuylkill River, a final speaker summarized the funeral proceedings as "one of the most distinguished eulogies that a people has ever pronounced upon one who claimed no distinction as a leader of armies or as a director in statesmanship."

The legislatures of Pennsylvania, New York, Massachusetts, Ohio, and New Jersey passed resolutions honoring the explorer. Condolences arrived from scientific societies around the world. From Great Britain, Sir Roderick Murchison of the Royal Geographical Society sent a eulogy in which he wrote: "The long procession of mourners, the crowded yet silent streets through which they move, the roll of muffled drums, the booming of minute-guns, the tolling of passing bells, the creped flags at half-mast, and all the solemn pageantry of the scene, proclaim that it is no ordinary occasion which has called forth these impressive demonstrations of public respect."

The most insightful summation came from Kane's friend John Pendleton Kennedy, formerly the secretary of the navy, who delivered a eulogy at the

Maryland Institute in Baltimore. Kennedy insisted that Kane's character and services were "worthy of being preserved in the memory of the nation." He praised his late friend as a gentle, brave spirit who combined the modest reserve of the student with the daring adventurousness of the chivalrous knight. "Such a character is a model for the training of youth and a subject for the applause of mature age," Kennedy declared. "The early death of Dr. Kane has been recognized as a national loss, and the honors which have been awarded to his memory, throughout the long journey by which his remains are conducted to their final resting place, are such as we have heretofore accorded only to the most eminent men of our country."

Yet perhaps those who best encapsulated the spirit of the times were the organizers of the obsequies in Cincinnati, Ohio. They wore badges announcing their mourning for Kane as explorer, scholar, and philanthropist, insisting that his very name added luster to the nation, and flatly declaring, "His memory shall be immortal."

Such was the judgment of 1857.

In Cincinnati, organizers of the funeral rites wore a badge insisting that the memory of Kane would live forever.

38

THE VERDICT OF HISTORY

In the century and a half since the death of Elisha Kent Kane, millions have visited Philadelphia's Independence Hall, where once his body lay in state. The building is the focal point of a World Heritage Site that comprises several city blocks. It includes monuments to dozens of figures, among them Benjamin Franklin, Edgar Allan Poe, and even a Polish military engineer named Thaddeus Kosciuszko. Yet a contemporary visitor will look in vain for a memorial to the Philadelphian explorer.

Once upon a time, Kane was an American icon. When he returned from his second expedition, the *New York Times* devoted its entire front page to the event. And the public mourning that followed his demise—a three-week funeral cortege, eulogies in six states, badges declaring "His memory shall be immortal"—can be compared, in that era, only with the national grief inspired by the passing of Abraham Lincoln.

For a while, with the backing of the Kane family, William Morton mounted a traveling exhibit called "Panorama of Dr. Kane's Arctic Voyage," for which he donned an Arctic costume and displayed one of the whaleboats (the *Faith*), Kane's rifle, and other artifacts. In April 1859, two years after the explorer's death, a group of New Yorkers created a Kane Monument

Association. They drew up bylaws, appointed committees, and undertook to see that "the monument shall be built within four years from the passage of this act." They began raising funds to build a bronze statue, but never did manage to get the job done. In the city of his birth, meanwhile, on June 5, 1857, a lodge of Philadelphia Freemasons honored Kane ceremonially. Then they moved on. Even here, in history-sensitive Philadelphia, this once-celebrated hero has left no permanent mark.

Today, a visitor to Independence Hall or to Laurel Hill Cemetery, where the explorer's remains are interred, essentially unmarked, in a family vault, will be driven to wonder: Did 1857 get it wrong? Did the explorer not merit the adoration he inspired, especially as he achieved what he did while waging a lifelong battle against debilitating illness? Are his accomplish-ments—geographical, anthropological, artistic, literary, survivalist—not worthy of remembrance?

If Kane did richly deserve a long goodbye, and if he did merit that unprecedented display of grief and public mourning, why does he now stand so completely forgotten? How can it be that only those with a passion for Arctic exploration even recognize his name? How has Kane become invisible?

Faced with this conundrum, the visitor to Philadelphia might specu-late about nationality and timing. Scholars of all nationalities tend to study their own. British authors have paid scant attention to Kane because they view Arctic exploration as interesting only insofar as it relates to their own imperial narrative. On the other hand, given that the polar route Kane dis-covered traces the northeastern coast of what is now Canada, certainly this story belongs to Canadian history. And yet, while laying claim to Scottish, French, and English explorers, Canadians have turned their backs on this inspirational American.

For Americans, the timing was wrong. Kane had scarcely been laid to rest when, in 1861, the Civil War erupted. That war was a watershed, a turning point that caused Americans to view unrelated events from around the same period as peripheral to the national narrative. In recent years,

This metal figurine of a bearded Kane with telescope and dog stands twelve inches tall. It may have been a model for a bronze statue that was never made.

American scholars have tried to situate Kane within a variety of secondary contexts—for example, within the histories of science, marketing, and even, negatively, Spiritualism. These studies have produced insights, but none of them has situated Kane as a central figure. None has succeeded in establishing him as a national hero.

Still, as explanation, context goes only so far. The visitor will turn to specifics, beginning with the men who sailed with Kane. Four of them— Isaac Hayes, Henry Goodfellow, Amos Bonsall, and Thomas Hickey—later wrote tributes to his leadership. Recent historians have paid scant attention, preferring to focus on negative accounts by John Wall Wilson, William Godfrey, and Carl Petersen. The criticisms of those three colored the portrait of Kane in *The Arctic Grail,* that classic overview of exploration published in 1988 by Pierre Berton.

Two later scholars, Chauncey Loomis and Constance Martin, have argued that "Berton does not take into account the fact that during the expedition Kane found all three [of those critics] wanting and let them know it." They have a point. John Wall Wilson kept a private journal during the voyage.

In it, he writes that Kane was "peevish, coarse, sometimes insulting . . . [he] thinks no one knows anything but himself." Wilson was furious about the leniency with which Kane treated William Godfrey, "a most audacious villain," and would have had the man flogged "until he could not stand." Wilson's anger derives from his own altercation with Godfrey, already described. And his feelings are understandable.

Perhaps Kane should have sent Godfrey home on a whaling vessel. But he remained desperately shorthanded, and he judged that Godfrey could make a crucial contribution as both the strongest man on board and a dog handler. And so he did. More to the point, Kane had felt compelled to reduce Wilson's responsibilities. To Cornelius Grinnell, even before reaching Melville Bay, he wrote that he had been forced to replace Wilson as second officer: "This I was sorry for; but I talked the matter over with Mr. Wilson, and he agreed with me that he had not experience enough in the duties. The fact is, he had no control over the men, and was deficient in seamanship as a deck officer. Ohlsen very modestly drew my attention to it; but I waited till we got among the ice, and then without hurting his [Wilson's] feelings, got him to withdraw from the watch as deck officer, on account of his eyes, he being very near sighted. Wilson is a good fellow, very pushing, but not reliable in emergencies. We are excellent friends, and he understands me I think perfectly."

Wilson understood, it would appear, less than perfectly. But some confusion attends his original appointment. While hiring officers, Kane drafted a letter of invitation to a sailor named Robert P. Wilson, "recently rated a master's mate in the service"—a man never heard from again. In his letter of application, the far less qualified John Wall Wilson had described himself: "I am 21 years of age, in good health, of ordinary physical endurance and have seen some sea service—one voyage up the Baltic, one to India, and two to London as third officer in one of my uncle's packets." Did the wrong man receive the appointment? Early in the voyage, Kane realized that as master's mate, Wilson was in over his head. And, with grace and sensitivity, he demoted the man. The resulting testimony must be assessed accordingly.

The second critic, William Godfrey himself, published his own counter-narrative of the voyage, as already indicated. A contemporary scholar, Mark Metzler Sawin, has established that the semi-literate Godfrey got help from ghostwriter Ella Lloyd, the wife of Philadelphia publisher James T. Lloyd. This couple produced Godfrey's book for commercial reasons, and its lack of credibility at crucial moments has already been demonstrated.

Clearly, the physically powerful Godfrey, hired off the docks by Cornelius Grinnell, lacked the vision, imagination, and sense of purpose required of those sailing on a voyage of exploration. The emotional truth about the man is captured in *The Voyage of the Narwhal* by Andrea Barrett. In that superb novel, Barrett's fictional narrator judges Godfrey to be a horrid man who "boils with resentment and self-interest." That narrator does wonder whether the rough sailor might not have some truth on his side.

But here we return to documentary fact. Was Elisha Kane angry, as Godfrey asserts, when half his crew defected, abandoning the sick to his ministrations, and possibly to death? Yes, and why should he not have been? Did he prove less than saintly, as Godfrey claims, in welcoming the defectors back on board? Yes—but they were lucky he received them at all. Certainly, Kane displayed an iron will after the return, and it's a good thing he did, or none of his crew would ever have escaped their frozen prison. Soon after publishing Godfrey's narrative, the opportunistic Lloyds brought out a book purportedly written by August Sonntag, though the astronomer himself immediately denounced the work as a fraud and disavowed any connection.

And so we arrive at Carl Petersen, the most credible critic. Five years older than Kane, and convinced of his own superiority as an ice expert, Petersen proved almost as problematic as Godfrey. Isaac Hayes, who would sail with him again, judged Petersen cautious, opinionated, and overly critical, "with somewhat of the persistence of a frontiersman's recollection of wrongs done to him." Writing in Danish, Petersen produced a 100-page account of the expedition. In the 1960s, a scholar named Oscar M. Villarejo translated, contextualized, and published this narrative as *Dr. Kane's Voyage to the Polar Lands.* Petersen's rendition, according to Villarejo, reveals "the high drama of the clash of the two strongest and most commanding person-alities among the twenty men aboard": Kane and Petersen.

After the withdrawal of Ohlsen, Petersen led the defection—an enter-prise that ended in defeat. And then he had to watch Kane demonstrate how such an escape could be achieved. As Villarejo observes, "the ignomini-ous manner in which the withdrawal party was forced to capitulate to the superior strategy of Dr. Kane must have represented a great loss of prestige to a person who had hitherto been considered one of the world's foremost experts in arctic exploration."

Elsewhere, Villarejo insists that "not many months after the failure of the withdrawal party to reach Upernavik, Elisha Kane successfully planned, organized, and executed one of the most remarkable journeys of escape in the annals of Arctic explorations (May 17 to August 6, 1855) when he con-ducted his sick and scurvy-ridden companions from the ice-bound brig in which the expedition had been trapped for two years and led his men to safety by means of sledges and open boats to the Danish settlements of northern Greenland." And he judges that, as a result of jealousy and resent-ment, "Petersen's manuscript fails to pay adequate tribute to Dr. Kane" for this accomplishment.

Petersen, it should also be remembered, blamed Kane for the deaths of Pierre Schubert and Jefferson Baker. He argued that March 19 was too early to dispatch a depot party from the ship, and that this premature sortie could only end in disaster—a criticism already answered and thoroughly rebutted by the experience of other explorers. In his unpublished journal, though not in *Arctic Explorations,* Kane provides a deeper analysis. First, he writes that, because he is obliged to comment unfavorably on the conduct of Mr. Brooks, "this journal is only for private and friendly eyes."

Writing before either death, Kane observes: "The practical error of the journey was in starting for the brig in a wind, instead of remaining housed in the tent until the weather became safe. The determination to return was made on the 29th, after a two days halt for a wind which still continued.

The party travelled nine hours with this wind on their backs and the ther-mometer at −40 degrees. Up to this time, the party in the midst of more severe temperatures (−43 to−48) were unfrostbitten. But on the evening of this unfortunate day, while camping, the disasters occurred which will cost us probably the lives of two of our party." He then notes: "I am obliged to comment unfavourably upon the conduct of this party in two particu-lars—of 1. loose tent and domestic routine 2. a grave error of judgment in starting as detailed (above). In all else Brooks sustained himself in my eyes. His well-known qualities showed themselves mostly in his determination, self denial, and endurance."

That Kane chose not to publish this convincing analysis, but rather to accept responsibility himself, speaks volumes about the character of the man. Fair-minded observers who peruse the record will conclude that, in Godfrey, Wilson, and Petersen, we are dealing with several varieties of sour grape. These three produced nothing that would account for the forget-ting of Elisha Kent Kane. And that leaves only the story of the woman he secretly married.

о   о   о

When Maggie Fox learned in January 1857 that her husband had fallen seriously ill, she tried desperately to reach him by mail. She received no response—her letters, suspiciously, went astray—and in February, increas-ingly distraught, Maggie booked passage from New York to Havana. With her mother, she began preparing to sail for the Cuban capital. Then, on February 17, as she sat at home eating breakfast, Maggie heard someone hollering in the street—a boy hawking newspapers. Catching a few words, she looked at her mother and her sister Kate, who jumped up and hur-ried downstairs. Two minutes later, pale and stricken, the young woman returned. With trembling hand, and without a word, Kate offered her sister the *New York Daily Times*.

On the front page, Maggie Fox found the headline she had been dreading: "Dr. Elisha Kane Dies in Havana." This first report carried few details, but Maggie read the short item twice. Then she folded the newspaper and placed it carefully beside her plate. Without meeting the eye of her mother or sister, Maggie rose and started moving toward the door that led upstairs to her private parlor. Before she reached it, the room went dark and she collapsed onto the floor in a faint.

With the help of her mother and sister, Maggie recovered sufficiently to adorn Kane's coffin with a magnificent wreath at Independence Hall. But after the funeral, she found herself in a dark place. Vowing to remain true to the romantic vision of her late husband, she built a shrine in a cupboard and sat in front of it for hours at a time, praying and weeping. To sleep, she started taking alcohol and then pain-killing drugs—and so began a long, slow decline.

Over the years, while Kate married and bore children, and her older sister, Leah, remarried and grew wealthy, Maggie spiraled into a maelstrom of self-destruction. At one point, in 1888, she would publicly denounce Spiritualism as a hoax, taking the stage at the New York Academy of Music to demonstrate how she and Kate and had created the "spirit rappings" by snapping their toes. Three years later, driven to desperation, she would recant this confession. In 1893, Maggie Fox Kane, age fifty-nine, would die destitute in Brooklyn, and be laid to rest there in an unmarked grave.

This depressing story has given rise to several books, all of them cited in the bibliography. These works strongly suggest, where they don't explicitly argue, that even though Maggie Fox lived for thirty-six years after Kane, the responsibility for her death can be laid at his doorstep. And they have been successful enough that, when people do recognize the explorer's name, they immediately mention the spirit rapper, comment on what a sad story it was, and blame the explorer. More than anything else, this chorus of condemnation has undermined Kane's reputation.

Yet documents held in the archives of the American Philosophical Society exonerate Elisha Kane. Those documents, which include Kane's will and a codicil to that will, not only show where responsibility lies—to the extent that it lies with anyone besides Maggie herself—but demonstrate that Kane himself was betrayed.

Following the death of her husband, Maggie Fox struggled to live up to his romantic ideals. Late in 1860, almost four years after his death, she would explain to a clergyman advisor, William Quinn, that she could not "turn spiritualist and make money in that way, as it was the doctor's sacred request that from the first hour we met, I should wholly and forever abandon the spirits and the followers of spiritualism. . . . I am sorry, but I shall die knowing on my death bed that I have lived as he would have me live were he living. In fact, I live to guard myself that I may meet him with no stain."

Having been reassured by Kane before he sailed for London, Maggie believed that, if he died, she would be made financially secure. Her mother, Mrs. Fox, wrote to Elisha's executor, Robert Patterson Kane: "A few days after the Doctor's death, Mrs. Grinnell called to tell Margaret that she had been 'remembered to the last.' And that he had made a bequest which was left with you to deliver to Margaret. Her trials have been (as you must already know) greater than she could bear, and we fear that unless changes soon take place she cannot survive much longer. I wish you would come at once."

But now there arose one of those protracted family squabbles that often ensue when money is at stake. Legally speaking, Kane had arranged—probably on the advice of his lawyer-brother Patterson—not for an outright bequest but for a trust. In his will, written at the Grinnell mansion in New York on October 11, 1856, and witnessed by three members of the Grinnell family, Elisha Kane declared that the first order of business should be "by sale or mortgage out of my said estate to raise the sum of five thousand dollars, and the same to pay unto my brother Robert P. Kane, or in case he shall not be living at my decease, then the same to pay unto my brother Dr. John K. Kane, within one year after my decease."

In a codicil to that will, also witnessed by the Grinnells and specifically designated a "declaration of trust," Kane further declared that "the sum of five thousand dollars named in the preceding will to be paid . . . to my brother Robert P. Kane . . . is to be . . . applied, used, employed and disposed of by the said Robert . . . in accordance with the trusts expressed by me in a paper writing to be found among my private papers at the time of my decease."

This sum—the equivalent, in contemporary terms, of roughly $115,000—constituted most of Kane's estate, as he did not foresee the magnitude of the success awaiting *Arctic Explorations*. The explorer could hardly have made his intentions more clear. Instead of honoring Elisha Kane's wishes, however, and handing over the money, Patterson stalled. He doled out small sums to Maggie, calling them interest payments, while withholding the principle and using it as leverage to extort Kane's love letters from her.

In acting as he did, Patterson may well have received encouragement from his father. The mature Judge Kane, according to at least one observer, the Philadelphia lawyer and essayist Sidney George Fisher, "had ability, acuteness, some learning, [and] plausibility, but he was without moral principle." In February 1858, however, one year after the death of Elisha Kane, the Judge passed away, leaving Patterson to chart his own course. And over the next few years, while *Arctic Explorations* generated the modern-day equivalent of millions of dollars, Patterson maintained his original tack.

Maggie Fox lacked allies powerful enough to force a settlement. Dependent on her mother and sister, she grew needy and then desperate. Sympathizers became outraged on her behalf. As early as the late 1850s, they were urging her to prepare Kane's love letters for publication as a way of forcing Patterson to do the honorable thing. In 1858, Maggie's most articulate friend, author Elizabeth Ellet, wrote directly to Patterson, charging that Maggie was being "very unfairly treated by the heirs of Dr. Kane." She said she had urged the young woman to hire a lawyer and "let her counsel arrange the business amicably and in a conciliating spirit." And she accused Patterson of tendering "vague expressions of brotherly regard" instead of a clear and businesslike statement of monetary matters: "When, instead of responding to the letter of her counsel, you went to her house, and as she said, loaded her with violent reproaches for two hours—then went to

Mr. Greeley, who had nothing to do with her affairs—and to her priest to induce him to use his influence to induce her to give up the letters—the matter certainly wore an aspect of intentional wrongdoing on your part."

Early in the 1860s, in a last-ditch attempt to help Maggie and avoid the publication of Elisha Kane's letters, Ellet sent an eloquent plea to the explorer's widowed mother, Jane Leiper Kane. The older woman was well known for her grace and generosity. After the death of her beloved son, scores of strangers had approached her with requests for Kane's autograph, and always she had sought to comply. From Cincinnati, for example, Emma Lou Sprigman had received one such sample and afterward sent a letter of thanks: "Your dear kind letter and precious memorial I received last evening and I must say unexpectedly. For I did not dare hope for an answer to my letter."

In her appeal to Kane's mother, Elizabeth Ellet wrote that Maggie possessed 134 love letters from Elisha. These left no doubt that she had become his wife: "I have read the letters, Madam, and I solemnly assure you their publication will bring a cloud of reproach on the memory of your illustrious son." Ellet noted that although Kane had left $5,000 in trust for Maggie, Patterson refused to give it to her: "I have seen a letter from him [Patterson] to said priest [William Quinn], in which he offers to give bonds for the payment of the interest of $5,000. Had these bonds been given, there would now have been no necessity for this communication."

For two years, Patterson had paid Maggie the interest on the principle amount. But then he stopped making payments, "leaving the poor girl destitute." A lawyer sought a settlement, but Patterson would agree to nothing unless Maggie relinquished the entire correspondence. Ellet observed: "This condition was not annexed to the bequest by the testator"—that is, by Elisha Kane. Nor did Patterson ever claim that it was. Ellet continued: "The young lady values the letters more than life; they are her only treasure." She wrongly asserted, although she doubtlessly believed, that Elisha Kane had wooed and won Maggie when she was fifteen. Yet she finished strongly: "I put it to you, madam, as a Christian: is not the money left to Mr. Robert

Patterson Kane as a verbal trust, for the lady's use, as truly and rightfully her own as if secured by legal documents. Is not withholding this money from her, a robbery?"

Jane Leiper Kane, who lived at Patterson's home after the Judge died, never received this plea to protect the honor of her first-born son "and prevent the scandal." Another member of the family intercepted it and delivered it to Patterson. That gentleman ignored it, and, in 1865, Maggie Fox, driven by looming destitution, and urged on by her outraged friends, published her late husband's letters in *The Love-Life of Doctor Kane.*

Initially, the book made few waves. And yet, over time, it has become like an albatross around the neck of Elisha Kent Kane, coloring all subsequent appraisals of the explorer. In it, the young Kane stands revealed as a besotted lover. He behaves foolishly, vacillating between declarations and renunciations, and condescendingly, as he seeks to educate the spirit rapper into Philadelphian respectability. Yet it is clear that he is unable to part from her.

Only the tragic demise of Maggie Fox casts the romance in a harsher light. And any fair-minded observer who scours the relevant archives will come away convinced that Kane deserves absolution. The sharp-eyed Elizabeth Ellet provided a superlative critique, but she did not see all the evidence. She did not understand, for example, that the explorer declined explicitly to name Maggie Fox in his will mainly to avoid subjecting his mother to a scandal that would have hurt her deeply.

The explorer can be faulted for believing in family and friends. He trusted his lawyer-brother to carry out his wishes. And so, unaware that during his second Arctic expedition, Patterson had colluded with Cornelius Grinnell against Maggie, Kane died believing his last will and testament was incontrovertible. Again, in the codicil, he stipulated that $5,000 should be disposed of "in accordance with the trusts expressed by me in a paper writing to be found among my private papers at the time of my decease."

No such paper survives, of course. For Robert Patterson Kane, its convenient disappearance meant that Maggie Fox could not legally prove the precise meaning of the will. By January 7, 1859, as revealed in a letter to William Quinn, Patterson had already taken up his legal position: "I have never received from the estate of the late Doctor Kane one cent of the five thousand dollars which by the terms of his will are a legacy to myself without words of trust and . . . if I should press my own claims independent of this legacy I could exhibit an indebtedness to myself on other accounts exceeding the above sum. I believe too that I have shown you that there is no estate of the late Doctor Kane."

Patterson's claim that Kane left him a legacy "without words of trust" is flatly contradicted by the codicil. If Patterson did not receive the stipulated $5,000 then he failed in his responsibilities as executor of the will. He prevaricated, seeking to avoid the formal "perfecting" of the will, though in fact Kane's estate automatically "vested" in him as executor. Finally, Patterson's assertion that Kane left no estate is ludicrous. By 1859, *Arctic Explorations* had sold over 100,000 copies while earning royalties at a rate of a dollar per book—so generating, in contemporary terms, more than $2 million. It continued to sell extraordinarily well, and earned, for the estate of Elisha Kent Kane, what can only be described as a small fortune.

The question remains: Why did Robert Patterson Kane behave as he did? Possibly, he acted out of simple greed, fearing that an initial payment might justify later ones. Probably, he believed he was serving the Kane family interest. Certainly, he did not act at the behest of his late brother. Elisha Kane had repeatedly refused offers from Maggie to return his letters, and at one point wrote that he never distrusted Maggie, "or even asked for those notes. . . . I only felt and feared that suspicious, designing friends or enemies might see and abuse these letters and give me pain and trouble."

From Canada, at another point, suddenly remembering the revealing letters, Maggie had written to Kane: "I wish that you would please go to our house, and request Mary [the servant girl] to put little Tommie in a room above, and keep my door locked all the time, so that Leah cannot read my letters. I wish that you would take my key and keep it until you go to England. Please do this; for there are many letters that I would not for worlds Leah should read." The author of *The Love-Life* notes that Kane already had the key to the box containing the letters, and rightly observes: "He could have taken away all his letters had he chosen to do so. . . . He at all times expressed a wish that they should be ever in her keeping; and sometimes reproved her for not being careful enough of them."

Robert Patterson Kane had long since decided that Maggie Fox was a reprehensible gold-digger who deserved no respect or consideration. Having inherited a streak of stubborn self-righteousness, Patterson believed that he knew better than his romantic older brother, and so felt justified in overriding Elisha Kane's last will and testament. The explorer had stipulated, as his first priority, that in the event of his death, Maggie Fox should be made financially secure. By repudiating that edict, Patterson betrayed his brother and sentenced his widow, Maggie Fox, to penury and destitution. As a result, posterity has condemned Elisha Kent Kane to obscurity.

o o o

When, some years after his death, Kane's Open Polar Sea stood revealed as a temporary *polynya,* some geographers dismissed his second Arctic expedition as a failure. Nobody thought to assess what remained unchallenged. But consider, first, that Kane discovered the world's largest glacier. That accomplishment went unrecognized for years because a scientist with better academic credentials, Dr. Henry Rink, contrived to steal the explorer's thunder. More recently, however, Edmund Blair Bolles has shown that Kane's vivid descriptions of Humboldt Glacier led scientists to conceptualize the Ice Age.

Consider, also, that while searching for the Polar Sea, Kane discovered a waterway leading north between Ellesmere Island (the Canadian coast) and Greenland. For explorers living in the late nineteenth and early twentieth centuries, before the airplane, the Kennedy Channel would prove the only feasible way to approach the North Pole. Those who followed Kane's route through Smith Sound included Isaac Hayes, Charles Francis Hall, George Nares, and Adolphus Greely. In 1908, when Robert E. Peary launched his final attempt to reach the top of the world, he too traveled Kane's route—the "American route to the North Pole."

While making these geographical contributions, Kane managed to create an alliance with Inuit who had never before encountered Westerners—a relationship that would save his own life and the lives of most of his men. By making friends with the people of Etah, learning from them, and emulating their adaptations, Kane established a foundation of trust for future explorers. By living among them, Kane also transformed himself. Having survived his ordeal, he painted a sympathetic, keenly observed portrait of the "Esquimaux" of Smith Sound—a contribution that laid the foundations for all subsequent appreciations.

Kane could accomplish this because he had a literary gift, one that remains grossly undervalued. Having honed his talent by writing of his early adventures in Asia, Africa, and Mexico, he brought it to maturity with his first book, then produced his two-volume masterpiece, *Arctic Explorations.* Previous biographers have stressed that Kane was a medical man and a scientist; but he was also, and more unusually, a man of literary sensibility. Of all the explorers who wrote first-hand accounts of northern adventures, Kane was easily the best writer. And so he inspired not only such explorers as Peary and Frederick Cook, but authors like Washington Irving, Jules Verne, and Henry David Thoreau. Kane's literary style, as Pierre Berton rightly observed, laid the foundation for his early reputation as "the outstanding polar idol of the mid-century."

Kane also proved a talented artist. Of nineteen paintings reproduced in his two-volume classic, seventeen derived from his sketches—and almost 300 woodcuts were based on his drawings. That Kane should have produced and refined these sketches while staring death in the face, as L.H. Neatby wrote, "speaks for the man's extraordinary courage, industry, and vitality. He was a striking and heroic figure."

Yet all these accomplishments pale in comparison with the achievement that made them possible, and without which none would be known. Elisha Kane led the most extraordinary escape in Arctic history. After surviving two horrific winters—seasons of darkness, starvation, disease, amputations, deaths, and a near-mutiny—he led that epic quest for survival. Traveling for eighty-three days, first by sledge and dogsled, and then in small, open boats, Kane journeyed more than 1,300 miles while leading fifteen men to safety.

His escape across the Arctic ice would not be challenged as the ultimate survivalist adventure until, six decades later, Ernest Shackleton led his legendary escape from the *Endurance*. But Shackleton worked his miracle at the bottom of the world. In the history of Arctic exploration, Kane's achievement stands alone. And so a visitor to Philadelphia will remain baffled. If the tragedy of Maggie Fox is only tangentially relevant, and Kane is absolved anyway, then should he not be celebrated as the Shackleton of the North? Should he not be recognized as the quintessential northern escape artist?

The Open Polar Sea, according to contemporary science, will eventually become a reality. This nineteenth-century American, a man far ahead of his times, went searching for it too early. A complex, challenging figure, he deserves to be remembered not just for his geographical contributions, empathetic diplomacy, and survivalist leadership, but as a top-of-the-world prophet. Elisha Kent Kane died in harness: the archetypal Arctic hero.

ACKNOWLEDGMENTS

Call it coincidence, synchronicity, serendipity, or kismet, but as a writing project, *Race to the Polar Sea* has benefited from more than its share of galvanizing good luck. In the prologue, I outlined the role played by chance in my discovery of the lost journals of Elisha Kent Kane—beginning with my impulse, while visiting Calgary, to call on Cameron Treleaven, a friend I had not seen for a couple of years.

Similarly, my discovery of two key Pennsylvania sites owes something to providence. Before traveling to Philadelphia to explore the mother lode of primary material held at the American Philosophical Society, I touched base with Meg Taylor, a book editor friend from Pittsburgh. Meg emailed her Aunt Elisabeth, who lives a few miles west of Philadelphia. The following Sunday, while out driving with her husband, Elisabeth Saxe spotted a library in Wallingford. The librarian had never heard of Elisha Kane, but another patron stepped forward: Angela Hewitt, a local historian.

Hewitt provided directions to Thomas Leiper House, where Kane's father courted his mother. Elisabeth Saxe relayed contact information, and Hewitt later provided a guided tour that included both Leiper House and

"Mrs. Turner's," where Maggie Fox languished while Kane explored the Arctic. No other author had ever visited either site.

At the American Philosophical Society in Philadelphia, Roy Goodman proved a gracious, well-informed guide, and Valerie-Ann Lutz did so much behind-the-scenes sleuthing that she deserves a medal—or at least a raise. At the Glenbow Museum in Calgary, Johanna Plant went beyond the call of duty. And in the High Arctic, the folks at Adventure Canada, led by Cedar Bradley-Swan and Clayton Anderson, proved inspirational: among the icebergs off north Baffin Island, they even allowed me to drive a Zodiac.

Here in Toronto, backed by the visionary David Kent, the peerless Phyllis Bruce led an extraordinary team effort at HarperCollins Canada. Kudos go to Noelle Zitzer, Rob Firing, Alan Jones, Neil Erickson, Colleen Clarke, and Sharon Kish. Sincere thanks, as well, to those who led the charge out of the trenches: Leo MacDonald, Terry Toews, David Macmillan, Doug Findley, Kathryn Wardropper, Mike Mason, Jennifer Flanagan, Shelley Tangney, Steve Osgoode, Deanna McFadden, Cory Beatty, Sandra Leef, and Michael Guy-Haddock.

My literary agent, Beverley Slopen, showed yet once more why she is renowned as one of the best in the business. And dealing with Jack Shoemaker at Counterpoint Press in California has proven a pleasure. From the jungles of Madagascar, Keriann McGoogan and Travis Steffens provided significant encouragement, while here in Toronto, Sylvia P. used Scrabble to keep me humble, and Carlin Fraser McGoogan stole time from practicing law to help me through a computer crash.

As a full-time writer, I welcome the continuing support of the Public Lending Right Commission, which owes its existence to The Writers' Union of Canada. Financial assistance from three agencies—The Canada Council for the Arts, the Ontario Arts Council, and the Toronto Arts Council—has proven crucial. Finally, without Sheena Fraser McGoogan, my life partner, artist-photographer, and fellow traveler, this book would not exist.

SELECT BIBLIOGRAPHY

Alexander, Caroline. *The Endurance: Shackleton's Legendary Antarctic Expedition.* New York: Knopf, 1998.

Barrett, Andrea. *The Voyage of the Narwhal.* New York: Norton, 1998.

Berton, Pierre. *The Arctic Grail: The Quest for the North West Passage and the North Pole, 1819–1909.* Toronto: McClelland & Stewart, 1988.

Bolles, Edmund Blair. *The Ice Finders: How a Poet, a Professor, and a Politician Discovered the Ice Age.* Washington, D.C.: Counterpoint, 1999.

Campbell, Joseph. *The Hero with a Thousand Faces.* 2nd ed. Princeton. N.J.: Princeton University Press, 1968.

Chapin, David. *Exploring Other Worlds: Margaret Fox, Elisha Kent Kane, and the Antebellum Culture of Curiosity.* Amherst, Mass.: University of Massachusetts Press, 2004.

Corner, George W. *Doctor Kane of the Arctic Seas.* Philadelphia: Temple University Press, 1972.

Elder, William. *Biography of Elisha Kent Kane.* Philadelphia: Childs & Peterson, 1857.

Fox, Margaret. *The Love-Life of Dr. Kane: Containing the Correspondence, and a History of the Acquaintance, Engagement and Secret Marriage between Elisha K. Kane and Margaret Fox.* New York: Carleton, 1866.

Godfrey, William C. *Godfrey's Narrative of the Last Grinnell Arctic Exploring Expedition in Search of Sir John Franklin, 1853–4–5.* Philadelphia: J.T. Lloyd, 1857.

Hayes, Isaac I. *An Arctic Boat Journey, in the Autumn of 1854.* Boston: Ticknor & Fields, 1867.

Kane, Elisha Kent. *The U.S. Grinnell Expedition in Search of Sir John Franklin: A Personal Narrative.* New York: Harper & Brothers, 1853.

———. *Arctic Explorations: The Second Grinnell Expedition in Search of Sir John Franklin, 1853, '54, '55 (2 vols.).* Philadelphia: Childs & Peterson, 1856.

Martin, Constance. *James Hamilton: Arctic Watercolours.* Calgary: Glenbow Museum, 1983.

McGoogan, Ken. *Lady Franklin's Revenge: A True Story of Ambition, Obsession, and the Remaking of Arctic History.* Toronto: HarperCollins Canada, 2005.

Mirsky, Jeannette. *Elisha Kent Kane and the Seafaring Frontier.* Boston: Little, Brown, 1954.

Nash, Gary B. *First City: Philadelphia and the Forging of Historical Memory.* Philadelphia: University of Pennsylvania Press, 2002.

Neatby, L.H. *Conquest of the Last Frontier.* Toronto: Longmans Canada, 1966.

Robinson, Michael F. *The Coldest Crucible: Arctic Exploration and American Culture.* Chicago: University of Chicago Press, 2006.

Sawin, Mark Horst. *Raising Kane: The Making of a Hero, the Marketing of a Celebrity.* Elisha Kent Kane Historical Society: unpublished doctoral thesis, 2006.

Smucker, Samuel M. *The Life of Dr. Elisha Kent Kane, and of other Distinguished American Explorers.* Philadelphia: J.W. Bradley, 1858.

Stuart, Nancy Rubin. *The Reluctant Spiritualist: The Life of Maggie Fox.* Orlando, Fla.: Harcourt, 2005.

Villarejo, Oscar M. *Dr. Kane's Voyage to the Polar Lands.* Philadelphia: University of Philadelphia Press, 1965.

Weigley, Russell F., editor. *Philadelphia: A 300-Year History.* New York: W.W. Norton, 1982.

ILLUSTRATION CREDITS

Images not credited below come from the author's private collection. The frontispiece—photo by Matthew Brady, engraving by John Sartain—derives from a print published in the 1850s and found in a Chestnut Hill art gallery. The other illustrations are taken from four volumes published that same decade and listed in the bibliography—three by Elisha Kent Kane and one by William Elder.

Photos by Sheena Fraser McGoogan: pages 20, 65, 125, 161, 343.
Photos courtesy of Cameron Treleaven: pages 5, 37, 92, 305, 311, 348.
Photo courtesy of Laurel Hill Cemetery, Philadelphia: page 344.
Original maps by Dawn Huck: pages xii, 130.

INDEX